Tyke on a Bike

D0494390

Author: John Priestley

Second edition

April 2011

By the same author:

Upward Road – first volume of autobiography
Get Rich Slow – second volume of autobiography
The Sword and the Claymore – a history of the British Isles to 1901 AD

Published by Lulu Books

© Copyright 2011

Lulu ID 1181782

ISBN   978-1-84799-144-7

CHAPTER 1

One day, I received a nasty shock, or shall we say a wake-up call. I was working as a computer consultant at Kelloggs in Manchester. I developed a frozen shoulder and had difficulty in putting on a jacket, so I went to see the nurse, a man called James. I took off my shirt and tie, and James poked and prodded at me, then recommended some exercises. However I had definitely been upset by all the finger jabbing, and shivered a bit as I started to get dressed. Suddenly I felt dreadfully faint and had to sit down - I almost passed out. James came clucking round.

"Is there something the matter?"

"I feel faint."

"Oh," said James, suddenly interested, "just come and lie down here for a while."

"I'll be all right in a minute."

"No no, you're my patient now, in my care, just lie down for a moment please."

James wasn't going to let me go so easily, and he duly took my temperature (normal) and then my blood pressure. His eyebrows shot up.

"Christ, that is high!"

"What is it?"

"185 over 90."

Stunned, I got dressed and got away. There was something wrong with me! I went back for another reading a week later and it was just as bad. A normal reading is said to be 120/80, and for someone middle-aged a figure of 140/85 is acceptable (it goes up as you get older). 235/120 would be catastrophic. So my figure was not life-threatening yet, but it was definitely time to relax.

This high blood pressure seemed to have other symptoms, firstly redness in the face. I dug out some old photographs, and this redness was there, going back five or six years. Before that, I had a normal complexion. There were other things - flushing round the neck, murky red eyes, and worse, every so often I could feel my heart go "thump". Things certainly did not feel – or look – right.

So I decided to take a break from work. I had few financial worries – no mortgage; my children's education was completed and paid for; also my wife Christine was still working, as a schoolteacher. I had built up savings. Another consideration was that I was out of a job anyway! Kelloggs offered me another contract, but the work would have been in Bremen in north Germany – two flights to get there and a 4.30 am start to be there on Monday morning each week. I refused this because I thought it would kill me. How serious was I about the blood pressure? I was offered a rate of £450 a day to stay at Kelloggs. Would you walk away from £450 a day? Most of my life I had earned nothing like this much money, but I did walk away. Having turned Kelloggs down, however, I couldn't find another job. Another American company, Honeywell, indicated that they wanted me to work at their factory in Scotland, and said they would get back to me. Well maybe they would. And maybe they wouldn't.

Earlier that year Christine and I had been on holiday with a tour party. One of our group was a man of 64 called Russell. Watching me light a cigar, he observed:

"I used to be a heavy smoker – 30 a day."

"You stopped then."

"Oh yes. I had a heart attack, you see!"

"Ah. How old were you at the time?"

"53."

"I'm 53!"

"There's one or two tips," said Russell. "Take a small Aspirin every day, 75 mg."

"Right!"

"And get some exercise to blow open your arteries."

Russell went on to tell me about some people he knew – college lecturers – who get beta blockers from their doctor and take them like Smarties. This is what I call the Elvis approach to medicine, and look what happened to him!

Russell had clearly thought a lot about his illness: "My idea is that the heart attacks that people get in their fifties are a warning that their lifestyle is wrong," he said. "Usually eating, smoking and drinking too much. But - " he continued, eyeing me carefully, "some people have lifestyles which are so drastically out of line that the first heart attack kills them." It was like the Voice of Doom. I think many of us know people who have been taken out by this cull, mainly of men, in their early fifties. The stakes were high. An acquaintance from school would die of this condition while I was writing this book. This was not a party I wanted to join.

"Well I hope I don't get a heart attack," I said.

"I expect you'll be all right," said Russell, smiling thinly.

At least I am not overweight, being five feet eleven inches tall and weighing in at twelve stones. The problem here is that I don't look that tall because I stoop, and this stoop has got worse as the years have gone on. I actually look as if I am about five foot eight with an S-bend in the middle, which people take for a paunch, but it isn't a paunch. I think the muscles that support me have just gone soft.

I discussed the problem with Christine.

"You need regular exercise," she said.

"I know, I know. Or a complete rest maybe."

"Well what are you going to do about it? What would you like to do?"

"Hmm. I think I would like to stop all work and spend my time lounging on a sunny beach in Spain."

"Without me?"

"I was thinking about nubile Lolitas ready to accommodate my every whim, while I drink gin and tonic and smoke cigars. But if you have any better ideas, I'm willing to listen."

"Why don't you buy a bike and get some exercise on that?" asked Christine.

Wives can be so crushingly unromantic.

"Round here? You are joking. It's too hilly"

"Go on the canal bank."

"Now I might just try that!"

What could be easier going than a canal towpath? Answer – a lot of things, especially for someone who had not sat on a bicycle for 37 years! But this form of activity had something else to recommend it – it would cost very little. When I am not earning money, I do not like to spend too much of it. I would need something to do all day, and this biking could use up a lot of time. The only costs would be the bike itself and some petrol money.

Anyway the first step was the purchase of a bicycle. Uncertain that the project would ever come to anything, I entered a bike shop, noting that the price of a bike ran from £229 to £999. I explained myself as best I could to a the proprietor, who did his best to keep a straight face. I am a Yorkshireman, as a breed some of the world's greatest skinflints, and I have brass in the bank to prove it. So it didn't take me long to select the £229 model, the "Mongoose".

"It doesn't look much different from the £999 machine," I observed to the shop man.

"Well everything around the expensive bike is better - the gears, the brakes, the weight."

Hmm! Well the Mongoose looked all right to me!

Would the bike fit in my car, I asked? Certainly sir, and in the unlikely event that it doesn't, you can unclip the front wheel, like so, said the bike man, effortlessly doing just that. So I said I would take the bike, plus a security lock. For the moment I took no other extras – no pump, puncture repair kit, panniers, pannier frame, mirror, mudguards, bell or helmet. They cost more money.

I picked up the bike an hour later after a "service", whatever that was, and gingerly pushed it out of the shop. Of course it would not fit in the car – I knew it wouldn't – so I set about removing the front wheel. This proved almost impossible but I got the job done after scraping the skin away from a few knuckles, swearing and cursing, much to the amusement of other callers at the bike shop. When I got the bike home I found it impossible to reassemble until I slackened a wire on the front brakes with an alan key. During his "service" the bike man must have tightened this wire. This is why I had made such a fool of myself trying to get the wheel off.

Looking at the bike with new eyes after all these years, I puzzled at that oddest of constructions, the bicycle wheel. Why did it have all these lightweight spokes? You would think it simpler to have three or four heavier ones. I also observed that the spokes of the wheel are not radii. They are fixed to the centre at all sorts of odd angles. It all looks purposeful and deliberate, as if designed to follow some recondite equation of aerodynamics, loadbearing and suspension, but would it carry Bessie Bunter?

Next I went out and bought a series of maps for the area, and started to read up on canals. In England, one canal generally joins up with another. So it is possible to construct a circular tour on what may look like one canal, but which is in fact a series of canals, built or restored at different times. In my local area there is the "South Pennine Ring", starting in Sowerby Bridge quite close to my home, going over the Pennines via the Rochdale Canal and descending into Rochdale and Manchester. To come back there is a reverse route via Ashton-under-Lyne and Huddersfield using the Ashton and Huddersfield Narrow Canals. The total distance would be about 75 miles, but obviously as the route would take me over the Pennines twice, it would not be easy – good! This would be my first objective.

However that would not take me all summer. My next best local route was to set off from Sowerby Bridge and head down the waterways of the Calder Valley and up those of the Aire Valley to Leeds. From here I could then take the Leeds and Liverpool Canal, 127 miles long, which heads north to Skipton and the Yorkshire Dales before descending through east Lancashire, heading for the coast. At Wigan a branch of the canal heads back to Manchester where it meets up with the Rochdale Canal, so I could find my way home over the hills again. And I had never been to Wigan either! This is the Central Pennine Ring. It's much longer than the first ring, maybe 150 miles. But basically there are loads of canals and if I finished that I wouldn't be short of a new route.

One intriguing aspect of the routes that I had chosen was that one of the canals, the Leeds and Liverpool, passes through the territory visited by George Orwell in 1936. He spent two months in the "industrial areas" of the north of England, and the result was his famous book, *The Road to Wigan Pier*. This is his description of conditions for the working classes in general and the coal miners in particular during the Great Depression. He concentrated on mining areas, particularly Wigan and also Barnsley and Sheffield, and it is a dismal picture that he paints – "labyrinthine slums and dark back kitchens with sickly, ageing people crawling round and round them like black beetles....monstrous scenery of slag-heaps, chimneys, piled scrap-iron, foul canals, paths of cindery mud criss-crossed by the print of clogs...belching chimneys, blast furnaces and gasometers." Was it still like that in Wigan? I didn't know, so why not go and see? It was to be a journey of many surprises.

My method of transport would be to load my bike in the back of my car and head off to a start point, cycle out for a stretch and then ride back. I never took a single taxi - Yorkshire people with any brass do not take taxis unless blood is spurting from an artery. Only those without the brass take taxis, that's why they have no brass.

From what I already knew about the canals going over the Pennines, some of it would be pretty rough going. I explained my plans enthusiastically to Christine.

"Do you think I'll make it?" I asked, tail wagging, as it were.

"If you do," she said, "you won't look the way you do now at the end of it."

Hmm! I would also have a very sore arse.

The Rochdale Canal in Yorkshire

NORTH   **SOUTH**

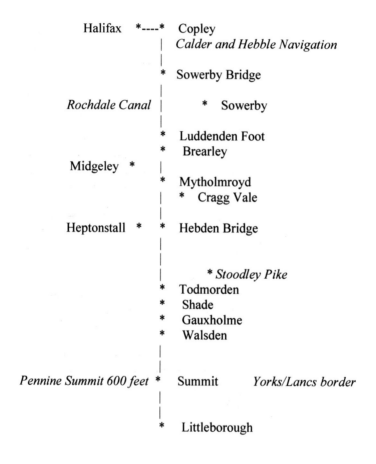

Halifax   *----*   Copley
                | *Calder and Hebble Navigation*
                |
                *   Sowerby Bridge
                |
Rochdale Canal | *   Sowerby
                |
                *   Luddenden Foot
                *   Brearley
Midgeley   * |
                *   Mytholmroyd
                | *   Cragg Vale
                |
Heptonstall *   *   Hebden Bridge
                |
                |
                | * *Stoodley Pike*
                *   Todmorden
                *   Shade
                *   Gauxholme
                *   Walsden
                |
                |
Pennine Summit 600 feet *   Summit   *Yorks/Lancs border*
                |
                |
                *   Littleborough

CHAPTER 2

My first difficulty was that Halifax is a town which sits on a hill, and a pretty steep one at that. The way into the Calder Valley where the canal runs is more or less straight down, no problem on the way out, but another matter on the way back. So I sailed downhill at first, knowing that the uphill part would have to be faced later, when I was tired. At the bottom of the hill I found the Calder and Hebble Navigation, the canal which runs between Sowerby Bridge and Wakefield.

The negotiation of the canal bank proved to be an obstacle course. First, the council or the water people or whoever runs these things had deliberately placed steel barriers across the path over the first mile of my journey, which involved dismounting and squeezing though. A cheery lad was cutting the grass with a strimmer.

"What are these barriers for?" I asked him. "To stop horse riding?"

"No, to stop people riding motor bikes on the towpath," he replied.

"Well they are stopping me as well!"

The next obstacles were the bridges, where the path narrows to a couple of feet of bumpy cobbles, the roof is low and the danger of getting pitched into the muddy water – only a matter of time, in my estimation – exceedingly great.

Have you ever read any of those books which are full of the names of exotic flowers and plants, redolent of the balmy Mediterranean air, the bougainvillea, eucalypts, oleanders, jacarandas and frangipani, the gentle chirping of the crickets? Well it is not like that here in Yorkshire on the Calder and Hebble Navigation. There is nothing but willow herb, nettles, blackberries, dock, common ragwort (a noisome yellow daisy) and Japanese knotweed.. In many places the path was only just over a foot wide and I feared for my bare legs brushing against the nettles. Again, the stench of the willow herb was a far cry from the aromatic shrubs of the maquis.

The canal runs in the bottom of the Calder Valley which is deeply incised at this point, with hillsides covered in oak woods rising away on both sides. On my right stood one of the great follies of northern England, Wainhouse Tower, built by one John Wainhouse in 1875. This phallic stone structure rises to 275 feet, its ornate top a gothic mixture of balconies and pillars. They say that Wainhouse built it to spy on one of his neighbours. It's a landmark for miles around, though it would have been a bigger one if it had been built on a hilltop.

I made my way up the Calder and Hebble Navigation to the canal basin at Sowerby Bridge, the end of this canal and the start of the trans-Pennine Rochdale Canal. Sowerby Bridge is an old, stone mill town. Until recently it was very depressed but it is now very much on the up and up, with the redevelopment of the canal basin and a number of good restaurants. In the world of canals, Sowerby Bridge is a metropolis and a mecca for boat people. There are always thirty or forty colourfully painted narrow boats in the basin at any time of year and on this day I counted a total of over 70 craft of all types, many of them in the red, black and blue livery of Shire Cruises.

The construction of the Rochdale Canal began in 1794. The route selected runs from Sowerby Bridge up the Calder Valley as far as Todmorden. From here the canal turns into a narrow, dank and thoroughly Wagnerian valley at Walsden, rising to a level of 600 feet above sea level. It then drops down to Rochdale and Manchester where it joins the Bridgewater Canal. Altogether 92 locks were built in the 32 miles between Manchester and Sowerby Bridge. That is a lot of locks, whether your are in a boat or on a bike All these locks are 14 feet wide, which makes the Rochdale Canal "broad" as its locks can accommodate two boats side by side. "Narrow" canals have a lock width of only 7 feet. The canal proved a commercial success, because a canal barge can carry 600 times the weight that a pack horse can, and also because it was the first canal to cross the Pennines.

After a long period of closure, the canal has been restored over recent years, at heavy cost. During the Sixties it was thought useless and a number of serious blockages were constructed over it. Restoration work started in the mid-Seventies and by 1986, £10 million had already been spent. One of the worst blockages was at Sowerby Bridge, where there is now a magnificent new lock, the deepest in the country (a drop of 20 feet), right by the Kwik Save car park. This was built in the late Eighties at a cost of £2.7 million. In 2000 £23 million was set aside for canal improvements, mainly on the Lancashire side, most of this money coming from the Millennium Commission and English Partnerships. The canal finally reopened along its whole length in the summer of 2002.

Today at the canal basin in Sowerby Bridge I was accosted by a perky little middle-aged man in shorts and boots with a pronounced Lancashire "bumpkin" accent. This was the summer holiday season and this man, with his wife, was enjoying a day in the sun in Sowerby Bridge.

"How far is it to Halifax?"

"Say three miles, two on the canal, then you have to turn off. A couple of miles by road up the hill."

"Three miles, that's not so far, is it?" said the man, looking hopefully at his wife, who was wearing a summer dress and shoes with heels.

"I suppose it's up to her," he added with a sheepish grin. I didn't say anything but the only way he was going to get to Halifax was on the bus.

At the canal basin I had to come away from the canal to cross the busy road to the new lock. This holds 170,000 gallons of water, or 500 tons of it! Water is heavy stuff. When the Health and Safety Executive heard about the 500 tons of water they insisted on a lock keeper. Over 1000 boats a year pass through here so he has something to do in summer at least.

Moving on under a tunnel past the centre of Sowerby Bridge, I could see the landmark tower of the parish church in the village of Sowerby, which sits high on a hill above Sowerby Bridge itself. Sowerby is the home of Leslie, my milkman back in the Seventies, who came from farming stock and had the broadest Yorkshire accent I ever heard, and who certainly believed that Yorkshire was God's Own County. Anyone unlucky enough to be born outside it, and especially if they had what he considered to be a poncey accent and came from the south, was a chinless wonder. Such a person probably had only half the normal number of testicles and an ancestry addled by inbreeding.

Having said that, the conception of northerners in the southern mind at the time was of huge, moronic and mud-bespattered rugby league players or grotesque wrestlers. Such people were barely able to articulate through their rows of broken or missing teeth, and had shaven heads and pot bellies due to massive consumption of beer. Their barely comprehensible speech consisted of guttural grunts, "thee" and "thou" and unmentionable oathings, interspersed with unpleasant wheezing from the over-consumption of Capstan Full Strength, untipped cigarettes of diabolical strength. Certainly no one with half-decent table manners could possibly be found north of Watford. Why, it was known that the only eating implement in the north was a wooden spoon and bathing was done in a tub in front of the coal fire once a month. The southerner could only suffer a nameless dread of the fiendish barbarian horde known as Yorkshiremen. At night they would lay down in the open on their barren moors in the howling wind, driving rain and miserable cold that are their normal climatic conditions, only occasionally seeking the shelter of a quiet night down a coal mine. Well Leslie the milkman was one of these.

Outwardly always cheerful, Leslie at one time took to selling eggs to supplement his income, but eventually gave it up as a bad job.

"It's a rum 'un, thegg job" he confided to me conspiratorially. I smiled back cheerfully, wondering what on earth a thegg was.

Leslie's wife was always pestering him to give up the milk round, which she did with him. It was not clear what he would do with himself if he did give it up until one day we met Leslie's identical twin brother Ronnie. He was doing the round to give Leslie a holiday, something I think only happened once. Leslie was the sort of man who would perform open heart surgery on himself with a mallet and a chisel rather than take a day off. Ronnie had apparently returned from farming on quite a large scale in Canada, but he regretted it.

"Our Leslie's the clever one," he opined.

"Really? How is that?"

"Asda," said Ronnie, emphatically.

"Asda supermarkets?"

"Aye," said Ronnie, "But Asda stands for Associated Dairies, and that's what they were when Leslie started buying shares in them. He's worth a half a million pounds!"

Just beyond the next village, Luddenden Foot, there was a field containing three carthorses - I hesitate to say huge carthorses, because all carthorses are huge of course. It was the size of their heads that impressed me, and their great shaggy ankles or fetlocks or whatever they are called. There can't be much for these animals to do but presumably they have an exciting time at the Sowerby Bridge Rushbearing Festival when there are carts to be pulled. I recalled reading that one of Spike Milligan's soldier comrades in the war was a ploughman in civil life. When asked how he liked the job, his response was: "How would you feel spending eight hours a day staring up a horse's arse?"

There were literally dozens of ducks in the water and then a large flock of Canada geese on the far bank. These are large, pretty birds with black beaks and a bad reputation. With them were two proper white geese with orange beaks. I wondered who if anyone owned these birds, and if anyone would mind if I took one home for dinner. In the water were a duck and a swan and I imagined a conversation between them would go something like this:

Duck: "Just look at that, Vestas! Two perfectly respectable white geese mixing with that riff-raff!"

Swan: "Yes, I know, ducky! The absolute dregs! I mean, they shit on the banks, don't they? Instead of using the British Waterways water closet like us! Shouldn't we tell the white ones to come away? There are some social distinctions which must be observed! I mean, it's not a colour thing, really! It's the way they behave!"

Canada Goose (approaching): "What are you saying about us, duck-heads?"

Swan: "Never you mind."

Canada Goose: "You just mind your mouths, I've a big gang here and we're having a good time trashing the place."

Swan: "Quite so my dear, that must be why they kicked you out of Canada!"

Canada Goose (walking away): "You can piss off, big bird."

Duck: "Illegal immigrants, typical!"

On my left, broad green playing fields opened out, dotted with rugby posts. I once played here. How I hated winter games with that thwack of wet leather on cold thigh! When I was at school, rugby was compulsory in all weathers, with its ghastly scrums and incomprehensible rules. We organized the soccer ourselves but even that could be a torment. In those days the ball was a soggy leather pudding which weighed about four pounds when wet. When I headed the ball, it always bounced straight off the top of my head instead of my forehead, an experience inducing a temporary form of Hutchinson's chorea. So much easier to let it bounce first.

On this first trip I only passed two moving boats, but there were plenty of other canal users, fathers with children, dog walkers and teenaged boys hopefully fishing in the muddy waters. As this was my first proper excursion I got to the lock at Brearley, outside Luddenden Foot, about five miles from home, and turned round. There is a good clear, wide stretch of towpath here and I made rapid progress at first, but I was soon slowed down by the muddy puddles. Of course you CAN go through these at top speed if you want – it just depends how quickly you want to get covered in mud. I passed through them slowly but by the time I got back to my starting point at Copley, both I and the bike were covered in mud anyway.

To get home I had to push the bike wearily up the one in six, half-mile long incline called Copley Hill. I looked a dreadful sight, covered in sweat with one dark patch of it down the back of my shorts. A couple of teenage girls stared at me – this was embarrassing all right, but what could I do about it? Frankly I hadn't expected to enjoy this part much and I was enjoying it a lot less than expected. Near the top I almost lost the will to live. Gratefully remounting when I finally reached the top, I wove groggily over the last stretch to my home in Halifax, arriving back utterly exhausted, not strong enough to open a bag of crisps and virtually unable to talk another two hours later. Because of muscular aches in my legs, forearms, shoulders, and even hands, a dreadful saddle-soreness and a general state of complete and utter knackeredness I wasn't able to get back on the bike for another two days.

So, I picked up the trail again where I had left it and headed into the next small town in the valley, Mytholmroyd. Here a beautiful branch valley known as Cragg Vale rises to the south. This was the home of the eighteenth-century Cragg Coiners, who made their living by clipping the edges from gold coins, reminting them and passing them back into circulation minus about 15% of their weight. The clippings were melted down and reminted as Portuguese guineas, which were acceptable as currency. The Customs men sent one William Dighton from London to investigate. He must have got too close because he was murdered in Halifax by the coiners. Four of them were eventually hanged, including their leader, David Hartley.

Each May, Mytholmroyd hosts the World Dock Pudding Championship. Made from the leaves of dock plants, this dish apparently tastes better than it sounds. Bernard Ingham, press secretary to Margaret Thatcher, comes from these parts, and he says it's good. It is not made with just any old dock leaf, but with the young shoots. Yet somehow I don't fancy it myself.

I soon arrived in Hebden Bridge, which is built on the steep valley side. As I approached the town centre I was stuck for a while behind an enormous equine backside, the horse being used to pull a Calder Valley Cruising tourist boat, the *Sarah Siddons*. It was led by a woman in traditional dress from some previous century.

"What is the name of the horse?" I enquired.

"Horny," came the response.

Well horses do have that reputation!

Hebden Bridge and the other towns in this valley are really creations of the Rochdale Canal. After it was dug and steam-powered machinery was introduced, requiring coal, there was only one place to be, right beside it. In the Sixties Hebden Bridge was just another blackened mill town, and many hippies settled here because of the ultra-cheap housing. The town then underwent a slow transformation into a tourist centre, a fact which amazes southern softies who expect it grim up north and still find it grim in Hebden Bridge. Yet it's an interesting jumble of building of different ages. There are plenty of shops, cafes and restaurants, and lots of tourists!

The towpath became much busier and I had some difficulty with the pedestrians, because they do not hear bikes coming. "Ting-aling!" I remarked as I went past a black woman in a motorized wheelchair, "I need a bell!"

"You do need a bell!" she replied.

A lot of the people I came across had cheerful Lancashire accents. Why are Lancashire people always so cheery? They have nothing to be cheery about! Others looked like backwoodsmen from North America with big check shirts and huge grey beards.

In the middle of Hebden Bridge I found one narrow boat actually occupied by hippies – they are still here, and looking just the way hippies used to look! There were two men, one playing a guitar, and a woman. She had a dreamy, faraway look in her eyes, presumably post-coital glow (three in a bed?) or narcotically induced, possibly both – after all, what are hippes for? Their boat was a scruffy affair with the smell of burning wood, cut logs on top, a couple of tatty bikes strapped to the roof and baskets full of herbs or pot scattered about.

Just on the far side of the town, the canal took the form of an aqueduct which carried it over the confluence or the River Calder and Hebden Water below. This stretch of the canal is associated with the murder of a girl called Lindsey Rimer, aged 13, who disappeared in November 1994 after going out to buy a packet of corn flakes. Her body was found in the canal, weighted down by a boulder, in April 1995. In 1998 a man called John Oswin of Halifax was convicted of the rape of two women and the indecent assault of two girls on canal banks. An attempt was made to link him with the murder of Lindsey Rimer, but insufficient evidence was found.

From the canal bank I could just see the top of the church tower in the village of Heptonstall, which stands on a hilltop overlooking Hebden Bridge, just down the road from a hamlet called Slack Bottom. Sylvia Plath (Hughes), the American poetess, is buried in the church graveyard at Heptonstall. She was of course the wife of Ted Hughes, who was to become the poet laureate. Ted was a local boy, originally from Mytholmroyd. Poor Sylvia put her head into a gas oven in 1963 when she discovered his affair with Assia Wevill, who subsequently suffered a similar fate; clearly, it didn't pay to get too close to Ted. I had read some of Sylvia Plath's poetry, because we had one of her books – "Ariel" – in the library at school. This is a couple of lines from "Ariel":

> Pillar of white in a blackout of knives
> I am the magician's girl who does not flinch

I wonder if this is what life with Ted was like – having knives thrown at her by the merciless magician, confident in his skill, working the crowd for money; a circus act that I could never bear to watch. One of those knives got her in the end.

Ted Hughes owned a property in Heptonstall for many years, Lumb Bank, which was put to use as a poetry writers' centre. Though he moved away himself, this valley with the moors above always remained his poetic inspiration. As a matter of fact, Haworth and "Wuthering Heights" lie only a few miles to the north of here, so this part of the Pennines has a significant literary heritage.

Beyond Hebden Bridge itself was a canalside pub, Stubbings Wharf, where four or five older men were sat out drinking beer in the afternoon sunshine. They nodded at me and my bike approvingly.

"Good fun!" I said.

"By the 'eck! Champion! Good for you, lad!" came the response.

Lad? I didn't feel one bit laddish, that's why I was there!

I passed into a country stretch of the canal beyond Hebden Bridge, where the gorge narrows and the steep hillsides are covered in thick woods. Passing a boat yard called Pickwood and Arnold, I approached the next town along the valley, Todmorden. Round here the valley bottom scenery deteriorates considerably and there is in fact a large sewage works which is old and tatty into the bargain. I know someone who lives near here, a teacher by the name of Jim. Not being sure exactly where he did live, I once asked him.

"Er, whereabouts in Todmorden do you live, Jim? Is it – er – near the – er…sewage works?"

"Not near the sewage works," came the reply, "At the sewage works! We live at the sewage works!"

I could see his house now, one of a stone terraced row. He was right. It is at the sewage works, no two ways about it.

CHAPTER 3

I rejoined the canal at a picturesque spot on the Halifax side of Todmorden, overhung by bare crags – probably an old quarry. The hills were beginning to rise steeply, and the River Calder fell over a stone weir just to my right. There were clean white geese in the water, and magpies and pigeons flitting about. Further towards Todmorden the view was less scenic, the towpath running behind many noisy engineering works and the like with barbed wire perimeters. It was slow going most of the way by bike, with cobbled overspill channels, difficult bridges and steep slopes by the locks.

It was a dull, overcast sort of day spitting occasionally with rain. There were one or two moving boats including one containing what I took to be a schoolteacher or youth group leader manfully trying to chivvy along a crew of sullen teenagers in kagools. The joys of watching endless locks fill under sullen skies just on from the expansive sewage works seemed to be lost on the youngsters.

Before undertaking this stretch I had decided that a further investment in biking gear was required – a bell and a set of mudguards. Creeping up on people on a narrow canal bank is easy on a bike, no one hears you if they don't see you. As soon as I set off I cheerfully rang my little bell. The pedestrian, a middle-aged man with a smart accent, said "Well done, having a bell! It's a very rare thing!" I felt so pleased. A hundred yards further on, the new front mudguard fell off - so much for that bright idea. The method of attaching it to the bike looked anything but foolproof and it came off over the first bumps.

High on the left Stoodley Pike was visible, a memorial built after the Napoleonic Wars, at a height of 1300 feet at the top of the Pennines above Todmorden. It is 112 feet tall and a landmark for many miles around. As it lies on the Pennine Way, many walkers pass this way, a lot of them ending up in Todmorden itself. From Stoodley Pike on a clear day you can easily see Ferrybridge Power Station, forty miles away.

At the marina in the town centre, a dozen narrow boats were moored up, and I passed two moving boats as well. Around here I noted some signs of new building and restoration. Clearly things are not standing still in old Todmorden. There were a lot of people about on the towpath – glum anglers, a couple of drunks knocking back Carlsberg Special Brew, dog walkers (one with five greyhounds) and a middle-class man pushing a buggy with a child in it, something you would never have seen back in the early Seventies.

Though Todmorden is old and still dirty, it does have a quiet charm of its own. There are quite a few dilapidated buildings requiring improvement, but I don't mind that. There are many unreconstructed terraced rows and mills, and also the odd mansion and old hall. Historically, Todmorden was dominated economically by one or two rich families – the Stansfields, the Fieldens, the Taylors – and they lived in the area, constructing large houses. A member of one of these families, one John Fielden, was the driving force behind the passing of the Ten Hours Act in 1847.

Beyond the town centre, proceeding on the canal, there is a huge embankment of blue brick supporting the railway, maybe 40 feet high and five hundred yards long. There was a frequent rattle, swoosh and toot as trains passed by – funny, that, I had no idea that the line was that busy. A lot of the traffic must have been freight – could it be nuclear waste? At this point I left the Calder Valley as the canal turns south-west into the Walsden Valley.

After a mile or so, I reached the suburb of Shade, where the uphill locks come thick and fast. A friend of mine from my time at Liverpool University had a house here, on Bar Street, right by the canal. His previous house, on North Street, had cost him and his three friends £600 in 1972. This one cost twice as much, a couple of years later. I had been to the North Street place as well. Half-way up a dank hillside, it has since been demolished, but I had some fun there at one time. I had a girlfriend there, a member of the hippie commune.

On this stretch today, the Canada geese were particularly vicious, every one of them hissing at me. There weren't many chicks with them – maybe a man on a bike came along one day and took their eggs. Good idea, stop the bastards from multiplying.

It isn't bad country round here if you are on a bike and the best bit was yet to come - a glorious, turreted and blackened railway bridge over the canal at Gauxholme which would not look out of place in the Rhine Gorge. It is wonderful and it is right here in the middle of nowhere. You have the feeling that when the Yorkshire and Lancashire Railway Company built this line, no expense was spared. Right then and there, I decided to open up a list of my Top Ten Sights of the North British Canals. This bridge would be the first entry.

Immediately beyond the railway bridge, the moors started, with bracken, heather, bilberries, cotton grass, peat bog and sheep. The sheep were a tatty-looking lot, but they are very hardy as they are left up on the moors all winter. Passing them by I soon arrived at Walsden, the next village in the direction of Rochdale. "Walsden" means "Village of the Welsh", "Welsh" being the Anglo-Saxon term for "foreigner", i.e. the "British", the people that were already here in this country when the Anglo-Saxons arrived. A house has recently been advertised for sale in here for £1.63 million! I could see it now – it is new, looking in fact like three houses rather than one. I doubt there are many houses in this village that would fetch a quarter of that – the median would probably be about £120,000.

I began to feel all alone on this towpath. There is no comforting job to go to, no one knows I am here, or cares where I am. Soon it started to rain fitfully and I began to wonder why I was there. The questions came into my head - why am I doing this? What good will come of it? God knows. I began to speculate – what does God know? Surely not everything. He can't possibly know how George W. Bush became President of the United States. Does He know why we had to wait until about 1997 for the invention of Viagra?

The going got tougher as I scrambled up past lock after lock, never passing a single moving boat. The canal opened out into pools big enough to turn a barge around, with ducks and reeds; it all seemed pretty enough given the background of overcast skies. However, the fields are small and full of rank grass and weeds, the hills loom on either side, covered with bracken and heather, and the scattered buildings are blackened with soot.

The stretch of the canal beyond Walsden is known as the Summit section because it reaches its highest point here, right on the boundary between Calderdale (Yorkshire) and Littleborough (Lancashire), at a height of 600 feet. One of the canalside notice boards here calls the construction of the canal to this height a "major feat of engineering". Now you may not consider that digging a large trench 600 feet above sea level IS a major feat of engineering. It just involves a lot of sweat, but there is more to it than meets the eye. At the bottom of the hill on the Lancashire side is a large reservoir know as Hollingworth Lake, or the Weaver's Blackpool. It was called this because it served as recreation for the weavers who could not afford to go to Blackpool. It was one of eight reservoirs which were originally built to supply the busy Rochdale Canal with water. These reservoirs and the massive stone-clad feeder channels around them are serious engineering works in their own right. They were all built as part of the canal infrastructure because the mill owners would not allow the canal company to use "their" water. Pumping stations used to carry the water from Hollingworth Lake, which lies on the Lancashire plain, right up to the summit pool.

Over to my left lay the escarpment of the Pennines, mountain streams tumbling down the flanks of the hills. The rocks in this central section of the Pennines are largely Millstone Grits, sandstones from the Carboniferous era laid down 350 million years ago. These are hard rocks to tunnel and dig, but they are impermeable, which reduces problems with leakage. On both the Yorkshire and Lancashire sides of them, the Coal Measures outcrop, and there were coal mines at one time on the eastern side of Halifax and Huddersfield and the western side of Burnley and Rochdale. One of the main functions of the canal was to be to move coal from the Coal Measures area into the Millstone Grit area. The geology of the area is of supreme importance, because the rainfall runs off the Millstone Grits in streams of some of the softest, sweetest, most beautiful water in the country, ideal in fact for use in the manufacture of textiles. To the north in the Yorkshire Dales, and to the south in the Peak District of Derbyshire, the Millstone Grit gives way to limestone. This dissolves to harden the water, and it is full of fissures and faults, so the rainfall sinks into it and streams run underground. The economy which grew up in these areas is completely different – there are no mill towns.

As I passed under the escarpment, the canal ran on a level for a mile or so, then I came to Summit village itself and hey! The lock here was downhill - I was over the top. Here was a café and a lock keeper's house. I later discovered that there has to be a lock keeper here to regulate the flow of water into the Summit Pool, which acts as a header tank or cistern for the whole canal. It was pretty bleak up here, they must have had a problem with the canal freezing over in the old days, quite possibly they still do today.

It was at this point that I did what no Yorkshireman does lightly (unless he is going to Blackpool) – I crossed into Lancashire. Now I know that Lancashire people are our fellow northerners, but you could not conceive of two more different sets of people or places. The plain of south Lancashire, where most of the people live, was until recent centuries nothing more than a bog. It was filled up very rapidly in the nineteenth century with sprawling towns and cities. You can tell it's a different sort of place because it has so many of the country's best football teams. As I write this, seven out of the top twelve teams in the Premiership are from Lancashire. Yorkshire has none, despite the fact that it contains some pretty mean large cities. Lancashire is like the Coronation Street I used to watch in 1963 with an infrastructure of tower blocks, urban motorways, supermarkets and fast food outlets grafted on top of it.

God's Own County, by comparison, is a cultured paradise, full of worthy, churchy, musical people and blessed with many lovely, historic towns and cities such as York, Harrogate, Beverley and Richmond. It has noble hills and moors and two large national parks. Compared to let's say Rochdale, even Halifax is a spa. (But compared to Widnes, Rochdale is a spa!) So I pressed on with that sinking feeling that I was about to learn a great deal more about the county of the red rose. Indeed, I was.

The reason for the absence of canal traffic became obvious when I started off downhill – half a dozen or more locks were under repair and the canal had been drained over quite a stretch. Passing a number of ugly old stone factories, in which this area specializes, a scrapyard and several towpath barriers kindly placed there for my inconvenience by the authorities, this did not feel like fun. A biker, I have found, likes to keep going – he does not like to dismount, and I had to do this repeatedly.

Heading rapidly downhill, I came to Littleborough, about four miles beyond Walsden. Here I turned round and headed back to Todmorden. It had been my intention to carry on to Rochdale and then take the train back to Todmorden. However the idea of climbing on a busy commuter train at 5 pm in my scanty biking gear and with a muddy bike did not appeal.

Back in Todmorden, I stopped to talk to a boater waiting for a lock to fill.

"Do you know anything about the closure of the Rochdale Canal at Summit?" I asked.

"Well, during the restoration, the lock gates were rebuilt using soft wood instead of oak, and they just rotted away," he explained. "In two cases the lock gates gave way while there were boats actually in the locks! They were left stranded and had to be winched onto lorries and taken away by road. A expensive business for British Waterways."

I was still finding bike riding an exhausting business. After two hours I ached everywhere and couldn't stand up straight, and I needed to take a day off before trying another stretch. My target mileage was beginning to look hopelessly optimistic – I had reckoned on biking every day.

Also bike itself was turning into a dangerous weapon for self-inflicted wounds. When I was almost back at my car I crossed one of the many cobbled overspill channels which provide amusing obstacles for the unwary cyclist. Thinking that I really should have made out my last will and testament before starting on the canals with such man-traps, I was surprised by a black dog swimming in the canal, being brought up short next to its owner, a woman in her thirties. At this point I cracked my shin against a pedal. Suppressing the desire to scream as I exchanged a few pleasantries with the dog owner, I furtively drew in a hundred yards down the towpath to observe the stream of blood running down my shin. Why am I doing this? I hadn't barked a shin in years before I took up biking and now it happens every week!

The Rochdale Canal in Lancashire

NORTH   **SOUTH**

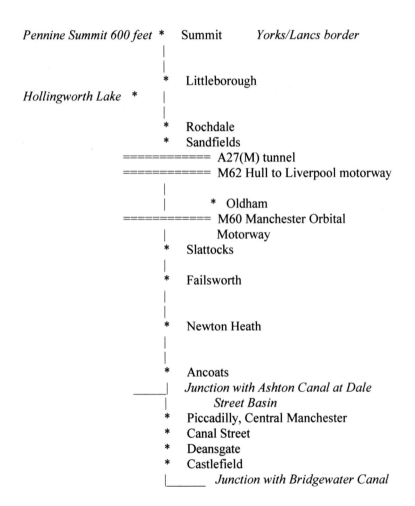

Pennine Summit 600 feet *   Summit   *Yorks/Lancs border*

               *   Littleborough

Hollingworth Lake *

            *   Rochdale

            *   Sandfields

============ A27(M) tunnel

============ M62 Hull to Liverpool motorway

              *   Oldham

============ M60 Manchester Orbital
                        Motorway

            *   Slattocks

            *   Failsworth

            *   Newton Heath

            *   Ancoats

              Junction with Ashton Canal at Dale
                    Street Basin

            *   Piccadilly, Central Manchester

            *   Canal Street

            *   Deansgate

            *   Castlefield

                 Junction with Bridgewater Canal

CHAPTER 4

My Encyclopedia of Family Health says that raised blood pressure (hypertension) seldom causes symptoms until secondary complications develop in the arteries, kidneys, brain or eyes (sounds dreadful!). By the time these symptoms occur, the affected person is in serious trouble. It also says that contrary to popular belief, it does not cause facial flushing. Well I have a question for the Encyclopedia of Family Health. If it does not cause facial flushing, why is my face so red this morning? Could it possibly be connected with a blood pressure reading of 175/90? Maybe it is another condition – after all my barber, a fattish man about my age, has a blood pressure of 235/105 and he is pale and pasty. (He's on the beta blockers now.)

The Encyclopedia goes on to say that sustained high blood pressure damages the blood vessels and that this leads to heart attacks and strokes. Quite so, quite so! Now that is what I want to avoid, of course. It adds that a reduction in blood pressure is a simple matter of stopping smoking and drinking alcohol, eating very little food, cutting out salt and taking regular exercise. Easy then! A straightforward change is lifestyle, any fool could do it! Would you like anything else, for example giving up sex and apple pie?

So there was to be no letup and it was back to the grindstone at Littleborough on the Rochdale Canal. I had to proceed carefully on the precarious, bumpy path right next to the canal with high nettle hazard and numerous midge clouds. However the way opened out eventually and the waterway began to assume the aspect of a lowland canal. There were no more hills, and no locks until I got to Rochdale. I was soon in the country. The canal was quiet – no boats at all and few dog walkers or anglers, though this number increased towards Rochdale. Fishing in the canal looks a pretty poor sort of pastime to me, and most of the men look guilty – probably because they are out of work (well, I was out of work!). There were one or two father-and-son combinations, the youngsters looking doubtful with brand new rods. Angling is the most popular participatory sport in the UK – two million people do it. Why, I do not know, because to me it looks like a pastime for the near-dead. Even daytime television might look lively after three or four hours of that – maybe that's it! Staring at an unmoving stretch of water for hours on end is better than watching daytime TV.

The dog walkers are a funny lot. They almost invariably stop and try to pull the dog away from the path, out of my way. However, I have no fear of dogs, in fact I like them very much, provided they belong to somebody else! At one time I used to live near Blackpool, a town which experiences surprisingly heavy seas in winter. Every year there seemed to be stories in the local paper about someone being drowned jumping in off the promenade after a dog. Sometimes it was the person who jumped in to save the person who had jumped after the dog that got drowned. Sometimes they both drowned but the dog crawled out anyway. When the spring tide is in, on the front at Blackpool, mighty waves crash into and over the sea wall. You can see that it looks nasty and only a supreme optimist would jump in to save his child, never mind his dog, which just goes to show what funny lot we are.

Back on the canal, I skirted past one or two modern industrial estates and seemed to be missing Rochdale completely, but sadly this was just an illusion. Then I passed one or two huge red brick mills, just the sort of thing one expects to see in Rochdale, at least one of them apparently at work. Here the canal became covered in green slime and there was much rubbish in evidence in the water, alleviated by the odd patch of water lilies. Coming up for air at a bridge I recognized immediately that this was an area of "urban deprivation", and indeed there was a sign indicating the "Sandfields Renewal Project". Immigrant youths drove past in battered Nissans, there were some skinheads at a lock drinking beer. Over on the other side were drug users, injecting themselves. Just down below me there was a large Kwik Save store. Time to get out! Happily the renewal project had provided a tarmac towpath – bliss after the stony, bumpy, nettle-ridden path I had just been on – and this made for a fast getaway.

I thought to myself, you know, a large amount of canal money has clearly been spent right here, yet no one would come here on a pleasure cruise. There was no sign of Donald Duck and Goofy. A trip out here would be on a par with a visit to the dentist or let's say an afternoon spent in an IKEA furniture store. Presently I was brought up short where the can dived underneath a nasty snarl-up of roads, traffic lights and a ruthless-looking retail park above, with no towpath. This was the start of the motorway spur connecting Rochdale to the M62. As I stood waiting to cross the road, I wondered (not for the first time) why the English language lacks a word for a set of vehicles released by a traffic light. I thought to myself – why don't I invent one? Say a "slarry". I'll just wait here while this slarry passes. There. Done it.

At this point I diverted into Rochdale town centre to take a look around. Here I found that there is actually one good building, the town hall, which is built to look like a cathedral, with a clock tower, flying buttresses and stained glass. It stands at the foot of the hill where the town centre, such as it is, is laid out. When completed the actual cost of the town hall amounted to over £154,000 which as overruns go makes the Millennium Dome look cheap. In *The Road to Wigan Pier*, George Orwell ruminates upon this type of construction: "One thing that always strikes me as mysterious is that so many of the northern towns see fit to build themselves immense and luxurious public buildings at the same time as they are in crying need of dwelling houses."

The town centre of Rochdale is a lot smaller than I would expect for a town of this size (94,000 people live here). There are a few banks at the bottom of the hill, then a single, rather mean street with two large indoor shopping malls off it - and that is all. I have never seen anything like it - outdoor shopping has virtually disappeared in central Rochdale. A former colleague of mine at a factory in Ashton-under-Lyne nearby lives in Littleborough and he was very interested to find out that I came from Halifax.

"Me and my wife go there every Saturday to do our shopping," he explained.

"But it must be 13 miles!" I said. "What's wrong with shopping in Rochdale?"

"Grim," he replied, shaking his head.

Some people would describe shopping in Halifax as grim but then they can't have been to Rochdale.

Rochdale will be remembered at the home town of the original Lancashire Lass, Gracie Fields. She was a star a couple of generations before mine, but in terms of looks, quality of voice and songs, it is somewhat difficult to discern exactly what the appeal was. I have no such problem with, say, George Formby. Anyway I'm not sure if Gracie was as popular as she thought she was. In the war she had moved to Capri in the Bay of Naples, and she would appear from time to time to wave at the English troops on the mainland, who would wave two fingers back at her. One more famous Rochdale person was its MP between 1972 and his retirement in 1992, Cyril Smith. No one ever had a bad word to say about Cyril, but, you know, would you get into a lift with him? No, of course you wouldn't. Whereas I would be only too happy to join Lisa Stansfield – another local – in a lift, or anywhere else.

Resuming on the canal, I was pleasantly surprised after the motorway tunnel to find that there was a distinct improvement in the environment. I almost immediately spotted a large grey heron. So! The anglers must be only slightly brain damaged after all, not completely doolally! That heron would not be there if there were no fish. Over the next five miles I saw three of these herons, or quite possibly the same one three times.

The towpath was tarmacked and overhung by leafy sycamores, with modern industrial buildings and red brick mills visible from the banks. Also there were some boats in the water, six canoes lashed together in pairs to form catamarans. Closer observation showed that these were occupied by youngsters with mental health problems, and their attendants. There were some more of these people on the banks, the badged minders looking sober and dispassionate as they always do. At this point I passed a group of four middle-aged joggers with running shorts and water bottles. I thought one of them looked rather fat for a jogger, but they were making a fair pace.

I soon reached the M62 where there is a new tunnel for the canal and a diversion of a quarter of a mile or so for towpath users. I was hoping for a magnificent flyover, but it was just a dingy bridge carrying the M62 over the road. After this the canal cut back out into the country and soon there was a range of five or six locks with some pretty, old bridges at a place called Slattocks. There should be other uses for this word, as in "What the slattocks was that?" or "Which silly slattock did that?" or even "She's a right slattock, she is!"

At this point there were four plump, grey-speckled birds by the side of the canal which seemed to belong to some sort of bird farm on the opposite bank, though they were obviously free to come and go as they pleased. These looked like the guinea fowl which I used to see so much of when I lived in Zambia in the Seventies, but they were quite a bit larger and they looked like pretty good eating to me. Could they be turkeys? Nah!

"Do you know what kind of birds those are?" I asked a passing couple. Nobody minds offering me help as cyclists are regarded as harmless, and middle-aged ones as probably eccentric.

"Grouse," replied the man confidently. "You often see them around here."

Now this proves to me that the English are just no good at birds because these fowl were absolutely nothing like grouse, which even I know are very colourful. Well, when I got home I looked up the strange birds in my bird book. I came to the conclusion that they were indeed domesticated guinea fowl, the picture of which mapped 100%.

The vegetation on the canal was the usual mixture of nettles and willowherb, in fact three different kinds of it - rose bay, great and broad-leaved. I found these in my flower book at home. This is very technical with much talk of stamens, sepals, stigma and so on: "Flowers 4-partite, to 3 cm wide, weakly zygomorphic, clustered in a terminal raceme." For Christ's sake, I'm not even sure how long a centimetre is. Well I know what ONE centimetre is but how long is 45 centimetres? However there are helpful photographs.

There were also a lot more anglers about, but then, this was a Saturday. Some of these people had very long telescopic rods.

"I hope you catch something with that," I observed to one of the anglers.

"I knock 'em on the 'ead wi' it."

I asked another if he had caught anything.

"Oh, aye."

"What sort are they?"

"Roach, tench, carp, pike. Some of them are big 'uns. I caught a seventeen pound tench here a few weeks back."

"Wow! Do you put them back, or what?"

"Oh aye, allus put 'em back."

As a matter of fact he had a net in the water, and if he put them back, what did he need that for? Maybe he just put SOME of them back. If it were me I wouldn't put ANY of them back, what is the point after all? I also noted that I never saw one of the dozens of fishermen pull in a catch so maybe the 17-pounder was an angler's tale.

In the vicinity of Chadderton I had the mortification of being overtaken by three of the joggers I had passed three miles earlier, while I was jotting down some notes. The fact is that you have to dismount so often that is it actually quicker to run! I passed them again shortly afterwards, one of them maintaining a conversation with me.

"We do 20 miles."

"Bloody hell!"

"Aye, we do it every week."

"You seem to have lost one." It was the fat one.

"He's not as quick as us but he'll still do 15 miles."

The fact is I couldn't do 20 miles on a bike.

Not far down the path I hit a vicious patch of nettles stretching over half a mile or so. It was so bad that I had to dismount several times. Shit! What if those joggers pass me again? Bullrushes were growing here and I did not immediately realize that they were in the water, and that if I stepped on them, I would be in it too. I then saw that I only had a foot or so of maneuvering room and that was overhung by nettles. A few of them got me but not as many as the previous day, truth be told. Those joggers must be getting close! However they didn't reappear, they must have turned off.

I also noted that there were more locks out of commission, one lock 61 (out of 92 on the way in to Manchester) and another lower down, where the gates were lying on the bank, rotten. Not long afterwards I met a British Waterways warden – I didn't realize such people existed. I asked him about the closures.

"Yes, four locks gave way completely."

He gave me the numbers – one of them was 86, which must mean that the canal is closed right up to Manchester.

"So the canal is closed to boat traffic?"

"Yes, we hope to have it open again in September."

By that time the season would be over.

"How long have these lock gates been in?" I enquired. Surely it is not beyond the wit of man in the white heat of the technological revolution to find a wood that does not rot in a few years when coated with preservative.

"Some of them, since the mid-Eighties. However the main problem is that people have been ramming their boats into them to try and make them close quicker!"

That's his story.

Near here I observed a field full of sheep racing towards the fence to a point not far in front of me. It is not often that one sees sheep behaving with such animation. When I arrived on the scene I found a middle-aged couple throwing pieces of Tescos Value sliced bread at a crowd of excited ruminants. They had several loaves and had clearly set out deliberately to feed these sheep. I mean you may call it sad and a funny way to get your kicks but after all, this is Lancashire. And I can assure you that the sheep appreciated it very much indeed.

CHAPTER 5

I picked up the canal where I had left it outside Oldham, finding many anglers on the banks. This was a Saturday and many of the men were accompanied by female partners, which I think says a lot for the long-suffering Englishwoman. Or perhaps they only do this in Lancashire. From the restored Failsworth Basin onwards the canal assumed a distinctly urban character and part of it even had street lamps. Passing through Failsworth, I came upon lock after lock. I thought I was on the Lancashire plain but there are more locks here than anywhere else on the canal. This was fine on the way down, but I knew that I would have to face them again going back when I was tired. The return journey was much more fun on the Yorkshire side when it was downhill.

I passed through some working-class estates of modern houses and the odd area that looking genuinely deprived. At one such spot, Newton Heath, I had to dodge a syringe and a lot of broken glass in a tunnel. I found myself singing a refrain from "All creatures that on earth do dwell" and it would have been "Nearer to thee oh Lord" if I had known the words. Some of the young men loitering on the bank looked as if they might mean trouble. Not the sort of trouble that implies say dropping a mouse down the back of Marya Sharapova's tennis dress, more something involving a Swiss army knife and my naked flesh.

Out of the blue I caught sight of the CIS tower, and it was quite close by, less than a mile away! Hey! I was getting somewhere! That is a landmark right in the centre of Manchester. As I worked my way through Miles Platting to Ancoats, formerly a major working class area, I could see waste land everywhere. It reminded me of the Gorbals in Glasgow where a lot has been pulled down and not much put back up to replace it. However, close to the city centre there were many signs of new building and restoration alongside the dereliction, "Luxury Waterside Apartments" being on offer at Dulcie Wharf.

At this point, called Dale Street Basin, the Rochdale Canal is joined by the Ashton Canal coming in from east Manchester. From here on I would be following part of a major tourist run, the Cheshire Ring, known as the Rochdale Nine – the last nine locks of the canal. By this time the towpath had been reduced to an obstacle course and I spent more time pushing the bike over flyovers, steps and steep cobbles than I did riding it. Then the towpath dived underground where a sign on a lock said "85 Piccadilly". I must be right under the middle of Manchester! Coming up again I found that that was exactly where I was. Unfortunately my way was blocked by a barrier with uniformed men guarding it.

"Ten pounds if you want to come down here," said a man.

"Why? I am riding my bike down the canal."

"It's the Mardi Gras Festival, £10 to get into Canal Street."

"Mardi Gras? That's Pancake Tuesday, the start of Lent! This is summer!"

"That's just what they are calling it, you'll have to ride round," said the man.

He directed me on my way. Round the corner I came into Whitworth Street and the massive and impressive buildings of UMIST (University of Manchester Institute of Science and Technology). I hadn't realized that the university was old enough to have building such as these, but it was founded in 1824! I tried to follow the instructions to pick up the canal again, but I lost it somehow, and no one I asked could help - it seems a lot of people do not realize that the canal is there. So I turned round at headed for home – it was already late and the last couple of miles of the Rochdale Canal would have to wait for another day. From this point I had to make my weary ride back all the way to the M60 near Oldham, six or so miles uphill. I am still so unfit, there is no point even taking a blood pressure reading until I can do better than this!

During this journey back I had a couple of mini-crashes, not coming off the bike, but stopping suddenly and sustaining damage to first my shins (as usual – those peddles and nettles again) and next my hand. This is what happens when you are either tired or you lose your nerve on a narrow ledge. You need a lot of confidence to ride a bike on a canal, and preferably all of your fingers, they come in handy when braking and changing gear. The dexterity of the human hand is a masterpiece of evolution unknown in any other creature. You can prove you are at the very pinnacle of the natural selection process by using your fingers to play Paganini on the violin or Bach on the harpsichord or even to embroider a tapestry. They are also very useful for picking your nose, so you really do not want to leave many of them stuck against a wall in Newton Heath. My cousin rides a bike on biking trails but daren't go on canals – "Too risky". Tinny bugger.

At one point I found a wreath attached to railings with the message "McNair, we shall alwayz miss you" in a girl's handwriting. It occurred to me that there must be disadvantages in having a canal run through a housing estate. I can only assume that there had been an accident here not too long ago. It can't happen very often that someone falls into the restored Rochdale Canal and drowns but, you know, if the canal had stayed filled in, it wouldn't happen at all. Pushing on up the hill, I eventually made it back to my car, predictably exhausted, in fact worse than I had been any day since the first.

So it was that the following day I returned to Canal Street in the centre of Manchester, this time on foot. From this point onwards the character of the canal changes again – it becomes a big city canal, or should I say a small canal in a big city. There are high-rise buildings to both sides, many still being built or refurbished, many to let, and lots of canalside eating and drinking places. On Canal Street itself there is no towpath and I had to make my way past many bars and clubs with outdoor tables. I couldn't help noticing that nearly all the clientele was male, and that there were a fair number of bare arms and shoulders and short haircuts. Also a lot of these men seemed to be sat alone, nursing a beer, and all of them seemed to be eyeing me curiously. Not knowing quite which way to look I moved along trying to look nonchalant. Given Manchester's reputation for gay bars, you will understand that I didn't dally too long in Canal Street. When I got home I looked it up on the Internet, where I found it is know as "Manchester's gay village" or "Gaychester". Harumph.

Back on the towpath I strolled past a guy sitting on the ground with a dog and a blanket, with the clearly ludicrous idea of parting the smart business people of Manchester from their small change, and not even offering an unwanted magazine in return. Just along from here a middle-aged man dressed in a very expensive-looking suit and gleaming shoes gave me a pleasant smile, as if he recognized me as one of his own, despite my casual clothes. Maybe I am one of his own, but I have certainly never spent more than £150 on a suit or £50 on a pair of shoes, and neither has my wife. She buys a lot of stuff from Marks & Spencer, and the next day takes half of it back.

I was passing a construction site at lock 89 when, on hearing a shout, I looked up to see a man tumbling through the air and into the canal! He was wearing a yellow T-shirt and a helmet and had evidently fallen from scaffolding next to the canal. He plunged straight in with an

34

almighty splash and after a worrying pause, emerged on the surface. By the time I arrived, he was already clambering out, a coloured man, about 20 years old. He immediately took off his helmet and emptied out the water. Several construction workers peered over their high fence and one jumped down to assist the young man.

"What is going on?" I asked.

"He fell in."

The young man looked extremely sheepish. "I fell off the scaffolding," he explained, "from up there!" He must have fallen 40 feet at least.

"Did you hit the bottom?"

"No, but I clipped the side."

He pulled off his T-shirt, with difficulty, and appeared none the worse for wear. "Stupid aren't I?" he said.

"You are a lucky man!" I said. One foot the other way and he would have been flattened on the towpath.

On Canal Street I had found evidence of someone who had not been so lucky. There was a plaque next to a bridge commemorating one Matthew Perrin, aged 21, who fell off the bridge and died on 8 May 2001.

I finally reached lock 92, the last lock, where the canal pours into the Bridgewater Canal in Castlefield. I had come to the end of at least the first part of my journey. I pottered about for a while in the canal basin here, one of the most impressive pieces of canal restoration work anywhere in England. The basin is overlooked by magnificent brick and ironwork railway arches converging on Manchester city centre from the south and west. Its various channels are criss-crossed with modern footbridges. At one end of the basin is a restored warehouse (the "Middle Warehouse") with round and arched windows, six stories high, with other new developments of smart flats either side of it. This place will definitely have to go into my Top Ten Sights of the North British Canals, along with the exciting run through Manchester, the Rochdale Nine.

So I had finished my first canal. What are the prospects for the Rochdale? There is never going to be much boat traffic with 91 locks in 32 miles. The reopening of the canal is supposed to create thousands of jobs – I read a figure of 4,000 direct jobs. The main thing must be the number of jobs created in the construction industry, with new building and restorations going on at many points along the canal. Also, you have to hand it to the Rochdale Canal for the tremendous variety of scenery that you see along the way. But I can tell you that if you are a novice 53-year old biker, it's a killer!

*   *   *   *

As I had never spent much time in Manchester city centre, I decided to take a look around. In 2002 the Arndale shopping centre in the middle of the city was voted the third-worst place in Britain, just behind the M25 motorway and the Sellafield nuclear power station. However, the giant IRA bomb which went off in June, 1996, created an opportunity to build much better buildings around it, including the new Selfridges, Harvey Nichols and Marks and Spencer stores. There have also been attempts to create new tourist attractions, including the Urbis Museum at Victoria, the museum of city life. This is a very good building, with an all glass exterior and a sloping roof line, having a pleasant grassy square in front of it. They will just have to find something better to put in it. The real Manchester disaster area is Piccadilly Gardens. Right in the middle of the city, it contains some truly awful Sixties-style blocks. I am thinking particularly of the unnamed monstrosity next to the Jarvis Hotel, which looked unfinished, as if it lacked cladding. They covered the worst end of this with a picture of an athlete for the Commonwealth Games, but the only real answer is dynamite.

However it is not all bad news in the middle of Manchester. There was one very pleasant area in St Anne's Square, which has the huge Royal Exchange Theatre, formerly a cotton trading building, down one side. At the end of the square is the lovely Georgian church of St Anne's. Albert Square was also impressive with its magnificent Town Hall, one of the greatest monuments of the Victorian era, built to Alfred Waterhouse's Gothic design of 1869. (Another Waterhouse building is the Natural History Museum in South Kensington.) I found another interesting modern glass building, fourteen floors of flats on stilts, at 1 Deansgate, the work of local architect Ian Simpson, who also designed the Urbis museum (which it resembles). However the thing I liked the best was the Manchester City Art Gallery on Moseley Street. This is free and has many well-known and wonderful Victorian paintings.

Manchester was much in the news in 2002 because of the Commonwealth Games were held there with great success during that summer. The city is never going to win any beauty prizes, but a lot of money was spent cleaning up and rebuilding ahead of these games, and it shows. The direct and indirect contribution of the Commonwealth Games to Manchester means that amidst widespread rejuvenation in the north, there is nowhere with such an exotic architectural cocktail of the old and the new. Manchester had been hankering for an event like this for years - it has bid for the Olympics, after all. No other provincial city in England has such delusions of grandeur.

Despite some rather strong claims from another place, Manchester keeps wanting to call itself the second city of England. In Victorian times it was the very epitome of the might of the Industrial Revolution. It provided the country one of its most important Prime Ministers, Sir Robert Peel (his family came from Bury), and the inventor of rugby, William Webb Ellis, so you could understand that. Since then the city has also given us L.S. Lowrie, Freddie and the Dreamers, Herman's Hermits, Oasis, John Thaw, Bernard Manning, John Stalker, Coronation Street and of course the Eccles cake, so I think this claim has got to be taken seriously.

The Ashton and Huddersfield Narrow Canals

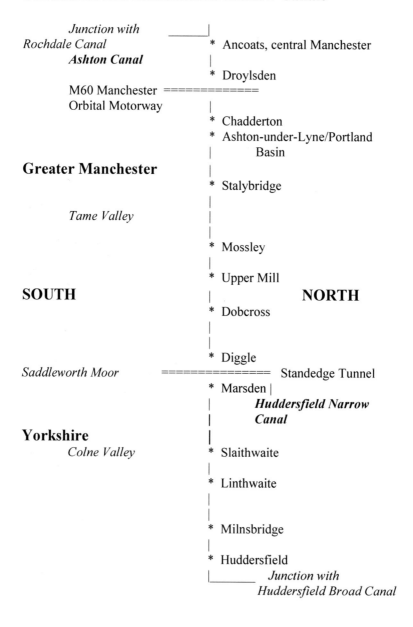

Junction with	⎤
Rochdale Canal	* Ancoats, central Manchester
Ashton Canal	|
	* Droylsden
M60 Manchester =============	
Orbital Motorway	|
	* Chadderton
	* Ashton-under-Lyne/Portland
	Basin
Greater Manchester	|
	|
	* Stalybridge
	|
Tame Valley	|
	|
	* Mossley
	|
	* Upper Mill
SOUTH	| **NORTH**
	* Dobcross
	|
	|
	* Diggle
Saddleworth Moor	================= Standedge Tunnel
	* Marsden |
	| **Huddersfield Narrow**
	| **Canal**
Yorkshire	|
Colne Valley	* Slaithwaite
	|
	* Linthwaite
	|
	|
	* Milnsbridge
	|
	* Huddersfield
	⎣____ *Junction with*
	Huddersfield Broad Canal

CHAPTER 6

Following my walking day in Manchester I was straight back on the bike, loading it into the back of my car and driving back to Manchester the next day. You may be wondering what kind of car this is. The answer is a VW Passat. You will realize by now that a Yorkshireman is very fond of his brass, always being reluctant to part with it. Not like these flash Harrys with BMWs, gigantic mortgages, super-duper holidays and gourmet eating tastes. However I will confess that I once did take a BMW out on a test drive. It was a 525 SE turbo diesel with leather seats and 190 horsepower. I stalled it three times, could not find reverse gear or stop the indicator, almost collided with a bus, drove at terrifying speed on a country road and ended up sweaty and shaken. I concluded that this is not the car for me.

So, to complete the South Pennine Ring I would have to go back to Dale Street Basin in east Manchester and head eastwards for seven miles up the Ashton Canal to the centre of Ashton. Then it would be back over the Pennines on the Huddersfield Narrow Canal. On this return journey I expected to see much the same scenery as I had the last time I had crossed east Manchester, but in its way it could not have been more different.

Approval to build the Ashton Canal was obtained in 1794. The Rochdale Canal and the Huddersfield Narrow Canal were also started in the same year. The 1790s were the peak years for Canal Mania and there were many competing projects. The Ashton Canal was completed by 1796. The driving force behind the construction was a man called Samuel Oldknow. I wonder what they called him at the time? Old Know-all probably.

It says something for amateur enthusiasm for canals that as early as 1968, a thousand volunteers from all over the country descended on the decrepit Ashton Canal to return it to navigability. Over the next few years the whole canal was cleared and restored. It was re-opened for navigation in 1974, 27 years ahead of the Huddersfield Narrow Canal.

The reason for this early restoration is that the Ashton Canal forms a part of the Cheshire Ring, an important tourist route for canal people.

I started out on the Ashton Canal at its Manchester terminus in Dale Street Basin, in an area of smart flats and huge building sites. Here I encountered a group of three young men, one of whom looked remarkably like the footballer Steven Gerrard – he can't live far away, after all! Almost immediately I found myself on a marked cycleway – yippee! This was luxury and it went on for two or three miles. By this time I had entered a surreal corridor of tall abandoned mills on either side of the canal, windows all broken, barbed wire on the walls, as if this was all that remained at the end of the nuclear winter. Just along here I encountered a group of half a dozen alcoholics, surrounded by tin cans. They looked very red in the face and unshaven and I thought they might make trouble, but no, far from it. They beamed at me groggily and one of them said "The force be with you." "It is!" I replied. "Pedal power!"

The locks came thick and fast – 18 of them, mostly very deep, and uphill all the way of course. Presently I arrived at a gleaming cluster of brand new buildings – aha! First was what I took to be the new stadium built for the Commonwealth Games. So it proved to be – the "City of Manchester Stadium", now the home of Manchester City FC. On the opposite bank was another modern monster, a velodrome – the National Cycling Centre. After this was a huge, shiny white Asda store, which looked more like an airport terminal than a supermarket.

I honed my technique for cycling up the side of a lock. This involves dropping my gears as I surge uphill, standing on the pedals, then idling at minimum speed at the top for a bit while recovering from the exhausting (for me) effort. At the top of one lock I chatted to an angler, my favorite pastime when trying to recover my strength.

"Caught anything?"

"Nah, not really. It's better about 5 or 6 when there's less light."

Presumably the fish can no longer see the line then.

"Do you put them back in?"

"Of course I put them back," said he, horrified, pointing at the muddy water. "I wouldn't eat ANYTHING that came out of that!"

Eventually I arrived in a relatively pleasant area, part of Droylsden. Here I came to the first of two huge new road bridges over the canal, and marveled at the cost. The first bridge, under the Manchester orbital motorway, and looking like a temple to Immense Ptah, was only 15 or so feet high, but that wasn't the half of it as the motorway ran a good 20 feet above the top of the bridge. It was about

120 yards long, really it was the biggest construction I have seen over or under a canal anywhere, it practically blocked out the sun and must hold some kind of world record. The second bridge, which also looked like a white concrete temple to the god Zog on planet Mars, appeared to be carrying no traffic. It must have been fifty feet high.

The last mile or so into Portland Basin in Ashton heading east was depressing territory, the remains of the urban jungle circa 1890. The banks were lined with old, decaying red brick walls, there were many old industrial premises, and the water was in dreadful condition. There was a film on the surface, many weeds both in and out of the water, tin cans, polystyrene burger boxes, traffic cones and plastic bottles, and at one point a dead cat floated past. Where oh where are the strimmer man and the net man? I'm sure that those thousand volunteers who gave their time and labour back in the Sixties would not be too pleased to see this sorry mess.

Here I was passed by two fast bikers. I thought I was dirty but they were just covered in mud. Serves you right for going so fast! Then, nemesis – brought up short by head-high nettles, aaargh! Shit! Again! Cracked my shin on a pedal. Now you may think that the most excruciating pain is to be obtained by stubbing a toe, or possibly by kneeling on a drawing pin, or if you are a man and don't happen to be wearing underpants, by catching your willie in a zip. But you have not ridden a bike for years, so you do not remember. Stubbing a toe has nothing on barking your shin on a bike pedal. Though I was wearing quite thick anti-nettle slacks, it seemed clear I must have broken the skin, and sure enough, blood began to ooze through. I hadn't barked a shin in years before I took up biking and now it happens all the time! I still had scars months afterwards. In fact, riding a bike on a towpath is a hazardous business. If you don't believe me, ask any one of the 379 people who were admitted to hospital – not to Accident and Emergency, actually admitted to a bed – in the UK last year for injuring themselves by riding a bike into a stationary object. Living with a bike is like living with a semi-house trained, eight-hundred pound gorilla. Even though it tries very hard to behave, you still end up with a lot of damaged flesh and covered in filth.

I finally arrived at Portland Basin, the eastern end of the Ashton Canal. Here it is joined by another narrow canal, the Peak Forest, in an attractive basin overlooked by the Portland Basin Heritage Centre. A helpful notice board explained that this handsome, new-looking building with a plaque stating "1834" is in fact a replica of the original which somehow got misplaced, and was built in 1999.

Ashton-under-Lyne itself is an unlovely but worthy old cotton town. Although it is physically contiguous with Oldham and east Manchester, it is in fact a self-contained town in its own right. It has everything that a town of 50,000 inhabitants should have – a town hall, a square, supermarkets, an inner ring road, a large Wilkinson's store and different grades of housing (none of them very good). In *The Road to Wigan Pier*, George Orwell sums up the social character of places like Ashton:

"In a Lancashire cotton-town you could probably go for months on end without once hearing an 'educated' accent, whereas there can hardly be a town in the South of England where you could throw a brick without hitting the niece of a bishop."

I had worked here for six months installing the Oracle computer system in a one-armed bandit factory, a fascinating place. It didn't take me long to find out that the younger end amongst my colleagues were wild clubbers. One night a group of them set off for the fleshpots of central Manchester, which is famed for its many clubs. One of the consultants was a diminutive Scotsman called Wee Dave. After nine or ten pints he lost contact with the others. Eventually he headed off back to his hotel in Ashton in a taxi, but there was a problem – he couldn't remember the name of the hotel. The taxi driver dropped him in what he said was Ashton, but Dave didn't recognize anything. Where the hell was he? He was alone in a deserted and unknown place at 2 am in the morning. So he decided to walk around and look for the hotel. However, this was not so easy. There were no hotels and no recognizable landmarks, just red brick mills, ring roads, supermarkets, garages and terraced houses – he could have been anywhere in the vast sprawl of east Manchester. As he staggered around, pairs of street lights seemed to merge into one. There was no one around to ask the way and he began to panic, walking faster and faster and getting more and more lost. After two hours he was no nearer, when he was stopped by a police car. By this time he had sobered up a bit.

"Would you mind telling us your business on the streets at four o'clock in the morning, sir?" asked the policeman.

"I am lost. What is this place, is it Ashton or what?"

"This is Dukinfield."

"Eh?"

"Dukinfield. Ashton is the next town along. You still haven't told us what you are doing."

"I'm looking for my hotel. I've lost it."

"Come off it, hotels don't move around do they now? What's the name of it?"

"I can't remember."

Policeman to second policeman: "We've got a right one 'ere."

"It's in Ashton is it?" said the policeman. "Could it be the Birch?"

"Nah," said Wee Dave, "Never heard of it. Know any more?"

"The Welbeck House?"

"Nope."

"York House?"

"That's it!"

"You're miles away mate, jump in the back and we'll run you home."

Dave hopped in and lived to tell the tale.

I wondered about calling in at the factory to see if they had any work for me now, then thought better of it. What would they make of this mud-spattered, sweaty biker with blood running down his shins – surely he couldn't once have been the Oracle consultant?

CHAPTER 7

The Huddersfield Narrow Canal was to be my return route across the Pennines, running as it does between Huddersfield in West Yorkshire and Ashton-under-Lyne in Greater Manchester, a distance of 20 miles. This canal is not like any of the other canals I have traversed so far, because there is something staggeringly, endearingly and utterly barmy about its whole conception. That something is called the Standedge Tunnel.

The story of this canal begins in 1794 at a time when the network of canals was being built through many parts of Britain. Shareholders of the Ashton canal saw the possibility of building a new canal to link their own canal with the existing Broad Canal at Huddersfield. This would provide a very direct link between Manchester and Leeds. The proposed route up the Tame Valley from Ashton and down the Colne Valley to Huddersfield follows an almost straight line between the two towns. The canal would need 74 locks over its 20 miles. The Rochdale Canal has 92 locks over 32 miles, so there are even more locks per mile on the Huddersfield Narrow Canal. As both canals were started in 1794, you could say that the race was on. It was a race which the Rochdale men were to win hands down.

The reason is that there was a big, big problem – the Pennines were in the way and no low-level way round was possible following this route, where Pule Hill rises to 1245 feet over the line of the canal. The maximum height of the Rochdale Canal is only 600 feet. So the plan envisaged the construction of a tunnel at Standedge at a height of 645 feet above sea level and 600 feet below the top of the hill. This tunnel, between Diggle in Lancashire and Marsden in Yorkshire, at three miles and 153 yards, would be the longest and highest canal tunnel in Britain by far. Nothing like it had ever been attempted previously, and not surprisingly, the project ran into trouble. Remember, we are not talking about digging out nice, soft clay, which was what the geology of the Channel Tunnel so sportingly provided. No, we are talking about 350-million year old, hard and solid millstone grit. Not as bad as granite, perhaps, but not exactly putty. They must have been mad even to think about it.

The engineer for the canal was Benjamin Outram, though he only lasted until 1801 when he resigned from ill-health. Even then, he had other projects and could not give this canal his full time. He encountered many construction problems with the tunnel, with water seepage, poor surveying and reservoir collapses, and in one year only 150 yards of tunnel was excavated. At one point it was realised that the two ends were not going to meet! Hence there are one or two unplanned bends in the tunnel. To this day these bends cause problems with navigation and boats are not allowed through unaccompanied as they must travel very slowly – one mile an hour - to avoid crashing into rocks at either side.

The method of construction involved sinking ventilation shafts which were then used for hoisting out the spoil. Holes were drilled into the rock and these were packed with explosives and plugged. The navvies then lit a fuse and ran off to what they hoped was a safe distance to await the explosion. In the case of the shafts, this was not of course possible, so the navvy would light the fuse and then call on his colleagues above him to hoist him out of the way. I can imagine that this was a precarious business:

"Dermot, have you lit that fuse yet?"

"Get me out of here now, you eejit!"

Bang! Bits of Dermot go flying past in the air.

"Always too hasty, that Dermot!"

The tunnel eventually took 17 years to construct. Fifty men had been killed in the course of construction. That may seem a lot but given the number of men involved, the long period of construction and the dangerous nature of the work, it doesn't compare badly with other engineering projects. For example, 57 men were killed during the construction of the Forth Rail Bridge which opened much later, in 1890. 28,000 men died during the construction of the Panama Canal!

Using the tunnel was not an easy option for the boatmen, however, because to keep costs down, it had been built without a towpath. While the horses were led over the hill, the boatmen had to leg the boat through the tunnel, by walking along the walls or roof of the tunnel, which took about three hours. As there were only four passing places, the tunnel became a bottleneck. Batches of boats would emerge from the tunnel only to have to queue to use the locks one at a time.

The Huddersfield Narrow Canal finally closed in 1948. As with the Rochdale Canal, serious blockages were created on it during the twentieth century, and again, these have been cleared at heavy cost. An organization called the Huddersfield Canal Society was set up to coordinate the work of reopening the canal in 1974. Working in association with the local authorities, British Waterways and property owners, the costly obstacles were one by one removed. Funding was again obtained from the Millennium Commission, English Partnerships and other sources to the tune of over £30 million! The whole canal became navigable once more in May 2001. After the completion of the restoration of the Rochdale Canal the following year, the South Pennine Ring was fully operational, whereby boaters could complete a full circle across the hills in both directions without retracing their route – a distance of 75 miles.

Before starting on the Huddersfield Narrow Canal, one Friday I took my bike back to the bike shop, as I had been instructed to do, for a free service. The bike man furrowed his brow.

"Might not have it ready for tomorrow, in which case it will be Monday."

I felt a sudden panic attack - three whole days without a bike? He could see I looked worried.

"Well I'll try and have it ready by tomorrow," he said, and indeed it was ready. But this machine which has tortured and wounded me – I can't bear to be without it now, even for a day!

So I began on the next leg of the South Pennine Ring, setting out from Portland Basin in Ashton and heading out uphill eastwards towards Mossley, a distance of five or six fairly easy miles (or so I thought). The path soon stopped so I diverted up past a huge red brick factory called Cavendish Mills, which has now been converted into flats. Plenty of these seem to be occupied, with curtains and lamps, so somebody must have persuaded someone that the centre of Ashton is a good place to live. This is a great tribute to clever marketing. Passing through the car park of an Asda supermarket I picked up the towpath again. Before long I came to a lock marked number 1 and a big sign saying "Welcome to the Huddersfield Narrow Canal!" so I was on my way.

As Ashton merged seamlessly into Stalybridge, there was one mill after another, and nearly all of them were working. Whoever said that British industry is dead cannot have been to Stalybridge! Along the canal in Stalybridge town centre there were three or four new bridges, smart railings, rough-edge paving blocks, all these stone tunnels – no expense had been spared. I must say the presence of the restored canal did seem to enhance the town centre, but maintenance was poor with many weeds, and the graffiti merchants had been at work. Then – a narrow boat – moving! This was the first moving craft I had seen on this canal. I enquired where the boatman was going: "Sheffield" came the reply – goodness knows how he would get to Sheffield from here by canal.

It had by now resumed raining, but I didn't mind. It always looks bad when you see all the raindrops falling on the surface of the canal but it was "nobbut a shower" as they say around here. I can't understand this obsession with Sun, Sand and Sea that you see in all these TV programs about people emigrating to Australia. I mean, everyone likes the sun to shine, but in moderation - this skin cancer thing is no health scare, it's for real. If you don't get that you could still end up with crocodile skin like Brigitte Bardot. As for sand, I mean, it gets everywhere doesn't it? So that's a no-no. And the sea, especially as portrayed off the coast of Australia with big breakers, poisonous jellyfish and hungry sharks, looks downright dangerous. So I shall put up with the odd shower and jolly well enjoy it right here in Lancashire.

I was soon sailing along an improved section through a rural stretch, when things suddenly took a turn for the worse. I entered Scout Tunnel, the existence of which I was previously unaware. It must have been at least two hundred yards long, it was very dark and the cobbles very rough. Water dripped from the low ceiling. It was impossible to ride in here so I dismounted and got my feet wet in the puddles. Largely unlined, I could see the blasted-out rock surface clearly enough, at least at first. This was the little sister of the Standedge Tunnel which lay ahead of me.

Amid the mud, puddles and nettles of an unattractive section of canal, I came to the small town of Mossley, built of stone but pokey and unattractive, though set in deepening hills. Oldham and Ashton must be bad if people thought this was a desirable place to live, which at the one-arm bandit factory, some did.

*   *   *   *

I took another blood pressure reading this morning on my little machine – 169/78. Now I like the 78, that is excellent, in fact absolutely normal, but what about this 169? Will it ever come down? Actually, it has come down, I've had a lot worse than that. I'm not exactly doing cartwheels yet, but this is progress.

So I set off back to Saddleworth to head upstream back to Standedge Tunnel. Until the 1974 local government reorganization, this area was part of Yorkshire. If you ask me, that reorganization has a lot to answer for. Saddleworth is an attractive place and its people did not warm to the idea of absorption into the Metropolitan Borough of Oldham, and who can blame them? They filled their gardens with white roses as a gesture of Yorkshire solidarity. Some of those roses are still there.

There were 20 uphill locks ahead of me, and the distance must have been about 5 miles, 10 there and back, but all Pennine and hilly. The small town of Upper Mill looked quite fetching from the canal, which runs through a park. The town strongly resembles Hebden Bridge on the other side of the Pennines, both in appearance and role in life. After a pretty run from Upper Mill I came to a sylvan spot at lock 23 with trees of many colours, framed by one of those massive stone railway viaducts which are so common in the Pennines, the Saddleworth Viaduct. This upland section of the canal was proving to be far more scenic than yesterday's section. Really it should be annexed back to Yorkshire. Just here was an aqueduct over the Tame which I later found out is called Old Sag because it droops in the middle. This place is another one for my Top Ten Sights of the north British Canals!

Presently I came upon a board giving some facts and figures about the canal restoration. It appears that there had been 19 separate projects, one of which was the cutting of the canal though the centre of Stalybridge! What? You mean the reason everything looked so shiny and new in Stalybridge was that the canal had previously been entirely obliterated? Yes, exactly!

After struggling up past all the steps at the many locks of the narrow valley, I found that the view suddenly opened out at lock 25 (only 7 to go!) and the clock tower at Diggle was visible, not too far away. The western portal of the Standedge Tunnel is at Diggle. However the path was blocked by two anglers, sat apart, each one with his chair right on the path, and no way round. I asked the first one if he had caught anything – he didn't have one of those nets that go in the water to keep the fish.

"Two mirror carp, about four pounds each," he replied.

"Did you put them straight back in?"

"Aye."

"Well how did you know that you didn't catch the same fish twice?"

"Well one of 'em spoke Lancashire and t'other one spoke Yorkshire."

I wondered what a mirror carp was so I looked it up when I got home. It seems that it is one of the most common types, having a few large scales, as opposed to leather carp, which have none. My dictionary says that carp are found all over the world, which probably means that they are a very ancient fish. As they live in fresh water and are found in both North America and Europe, their ancestors must have been around when those two continents were joined together, and that is going back a bit.

Passing a sign that said "No keepnets", I came to the second angler, an older man. Approaching, I rang my bell five separate times, the last time when I was right on top of him, but to no avail.

"Excuse me!" I exclaimed.

He nearly jumped out of his skin.

"You frightened me to bloody death!"

This man was not deaf, just bell-deaf. I asked about the "No keepnets" sign.

"It's to give us anglers a chance," he said. "Otherwise some bugger will get here early and fish out the lot."

"Does everyone put them back in?"

"One or two take 'em home and put them in the pond."

"What sort are they?"

"Mostly carp, four or five pounds each."

"Caught anything?"

"Nah. They're taking my bait all right, but not getting hooked."

A heron flew past on the opposite bank. There must be some experienced fish in this canal, but in their place I wouldn't take any chances with that heron, he wouldn't throw them back, for sure.

Above me now loomed Saddleworth Moor, conveniently close to some pretty rough areas of Manchester and its suburbs and the scene of some dreadful crimes, including the Moors Murders perpetrated by Ian Brady and Myra Hindley in 1963-4. Ian Brady was a stock clerk from Glasgow, and Myra Hindley was a shorthand typist. They moved into a council house at 16 Wardle Street in Hattersley, on the outskirts of Oldham. Before long the Manchester police became alarmed when four youngsters disappeared without trace, but there were no clues. However Brady murdered one boy, Edward Evans, who was 17, in full view of a man called David Smith, Myra Hindley's brother-in-law. Frightened and horrified, Smith informed the police. Photographs of Brady and Hindley having picnics on shallow graves were found. The police subsequently discovered two graves on Saddleworth Moor belonging to Lesley Ann Downey, who was only 10, and John Kilbride

(12). Another was found over 20 years later in 1987, that of a girl called Pauline Reade (16). The pair are also thought to have been responsible for the disappearances of another boy, Keith Bennett (12).

All the victims had been sexually assaulted and the court had to listen to a tape recording of the last moments of Lesley Ann Downey, who was also tortured before being strangled. Brady and Hindley were eventually convicted of the murder of Edward Evans and Lesley Ann Downey. Brady is still in jail, his "right to die" plea being rejected by the High Court in 2001. Myra Hindley's 30-year sentence expired in 1996 but public opinion was still strongly opposed to her release, so she stayed in jail where she died, aged 60, in November 2001.

Moving close to Saddleworth Moor, I arrived abruptly at the entrance to the Standedge Tunnel, which was gated and padlocked. A train suddenly materialised out of the hillside, coming out of one of the parallel railway tunnels and giving me a shock. There was a merry game of hop-scotch laid out in the park with the paving stones telling the history of the canal:

"1824 first shareholder dividend"

"1801 engineer Benjamin Outram resigns as costs rise"

"Tunnel cost £123,804, nearly twice the original estimate"

"1948 Ailsa Craig last boat through"

"3 September 2001 re-opened by the Prince of Wales"

The Prince of Wales! This is just his sort of thing. Personally I can never really understand the public fascination with the monarchy, it is just as much a mystery to me as let's say the sex appeal of Michael Douglas, Alan Titchmarsh, Nicole Kidman or Geri Halliwell. However at least when it comes to environmental matters, Prince Charles is generally on the right lines. If he thinks it is a good thing to spend £30 million reviving a canal which no one is going to use then who am I to argue?

CHAPTER 8

The Standedge Tunnel has no footpath so I headed off to the far end of it, the eastern portal, aiming to get down to Huddersfield, a distance of about 8 miles. It was certain that there would be a lot of locks, I wasn't sure how many, but a lot. But at least I was back in Yorkshire.

Standedge was a fascinating place. There are actually four tunnels here, all entering the hillside at the same point – one canal, two single-track railway and one double-track railway. Boat trips were available in the canal tunnel from the Standedge Visitor Centre where the admission price of £4.50 includes a journey a short way inside on the "Pennine Princess", a converted narrow boat. Our guide, Stuart, a man of about 35, was suitably instructive.

"At the height of the summer we run trips right through for £6, known as a hiker's ticket. Most people ride one way and walk back."

"Couldn't they ride both ways?" I asked.

"Well yes, they could pay another £6 and ride back, but most people don't fancy the idea of spending six hours underground."

He continued: "The temperature is a more or less constant six degrees Centigrade."

This statement caused a flurry of consternation on the boat – what did it mean? There were various guesses – fifty, fifty-five degrees – because the fact is that after 25 years exposure to it, we still do not understand Centigrade (the answer is 43 degrees Fahrenheit but nobody got it right).

Stuart went on: "It was a foregone conclusion that the railways would eventually ruin the canal. It only takes ten minutes to arrive at the tunnel portal on the train from Huddersfield. On the canal it could take a couple of days to get up here, what with queuing at the locks."

The start of the tunnel is brick-lined but even on the short trip you do get glimpses of the living rock from which it was carved. We could see shafts dug through to the rail tunnels and hear the rattle of the trains themselves. We soon came back out of the tunnel, and I went into the visitor centre at Standedge, a converted shipment warehouse.

When I had finished looking round the complex of building here at Standedge, I began to think there is something funny about the "Seven Wonders" of the British canal system. These are the engineering marvels of their era, some of which I planned to visit later in the summer. The Standedge Tunnel is twice as long as one of them, the Harecastle Tunnel on the Trent and Mersey, and constructed very high up. My vote would go to the Standedge every time. I found the whole place pretty and interesting and it gets a place in my own Top Ten Sights of the North British canals.

Standedge is situated in a large village, Marsden, which I happen to know has its own Gilbert & Sullivan society. Even villages have their own choirs in these parts. I am sure there are more choirs per head in West Yorkshire than any other part of the country. If you read the obituaries in the local papers, it seems that a very large part of the population has sung in a choir at some point in their lives. The old mill workers would heave giant bundles of wool about all day singing "His yoke is easy, and his burden is light!" from Handel's *Messiah*. Well, I had the feeling that the burden that lay ahead of me was going to be anything but light. It turned out to be one of the most difficult days I ever had on a bike.

So I set off down the scenic Colne Valley. "Colne" has nothing whatever to do with the town Colne in Lancashire but they share the same ancient British name. I noted with interest that the first lock was number 42! So I made my way downhill, recognising with mounting concern that every lock I sped past would have to be renegotiated of rather different terms on the way back. On and on they went, one lock after another, would they never end? Narrowly avoiding a collision with a fork-lift truck (no really, after you!), I soon arrived at the village of Slaithwaite. It had something of a toytown appearance, not because of its size but because of the way the big old mills, all humming with industry, juxtaposed with the houses and canal in a kind of artist's impression of an old mill town. The canal looked very smart as it passed through the village. Here were three shiny canal boats, moored up with people having lunch. Perhaps they were actually using the canal!

I had been wondering if a Yorkshireman would ever purchase a narrow boat. There is no item of expenditure more conspicuous, lavish and wasteful than a big yacht, so he wouldn't buy one of those. I'm sure flash boats depreciate very quickly indeed, but a narrow boat is not a flash boat.

In Slaithwaite I found a woman I could ask. She was tending a tiny garden by the side of her boat. She was a middle-aged, wore a headscarf and spoke with a strong Yorkshire accent. You may not find that surprising in Slaithwaite, but boaters can come from anywhere.

"Do these narrow boats depreciate then?" I asked.

"Not really, not if you look after them."

"What about if you buy a brand new one?"

"No, again, not if you look after it."

"I suppose it's an alternative to a house."

"Ah yes, but owning a boat isn't like owning a house. You've a lot more maintenance to pay for on a boat. It has to be painted every five years, and if you're moving, every three years you have to put it into a dry dock to get the bottom scraped. They are very damp and the wood – the exposed floorboards for example – needs to be replaced every so often. The engines need a lot of maintenance as well. But the boats keep their value – I've had this one valued for more than I paid for it."

"What about licence charges?"

"It all depends on the size of the boat."

"Well what about mooring fees, they must cost a bit?"

"No, the moorings are often free, if you stay for less than 24 hours. I pay £2000 a year because I'm commercial."

"You rent it out then do you?"

"No, I'm a tearoom!"

Sure enough, the boat had been equipped as a tearoom. They must get enough tourists in Slaithwaite to justify a tearoom. The boat was called the Mayflower. Another boater I spoke to later said that narrow boats do depreciate so I don't know who is right about that.

I moved on. The countryside opened out into a broad meadow with a vast stone mill at the far end of it, undergoing conversion into flats. As it was in such a nice place I was not at all surprised to see this. I asked a dogwalker its name – "Titanic Mills" – you don't say! My Dad later showed me an advert for this in his Saga magazine – these flats are being marketed nationally as retirement homes, and they are not cheap, you can pay £325,000. Across the canal I saw some unusual large black ducks with red faces, and behind them in a field some domestic animal which looked like a cross between a pig and a rhinoceros, God knows what it was.

At lock 11 I found two British Waterways men filling the lock, though there was no boat in it. Always curious about this type of thing, which you do see quite often, I asked them why they were doing it.

"We've three boats stuck short of water at lock 6," came the reply, "so we're just trying to speed up the flow a bit".

So! There is more to canal management than you think. I personally had not seen a single moving boat on the Yorkshire side of the Huddersfield Narrow Canal – and this at the height of the summer – but they are out there somewhere!

At this point I decided to turn round, having become distinctly nervous about the shear number of locks I would have to climb on the way back. 31 was quite enough, never mind the full 42 into Huddersfield. (What a wimp!) The return journey was predictably painful. Uphill, you can see the lock gates ahead of you. Every one of these was eight or ten feet deep – very deep; they didn't mess about with shallow locks on this canal. It was slow going scrabbling up cobbles past the locks, so much easier on the way down! However I had plenty of time to appreciate the scenery, which I had whizzed past earlier. After Slaithwaite the way became very pretty, even under lowering skies and threatening rain. There were blackened stone cottages, green fields, there was heather on the moors and sheep gently bleating. I could see the high moors looming ahead – the tunnel could not be far away now. The sylvan glade at lock 35 was very scenic, the old lock and the pool below it framed by trees. This was the outskirts of Marsden, the last village in the valley. Really I will have to link this top end of the canal with the Standedge Tunnel in my Top Ten Sights, who would want to emigrate to Australia or to a ghastly development in the Costas if they could live here?

I finally made it back to lock 42 and the Standedge Tunnel. Phew! Stopping here and there to take notes or ask questions, it had taken me one hour and fifteen minutes – not bad, not bad (it had taken me 40 minutes to get down). Mind you, I was still seriously knackered when I got home (in fact unable to move). The idea of any rapid improvement in my fitness seems laughable now.

I restarted on the canal where I had left it at Milnsbridge, a couple of miles outside Huddersfield town centre. I retained my nagging doubts about this canal. All the way into Huddersfield there was only one boat, and that was a small launch, not a narrow boat. £30 million for this? The route into Huddersfield was tatty in the extreme though there were some nice mill conversions. Even here, however, there were short wooded country stretches with ancient bridges curling over the canal with its blackened locks beneath. I had the feeling, not for the first time, that things would not have looked much different back in 1820. That is one of the things about canals – once you get away from the roads and city centres you take a gigantic step back into the past. The ambience is old because everything around you is old – the farm buildings, the field boundaries, the canal architecture – or looks similar to the way it would have looked two hundred years ago.

The blackened little bridges caused the towpath to narrow alarmingly and I was constantly revisited by fears of falling in. That would certainly make me look foolish, but I did wonder what it would do to my mobile phone. I always carry this on canal trips, not for fear of needing assistance but in case I get a call from an agent with some work for me. Today the phone actually rang, startling an angler.

"Hello, it's Nigel from Proactive!"

These people are always called either Nigel, Louise or Prakesh.

"We might have something for you in Amsterdam! How are you fixed?"

"Still available."

"Right, I'll get your CV out to Holland tonight. What is your rate?"

"Five hundred and fifty pounds a day then."

"Might be a bit heavy for them."

"I'm not going out to Amsterdam for any less."

"Fine, I understand, I'll keep you in touch!"

Of course that was the last I heard about it.

There was a new and very expensive-looking tunnel at Sellers engineering works and here I had to take a long diversion in the direction of the town centre. The diversion took me right up to and round the Huddersfield Inner Ring Road with its multi-storey car parks, multiple traffic lights, and pedestrians, not exactly the sort of place a chap wants go in his T-shirt, shorts and bike on a Saturday afternoon, but never mind! There were several flights of stairs to negotiate, one a particularly steep and menacing set made of steel, but I made it back to the canal in the end. By this time I was reconciled to the fact that you need True Grit to be a biker on a canal. Otherwise you will never make it amongst the muck and nettles at Oldham, the concrete flyovers, vicious steps and cobbles, man-trap "speed" barriers, the leering yobbos of east Manchester, the idiotic pedestrians, the thorns and the generalised fuckwittage, buggeration and gruntfuttocks.

The Huddersfield Narrow Canal finally passed into the Huddersfield Broad Canal at Aspley Basin. Here I found a short, rather stout man of about 65 was stood at the helm of one of the boats.

"Come far?"

He pointed to the markings on the side of the boat – Montgomery, in mid-Wales.

"How do you get to here from there?"

He reeled off a string of canal names, of which I caught the Llangollen and the Shropshire Union, and also mentioned the Sowerby Bridge canal basin – "Amazed at the progress there, that Salt Warehouse!" He spoke with a smart southern accent and clearly warmed to his theme.

"We sold up three years ago and have lived on the canals ever since."

"How much do these boats cost?" I asked.

"You can reckon on the basis of a thousand pounds a foot. This is a 57-footer and it cost £62,000, but it has a lot of extras – a big generator, for one thing. We use the alternator for a lot of things, such as the washing machine – the alternator powers things when the engine is running. We use the generator to store up power to watch the tele in the evenings.

Washing machine? Tele? Clearly, I had a lot to learn about life on a narrow boat.

"What do you do in winter? Don't they close the canals? Do you just moor up in a basin?"

"No, no, that's dull. We find a stretch which has a string of pubs on it and pick the ones where they put on live music in the evenings, they are always the best. You do get stuck because British Waterways use the off season to repair the locks, so you need to plan it out carefully. Last winter was quite a hard one, but it felt very nice and snug in our narrow boat. Anyway we have to keep moving because of our licence - ten miles or ten locks or a combination of the two every two weeks."

"And how much does that cost?"

"£509 a year."

So! I came away as an engineer appeared to fiddle with the boater's engine.

I had now reached the end of the Huddersfield Narrow Canal. By this stage I had come to really appreciate these Pennine canals. If you don't mind the locks and the unlit tunnel, the Huddersfield Narrow must have just about the most spectacular and varied route you will find on 20 miles of canal anywhere in England.

Some time after my initial visit, I found myself back at Standedge, and I came upon a British Waterways employee who was able to satisfy my curiosity about the tunnel and the canal traffic. He was a handsome and helpful man of about 35 with dark hair and clear blue eyes.

"Well this is our first normal year, because the first two years weren't typical," he said. "In the first year the National Waterways Festival was held here and we had over 500 boats through. In the second year the Rochdale Canal was closed, and so was the Leeds & Liverpool for part of the time, so we were the only trans-Pennine route available and we got a lot of their traffic. This year we expect about 120 boats through."

Not many, is it? Less than one a day in the season. The boaters had been there for the grand opening, taken it all in and not returned. It was the same story at the Visitor Centre – it was much quieter and the stalls had disappeared from the ground floor. Clearly the Standedge Tunnel and the Huddersfield Narrow Canal with it were settling down to the quiet life.

        *   *   *   *

Huddersfield itself is a big, stone town, but unfortunately it seems to suffer from architectural fadism. Every latest craze is immediately seized upon and the result is that there are few decent buildings left in the town centre. I used to think of Huddersfield as Halifax's big sister, but it isn't at all, because in Halifax, hardly anything of significance has been knocked down and some of the new buildings are good. The Piece (cloth) Hall has been there for over 300 years and the original Borough Market, a magnificent building, is still there. I understand that Huddersfield also had a Piece Hall and a Victorian Borough Market, but they've gone now.

Still, for all that, Huddersfield retains a prosperous, confident air. There is a large university (with over 8,000 students) which is one of the least popular in the country (just ahead of Teesside), but it does bring a lot of people and work into the town. The Huddersfield area is also well-know as Last of the Summer Wine country. The long-running comedy series, featuring Norah Batty of the wrinkled tights, was filmed in the Holmfirth area south of the town.

I once worked next to another Oracle consultant, one Jeremy. I found out that he hailed originally from Huddersfield.

"You never went back to live there, then?" I asked.

"No," said Jeremy, "it's a dump!"

"I quite like it – there is some very good country around it."

"Around it, yes, but the town itself is still a dump! After I could choose where I wanted to live, I spent seven years in Edinburgh, then moved to Richmond on Thames. You have to go where the work is."

We were working in Accrington at the time. It used to take Jeremy seven hours to get there on a Monday morning so maybe he should have stayed in the Huddersfield.

Huddersfield's most famous son is the former prime minister Harold Wilson. Although he moved to Merseyside at the age of 11 and then to Oxford and London, a Yorkshire twang remained in his accent all his life. He never really mastered BBC pronunciation, though he tried hard enough. For that matter neither did his colleagues Dennis Healey (from Keighley) or Barbara Castle (MP for Blackburn, but from Bradford). Wilson's 1964-70 and 1974-6 administrations were the first and last real attempts at government by the people – that is the sort of people you might expect to find in a local council rather than in the national government. As W.S. Gilbert observes in *Iolanthe*, with none of the Cabinet "with grandfathers worth mentioning, the country must go to the dogs!", and so it did. With people like the drunken George Brown and the Brummie unionist Frank Cousins in senior cabinet positions, what can you expect?

To complete the South Pennine Ring and get back to where I had started, I would now have to carry on downstream on the next canal in the network, the Huddersfield Broad Canal, also known as Sir John Ramsden's Canal after its eighteenth-century sponsor. This canal is just under four miles long and connects up at the other end with the Calder and Hebble Navigation, dropping down over nine locks as it does so. Like the Calder and Hebble and unlike the Huddersfield Narrow, it was one of those early waterways that made plenty of money.

Getting going on the Broad Canal, at first I passed the predictable town centre shopping malls, supermarkets, gasometers, retail parks and brand new football stadium. However I was soon into industrial territory. If you thought all our industry had moved offshore to China, you should take a trip down this canal in Huddersfield. However there were also broad parks and playing fields with a cricket match going on, and at one point a huge dark-brick railway viaduct with a crumbling parapet. Clearly this was disused but I dare say no one has the heart to demolish such a lovingly built structure. There was also that other urban feature, the downstream sewage works, which the citizens of Huddersfield have kindly donated to neighbouring Colne Bridge.

The canal terminates at lock 1, overlooked by a pretty lock keeper's cottage, where it tips into the River Calder at Cooper Bridge.

To compete the South Pennine Ring I would have to head back up the Calder and Hebble Navigation from here to Sowerby Bridge, a distance of ten or twelve miles, but I wasn't going to do that, because that stretch of canal also forms the first part of my next circuit, the Central Pennine Ring, and I would be riding out on that tomorrow. So I headed for home.

I don't think the Huddersfield Broad Canal ever closed so it would not have needed the full restoration works like its baby sister upstream. However I saw no residential development or mill restorations by this canal, and there were no moving boats. It's just a fact of life. Huddersfield does not attract tourists. But if there were no boats on this canal, it's not surprising there were so few on the expensively restored Narrow Canal either.

As far as the South Pennine Ring is concerned, all I can say is that if I had known how tough it would be – anything like how tough – I would have started somewhere else first. It had turned out to be a masochist's choice for a novice biker. You are talking about close to 200 uphill locks in 150 miles there and back, and that is a lot of locks by anyone's standards. On a bike it was hard, very hard. In a boat I would guess it would be a complete no-no. What is more there were few fast towpaths. A lot of them were bumpy, stony and nettle-infested. I was about to find out that they are not all like that.

The Calder and Hebble Navigation

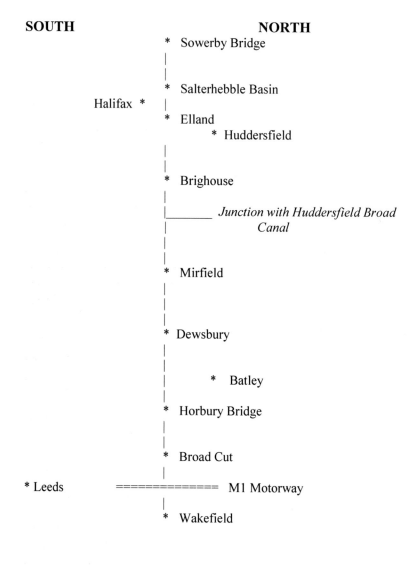

SOUTH   NORTH

* Sowerby Bridge

* Salterhebble Basin

Halifax *

* Elland

    * Huddersfield

* Brighouse

|_____ *Junction with Huddersfield Broad Canal*

* Mirfield

* Dewsbury

    * Batley

* Horbury Bridge

* Broad Cut

* Leeds   =============== M1 Motorway

* Wakefield

CHAPTER 9

My doctor's rule of thumb is that for every year his patients retire before the age of 65, on average they live a year after it. So a patient retiring at 55 can expect to live to 75, and a patient retiring at 65 has a life expectancy of less than a year.

"They wait for that pot of gold at the end of the rainbow," he says. "Not that many have enough money to stop working. So they carry on until they're 65. Six months later, I am signing the death certificate."

This is the most powerful justification I have heard yet for doing what I am doing. Because the fact is, there is more work about now, and if I was prepared to sign up to some deal which would involve me flying out to say Hungary every week, I could be working. And what am I doing? Cycling, of course. It's a question of options. I'd be a fool not to but it is surprisingly difficult to turn work away.

Tiring of the rocky towpaths over the Pennine Moors, today I start on my second objective, the Central Pennine Ring. This would take me on the boater's route eastwards down the Calder Valley and back up the Aire Valley to Leeds, then across westwards to Skipton on the Leeds and Liverpool Canal. Descending into Lancashire by a relatively easy route I would eventually turn at Wigan and head for home via Manchester. The distance would be much greater than my first ring, maybe 150 miles (300 there and back), but there would be fewer locks. However by now I would be a fool not to expect some problems and indeed I was not to be disappointed.

The Calder & Hebble Navigation runs between Sowerby Bridge and Wakefield, a distance of 23 miles. The term "Navigation" has a distinct meaning – a navigable waterway which may be part river, part canal. I was to find out that this has its disadvantages from a biker's point of view. Navigations were in general competed before the canal era itself got going. The Calder and Hebble was finished by 1770, under the direction of the man often considered the first civil engineer, John Smeaton of Leeds. He was also responsible for the third Eddystone lighthouse, which stood for over a hundred years.

The Calder & Hebble provided commercial access to the area of the Calder Valley around Halifax with its textile and coal industries. The navigation was highly successful and profitable, having a good long run before the railways arrived and even then thriving until well into the twentieth century. It remained open longer than most canals, finally closing to commercial traffic as late as 1981.

One early investor in the Calder and Hebble Navigation was the Halifax heiress Anne Lister (1791-1840), who also owned the magnificent Shibden Hall outside Halifax. She inherited shares in the navigation it from her uncle and was surprised to find them extremely valuable. The life of this woman has attracted a great deal of attention in recent years as she was an unrepentant lesbian who, in defiance of the social norm, refused to contemplate a marriage of convenience. From her portrait at least she was a handsome if masculine woman, though apparently a tremendous snob (in an era when snobbishness was normal). She left a diary of four million words, written partly in code, which is of great interest to antiquarians, especially lesbian antiquarians. It appears that Anne Lister and her lover, fellow heiress Ann Walker, did quite a bit of good grubbling together. I'm not exactly sure what that might be, it sounds like the sort of thing Rambling Sid Rumpo used to get up to on the Watford bypass-o, but I don't think it was, somehow.

I thought the Calder and Hebble would offer a broad and easy towpath, but I was learning that there aren't too many of those. I took a route starting from Copley outside Halifax, where I had begun my travels, and heading downstream in the opposite direction to my first journey on a beautiful sunny afternoon. Following the river Calder down-valley past an extensive but well-screened sewage works I arrived at the basin at Salterhebble in Halifax itself, where a branch canal takes off towards the town centre. This was built much later than the original canal (completed 1828) and was little more than a range of 14 locks. This took the navigation the mile and a half to the railway station in Halifax a hundred feet higher. Closed in 1944, it is now little more than a stub, but the basin is interesting with a keeper's cottage and green lawns.

One famous feature of Halifax is the Gibbet, which is actually a guillotine, now reconstructed. It was used to chop people's heads off until some incredibly late date like 1925 and is remembered in the saying, "From Hull, Hell and Halifax, the Good Lord preserve us."

This really means that if you were caught stealing a sheep, you would be better off in Bradford.

Moving away from Halifax towards Elland, the configuration of road, canal and railway became interesting to say the least, all of them converging at Elland Wood Bottom in a tangle of bridges, tunnels and aqueducts. Emerging from this I found myself on a much broader canal than the toytown Rochdale, over-arched with elegant oaks and willows. However there was a stench of willowherb which when commingled with the whiff of sewage made this a poor spot in an olfactory sort of a way.

The rumble of traffic heading in and out of Halifax and the huge flyover carrying the Elland bypass over the canal made this seem a very different world from the Pennine canals, where from the towpath there is little to indicate that one is not in fact in the nineteenth century, even the eighteenth. From the point of view of the towpath, Elland looks like a boom town, with an industrial estate bristling with big new commercial premises and a mill restoration going on across the canal. A sign hanging outside this said "Penthouse flats available, £390,000"! What? Here in Elland? I stopped at Elland lock where two narrow boats were packed like sardines, waiting to ride upstream. The crew pushed the lock gates closed using the balance bars, those heavy beams that stick out sideways, invariably painted black or black and white, and the operation was ready to begin. It took literally five minutes – I timed it. However, the locks on this canal are only 58 feet long. On the Rochdale Canal, for example, they are 70 feet long, they hold more water and take longer to fill.

I struck up a conversation with one of the boaters. A man of about 30, he said he had come from Hebden Bridge and was heading for Lincoln. He was sharing a boat with his father.

"My dad sold up and bought this boat," he said. "He lives in it now, based in Lincoln. I'll travel with him as far as Castleford – we should get there by tomorrow lunchtime. Then I'll travel back overland to work and he'll carry on, on his own, to Lincoln. It'll take four days from here."

"Four days!" It sounded quite a long time, it can't be more than 80 miles by road, if that. "How will he get there?"

"He'll join the Trent at Keadby lock."

I had no idea where that was - these canal people have a geography all of their own. Places that don't matter much to you or I, such as Castleford, are very important in their world.

Over to my right I saw a herd of cows standing in the water on a bend in the River Calder, a sight which, not unexpected in say Africa, is somehow not quite normal for Elland. Mind you I can see the advantages from a cow's point of view. Those horrid hot hooves! Those hot udders! Nice cool water! Further down the valley towards Brighouse I passed a number of lagoons in the valley bottom, which have a certain amount of water sport. One of these lagoons now boasts a restaurant called the Casa del Lago, which is stretching it a bit for Brighouse. Along this section I kept having to change canal banks on "turnover" bridges, where the path, for reasons of local topography, changes sides.

There were a number of anglers fishing in the canal, I suppose it was just the day for it. One of them, a young man of about 28, grimaced as I passed by.

"The one that got away?" I enquired.

"Aye, he's taken the bait and hopped it!" replied the angler.

"Are there many fish in the canal?" I asked.

"Oh aye, given the volume of water, there are fish here all right, but they're proper wild, like, wily and careful. It's not like fishin' in a stocked lake here."

"No? I don't know much about it," I said.

"Well a landowner will fill a lake with carp and then you can pay to fish 'em 'art," he said. "I do that on my holidays – I went fishin' for carp in Belgium a couple of months back. Look here."

Without further ado he reached into his bag and fetched out his holiday photos. They were all the same – him holding up a large, floppy golden carp with a soppy grin on his face.

"They are big fish," I said.

"Oh aye, forty pounds each!" he said. "But they're fished out so often, they get damaged, battered, you might say. I prefer this type of fishin', it's more of a duel between you and t'fish."

"You do it a lot, then?"

"That's right, I work as a barman in a hotel, I have to work most evenings but I do get some afternoons off, then I come down here."

"Hope you catch one anyway."

"I will, I will!"

I carried on down the canal as far as Brighouse. This town revived from its moribund condition in the Sixties and Seventies due to its position at an important junction on the M62. It is no beauty spot but it is built of stone and it does have one area of excellent housing. As a matter of fact I have devised a simple prosperity index based on the supermarkets I find in a town. The scoring system works like this: one point for Aldi, Netto and Lidl. Two points for the Co-op and Kwik Save. Three points for Asda, Sainsburys, Morrisons and Tesco. Those are the only ones found in this area. Add up the score and divide by the number of supermarkets in the town. Sowerby Bridge has a Tesco, a Kwik Save and a Lidl (2). Todmorden has a Morrisons, a Co-op and a Kwik Save (2.3). Brighouse has a Sainsbury and a Tesco (3). Need I say more?

Brighouse was put on the map in the 1977 by the release of a record, *The Floral Dance*, by the Brighouse and Raistrick Brass Band. There was something tremendously catchy about this and it sold in large quantities over one Christmas, being taken up on Radio 2 by Terry Wogan, who eventually released his own version of the tune. The record went to number two in the hit parade and stayed there for six weeks (stuck behind Wings and *Mull of Kintyre*). The brass band, used to playing second fiddle (as it were) to the Black Dyke Mills Brass Band from nearby Queensbury, suddenly found itself catapulted to fame and inundated with offers, appearing on Top of the Pops.

Just after Brighouse town centre the canal widens into another lively basin, full of boats with people disporting themselves in the afternoon sun. The basin is overlooked by an old mill, Millroyd Island, which has been converted into flats with balconies. Nearly all the development sold off-plan in one evening, which tells you something about the state of the housing market because it is the ugliest mill conversion I have ever seen. At the exit lock of the canal basin I was in for a disappointment – the canal ends abruptly and the boats carry on directly in the River Calder, with no towpath. Despairingly I called after a departing boater:

"How do I carry on from here?"

"Can you walk on water?"

So I had to skip a stretch, Still, I found I could resume on the canal a couple of miles downstream at Cooper Bridge, outside Huddersfield, so off I went. This is the point where the Huddersfield Broad Canal joins the Calder and Hebble Navigation so hey! I had finished my first ring. Repeatedly swapping between river and canal, I eventually arrived at the whimsically-named Battyeford, outside Mirfield, where there were moorings and quite a few narrow boats. I carried on a little further but was faced with a long run of river ahead. Though the path continued, I turned round, lacking the willpower and moral fibre to continue on the unattractive towpath ahead. I'll never do this ring at this rate. Back at Battyeford I chatted briefly with a boat owner who was polishing the brass on his gleaming narrow boat. It was a stretch-limo job with four sets of windows, a polished interior with copper kettles, and roses and castles painted on the outside which probably set him back £75,000 or so – a BMW of the canal world and just the sort of status symbol a Yorkshire miser would avoid.

Downstream there are further canal stretches of the Calder and Hebble Navigation and so it was that gritted my teeth to attempt the stretch between Broad Cut, not far from Wakefield and close to the M1, and Battyeford seven miles or so upstream. I chose to go upstream because of easy access to the canal from the M1. The canal was big, broad and straight and I soon picked up speed, sailing along on the broad towpath at what seemed like a terrific rate after scrambling up the Pennines. Little did I know I was being lulled into a false sense of security.

I came across a man with a strimmer – aha! Maintenance! There had been no problem with nettles on this canal. The man was tattooed and spoke with an Irish brogue, but seemed pleasant enough, telling me that the work was contracted out by British Waterways. However from this point on the path was strewn with strimmer debris, and some of it looked quite nasty. I came to second strimmer man, working half-naked in a cloud of dust. It was very hot. He stopped for a drink and pronounced himself "fucking knackered". Well yes I suppose so! It looked terrible work on a day like this.

Pretty soon I found a canal spur leading into Dewsbury and I took this, riding for a mile or so to a basin where I was rather surprised to find about 20 narrow boats moored up – surprised, because Dewsbury isn't what you would call a tourist spot. Resuming on the main line I eventually got back to Battyeford and turned round. After I had got past Dewsbury, disaster struck! Near a place called Figure of Three locks, I heard a noise coming from my front wheel – there was strimmer debris stuck to it. I pulled this away and hiss! Shit! A puncture! A thorn!

It was a long and sorry way trudging back in the wearisome heat – over three miles. Once the air has gone out of a tyre you cannot ride a bike, because the tyre slips over the wheel rim and sticks in the brakes – you cannot ride even a yard. In my case I could not even push the bike because the tyre kept slipping out and jamming, so I had to carry the front lifted slightly off the ground. This was backbreaking work, far worse than riding the bike, and soon I was covered in sweat. Just think, I could have been sat at home in the garden, basking in the sun, and here I was being tortured on the Calder and Hebble! Am I doing the right thing? Yes! Will I give up? No!

I felt like a child with a broken toy. You do not want to be seen pushing a bike. People instantly realize that something is wrong, either with you or the bike, but I must say the ones I met were very sympathetic. A friendly biker, grey-haired and middle-aged, who was coming the other way, shook his head when he saw me. He observed that thorn punctures were common on this stretch.

"I carry a spare inner tube, I need it because I bike everywhere these days," he said.

"Good for you!" I observed.

"Aye, since I smashed up my car." He smiled ruefully.

"Ah."

I drove home and went straight to the bike shop.

"Are punctures common?" I asked my cycling consultant, the proprietor.

"You might get two in a week and then go twelve months before you get another," he said.

So, he fixed me up with a new inner tube and a working bike in five minutes at a cost of £4, and I was ready to go again.

Aire and Calder Navigation

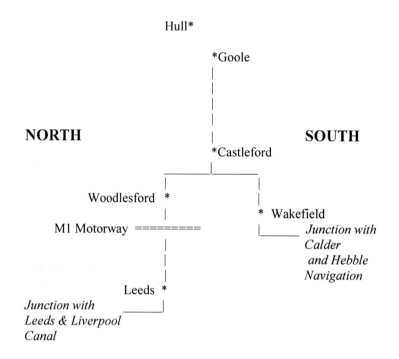

Hull*

*Goole

NORTH   **SOUTH**

*Castleford

Woodlesford *

* Wakefield

M1 Motorway =========

Junction with Calder and Hebble Navigation

Leeds *

Junction with Leeds & Liverpool Canal

CHAPTER 10

I picked up the canal boater's route to Leeds again on the Aire and Calder Navigation. This waterway is made up of three stretches of canal, one down the Calder Valley from Wakefield to Castleford, another converging route down the Aire Valley from Leeds to Castleford, the joined-up canal then continuing on to the port of Goole on the Humber. I would be following the first and then the second of these canals.

Built on a grand scale, the Aire & Calder Navigation is a different kettle of fish altogether from the Rochdale or the Huddersfield canals. It is much older (work on it began in 1699) and much larger. Improvements continued on this highly profitable canal well into the twentieth century, so that the locks can hold the equivalent of 20 double-decker buses and allow cargoes of 700 tons. This is a king amongst British canals, the Yorkshire equivalent of the Manchester Ship Canal. After the canals were nationalised by the Labour government in 1948, this canal was British Waterways' greatest moneyspinner by far.

So it was that one afternoon I picked up the southern arm of the Aire and Calder, which stretches along the lower Calder Valley from Wakefield to the confluence of the two rivers in Castleford. I started at a place called Stanley Ferry Marina outside Wakefield, about five miles from the confluence, aiming to get there and back in a couple of hours. However, I was in for a disappointment.

Stanley Ferry Marina was a very busy place, fronted by a giant modern pub with a full car park. Here were British Waterways workshops and two aqueducts over the River Calder, one an old and elegant, the other new and brutalist. There were lots of launches and narrow boats moored up and the whole place, previously unknown to me, looked a hive of activity. I set off towards Castleford through green fields and pleasant countryside, criss-crossed by pylons emanating from the nearby power stations. The canal was beautifully clean with no weeds. Its locks were big, each one with a lock keeper's house and warnings about 24 hour CCTV surveillance. There is clearly a problem with the locals here, in the middle of the old Yorkshire coalfield, and though I wouldn't like to be derogatory about my fellow Yorkshire people, some of those I saw on the towpath looked a rough lot. The coalfield with its whippets-and-pigeons culture was always a different world to the "woollen" towns of the West Riding, whose music-loving, churchy citizens never really understood it.

At school I played ruby against a team from a coalfield grammar school at Hemsworth and I remember being bemused by the vocabulary, which strongly featured the words "thee", "thou", "thine" and "fucking bastard". Rugby was supposed to be a means of channelling the aggression of young men. All I can say is that it terrified me, especially when the opposition came from the coalfield.

Passing under the M62, where there was heavy graffiti, I was soon balked again at a lock. In front of me was the river, broad and swirling, no canal at all and definitely no towpath. So this was another navigation, just like the Calder and Hebble at Brighouse, with river sections. I wouldn't be able to get to Castleford, still a couple of miles away, so I had to turn round and go home.

On the way back I was charged down by an alsatian. It came at me at terrifying speed and looked as if it meant business. It did, but it was muzzled. Had it not been, I think I would by now be missing a large and important lump of flesh.

*   *   *   *

Careful study of a large-scale map at home made me realise that I was not going to get to Castleford on my bike, because the junction of the northern and southern of the branches of the Aire and Calder Navigation is a confluence between two rivers, not canals. So it was that I picked up the Aire and Calder again the next day downstream from Woodlesford Lock, six miles or so from the centre of Leeds, and now heading north-westwards. It was a grey and overcast sort of afternoon. The canal lay before me, huge, broad and straight, really a monster compared with say the Rochdale or even its little sister branch I had been on the previous day, and much more impressive than the river Aire to one side. It was covered in green amoebae, far more of them than I had seen anywhere, could it be genetic engineering? These were being greedily sieved off by swans which obviously didn't mind in the least. However, amoebae floating on the surface of the canal was hardly a promising sign, indicating stagnant water. I used to work near here back in the Eighties and there was plenty of commercial traffic then, and I had read that the Aire and Calder still carries millions of tons of freight annually as well as leisure traffic. However it looked to me as though that was a thing of the past and in fact I was not to see a single moving craft of any type all day. How sad for a mighty waterway like this. I guess that most canals were really built to carry coal, and that trade here would have packed up when the Yorkshire coalfield was virtually closed down.

The canal and river lie side by side in a trench perhaps 50 feet deep, with the main flood plain above that. This trench opens out from time to time with lagoons, and is overlooked by desiccated bluffs. It has an air of greyness and desolation – there are few signs habitation and the vegetation is largely thistles, dock, nettles and willowherb. Could this be the same river that tinkles so prettily through the green fields round Gargrave and Skipton in the Yorkshire Dales? Evidently, however, this area has been landscaped. I talked to a boater months afterwards who said that four years previously, this run into Leeds was the worst stretch of canal all the way from Sowerby Bridge to Burnley with nothing but derelict factories and piles of old rubble.

Arriving at Woodlesford lock I was astounded at the size of it. Fronted by a traffic light and overlooked by a control tower, it has its own lock keeper with his own house right by the lock. It was the same at the next lock up, Fishpond; one lock, one lock keeper. The reason seemed clear – someone must be present to look after the lock, because a serious amount of water is displaced every time the lock gates are opened – by my reckoning, 25,000 cubic feet, knocking on for 2,500 tons of it! You would not want to stand in the way of that lot, or accidentally lose it by leaving the lock gates open.

Moving along the broad, well-maintained and clean cycleway I soon passed under an immense flyover carrying the M1 past Leeds. The cycleway was good but much disturbed by tiresome crossover bridges and barriers. There wasn't much sign of Leeds for quite a long time, although there was an industrial smell in the air, as one finds when walking through an engineering workshop. At one point there was a diversion away from the canal, round two roundabouts, where I was told the canal bank had collapsed. Rejoining the canal after the diversion at a derelict mill ("Sidney Smith & Co, Manufacturers of mantles and skirts"), I observed that the canal had disappeared! Here there was only the river, looking much larger. On the way back this was clearer – at this point the river splits into river and canal. There is no lock – the canal just backs up as far as the first lock at Knostrop half a mile downstream.

The city centre was now close. Industrial premises sat cheek by jowl with modern flats on the canal bank and I received an unpleasant spray (probably radioactive) from one factory. There were new blocks of riverside flats everywhere. To my left on the bank was a very large new angular building in variegated grey granite. Rounding the corner into Clarence Dock, I found that I had stumbled upon the Royal Armouries Museum.

Outside this building was a man in a suit who appeared to be selling balloons. Other people dressed as waitresses and waiters were standing about ready to serve orange juice and champagne, but to whom? Suddenly it became clear as a large, smartly dressed party poured out of the Royal Armouries. Mainly women, they were all wearing badges and carrying clipboards and identical brochures. Each one of them got a drink and a balloon. This would be one of those ghastly corporate get-togethers I used to endure when working for Oracle. We had to sit and watch videos of Larry Ellison (the chairman) making ra-ra speeches and would be given goody bags filled with ra-ra literature, which we would dump in the lobby on the way out. Even worse, we might be asked to bond by participating in *It's A Knockout* or competitive games. I recall at one function in central Birmingham, one of Larry's men got on the stage at the front and came out with some inane phrase which we consultants were asked to repeat:

"We love it and we know! We love it and we know!"

Most of the consultants were middle-aged accountants and the like. One of these, in fact an accountant aged about 38 from Newcastle, turned to me and said:

"I know why we have got these goody bags now – so we can puke into them!"

When driving to Woodlesford earlier that day I had been listening to the radio, where they were discussing the case of one Steve Gough, who was trying (with difficulty) to walk naked from Land's End to John O'Groats. Two people were interviewed, a naked walker and a naked cyclist, the latter of whom said that he cycled naked through the centre of Cambridge and nobody bothered him. Cycling back from Clarence Docks through the semi-landscaped, dusty, grey, weedy and generally unpleasant Aire Valley, there was no one about and I thought, you know, this wouldn't be a bad spot for a bit of nude cycling! Shall I try it? Shall I?

The Leeds and Liverpool Canal in Yorkshire

NORTH   **SOUTH**

```
                              *  Leeds
                              |
                              |
                              *  Apperley Bridge
                Shipley  *         *  Bradford
                              *  Saltaire
                              *  Bingley        *  Denholme
       *  Ilkley             |
                              |    *  Keighley
                              *  East Riddlesden
                              |
                              |
                              *  Bradley
                              *  Skipton
                              |
                              *  Gargrave
                              |
                              *  Priest Holme
                              *  Newton Locks
                              |
                              *  East Marton
Summit Pond Pennine crossing  *  Greenberfield
Yorkshire/Lancashire boundary |
                              *  Barnoldswick
```

73

CHAPTER 11

Ah well, another day, another canal. It was finally time to get my teeth into the Leeds and Liverpool, 127 miles long (the longest in Britain). This canal links the port of Liverpool with the Aire and Calder Navigation at Leeds, forming the major part of a through route between the Irish Sea and the North Sea. Just like the Rochdale Canal it has 92 locks, but as the Rochdale canal is only 32 miles long, there are obviously many fewer per mile. The canal takes the long, low-level route through the Pennines at Skipton known as the Aire Gap, and has a long tunnel at Foulridge near Colne in east Lancashire. It took 46 years to complete, partly because the British Government kept getting involved in wars which sucked up free cash (does nothing change?).

Canal builder: "Hey, can't you stop fighting, we're trying to build a canal here!"

William Pitt the Younger: "No."

Canal builder: "Who are you fighting anyway?"

Pitt: "Napoleon. It will take time. 23 years."

Canal builder: "I shall be dead by then!"

Pitt: "So will I."

He was.

Although the Leeds and Liverpool is England's longest canal, it does not compare with some continental canals, for example the Erie Canal in the United States. Built to connect the Hudson River (upon which New York stands) at Albany and Lake Erie at Buffalo, it is 363 miles long! It was a very important canal, giving New York direct access to the Mid-West and enabling it to power ahead of rival cities on the eastern seaboard of the United States. This gives you an idea of just how big the United States actually is, because the Erie Canal was built entirely within New York state, just a small block in a map of the whole country. Yet even that canal is small fry next to the Grand Canal of China, at 1114 miles the world's longest man-made waterway, connecting the Yangtze and Hwang-Ho rivers. That was begun in 486 BC!

So I suppose you might say that the Leeds and Liverpool is a bit of a late-comer in the canal world! Mainly used for the transport of coal, it was a very successful and efficient carrier, well able to survive railway competition. It was only when road transport developed after the First World War that trade on the canal really declined and regular traffic continued right up until 1972. This canal had a longer commercial life than most, and the reasons for that became clear when I biked along it.

I began my journey at the eastern end of the canal in Leeds, electing to walk into Leeds from the Industrial Museum at Armley Mills about two miles out of the city centre. I did it this way round because it is much easier to park and because the best way to find the terminus of a canal is to walk along the towpath until you run out of canal. Also after my experiences in the centre of Manchester I thought (rightly as it turned out) that the bike would be a liability. A light rain was falling on a grey sort of day but there was an excellent sand towpath, with the River Aire and industrial buildings effectively screened off by trees for the first part of the walk. The landmark clock tower of Leeds Town Hall soon came into view, along with many new tower blocks in red, blue, white and grey in the near distance.

When I reached the first of the tower blocks, I found they were situated overlooking the River Aire and the canal at a particularly murky and weed-ridden stretch. It just goes to show that when the phrase "waterfront development" is used, you cannot jump to any conclusions about the scenic value of that waterfront, and you have to think about the flood risk as well. (My rule of thumb is that all rivers flood sooner or later.) I remarked upon the flats to an angler.

"A lot of building been going on."

"Aye, boom-town Leeds!" he replied.

"Some of them look less roomy and comfortable than a narrow boat."

"I know what you mean, but they've been snapped up anyway and you should see the prices," he replied.

The canal terminated at Granary Wharf, under the railway station. Not wanting to give up just yet and with some ambition to at least locate the Royal Armouries Museum from the other side, I attempted to carry on. Following the river downstream, I passed the head offices of Asda Supermarkets, then the steaming Tetley's Brewery also hove into view. However I found my way barred by private flat developments by the side of the river. What right do these people have to privatise the waterfront? With difficulty, I eventually got back to the

Royal Armouries. The river Aire swirled below, muddy and totally unattractive. There was a barrier across this made up of orange barrels and an accumulation of debris up against it – where's the net man then?

But the worst thing of all was the mad over-development of high-rise buildings, mainly residential and concentrated around Clarence Dock. There were absolutely no green spaces, public facilities, cafes, pubs or shops in this area and it seemed that pure greed on the part of the developers (for the sales) and the council (for rates) had been allowed to dominate. Virtually no sign was left of whatever had been there before. This is the urban jungle, twenty-first century style, and what a disgrace it is.

Leeds is the principal city of West Yorkshire and unlike the unloved Bradford, it has every appearance of prosperity. I took a temporary job here with British Gas at the end of 1994. At the time, the city seemed a glamorous, grand sort of place, but as I looked at it today, with its functional shops on Briggate and Boar Lane, the brewery and the muddy river, it did not seem at all glamorous, and with the exception of the Town Hall, the City Markets and the Corn Exchange, not very grand either.

For all that, Leeds can be considered the beating heart of West Yorkshire and it is a magnet for people from outside the region. A lot of southerners are drawn to the universities. Quite a lot of these people like the city so much they never leave it. I met some of this type when I worked at the gas board.

Leeds' most famous citizen is the disk jockey and TV personality Sir Jimmy Savile – "Now then Now then! How's about that then, guys and girls? Clunk click every trip!" Jimmy started work down a coal mine at the age of 14 and used to do all-in wrestling two nights a week before finding his true métier behind a microphone, which set him on his path to the cigars and Rolls Royce. He worked part-time as a hospital porter at Leeds Infirmary for years after he became famous and is said to have raised £40 million for charity over 40 years. However there was always something rather ODD about him, wasn't there? I mean it's OK to act the lovable eccentric, dye your shoulder-length hair and so on, anything to escape the coal mine, but what about his relationship with the "Duchess", his mother, whom he worshipped? It was just too serious for his image. You could see behind the mask.

Back at Armley Mills, I took the bike out of the car and continued westwards on a promising-looking towpath as the sun began to break out. The sight of this part of the canal filled me with alarm. There were millions of midges, whole clouds of them, over the surface of the water. What on earth do these tiny creatures feed on? How many were going to end up in my eyes?

Apart from a large electricity installation and the odd factory, there wasn't a lot to suggest that I was in fact near the centre of a major metropolis, an illusion which persisted all the way out of Leeds. Not a bit like say Manchester where you are only too well aware of the inner-city suburbs. As the valley opened out to a broad meadow, I could clearly see the mediaeval ruins of Kirkstall Abbey. As the sun shone I began to feel much better about Leeds. I take it all back. Finest provincial city in England.

A number of cyclists whizzed past - how do they go so fast? I still haven't worked it out, but whatever they are taking, I need some of it, a lot of it in fact. Eventually I arrived at a place called Rodley, from the number of people here obviously a local beauty spot. It didn't look that beautiful to me, but then I don't live in Bradford, the next city along. One towpath user congratulated me loudly for having a bell:

"Brilliant! You're the first one!"

Why don't the other bikers have bells?

The towpath was good and I eventually went mad and risked high ratio. There are three ratios on my bike but up to now I have only ever used the middle one. In the high ratio I began to whiz along – whehey! Middle ratio is for wimps! This is how the other guys do it. The next place of note was Apperley Bridge, about six miles by now from Armley. As I approached I could see a tremendously smart school with wonderful green lawns off to the north, with a cricket game in progress in the grounds. Clearly a public school, there is an obvious market for it. After all the comprehensives in Bradford must be fearsome. I found the school later on my map: Woodhouse Grove Public School.

I did rather wonder what George Orwell, would have to say about a place like that. Orwell had the misfortune to attend both preparatory and public school (Eton) as a scholarship boy. The fact that the other children came from families much better off than his left him with a gigantic and unerasable chip on his shoulder. Partly this explains his disdain for English civilization, which he described in *Homage to Catalonia* as sneering, hard-boiled and class-ridden. But he put his own adopted son down for Eton.

Soon I arrived at the canal basin at Apperly Bridge where there is a whacking great stone mill of the type in which the area specializes, right next to the waterway. Were it not for that you could pass by here on the Leeds & Liverpool blissfully unaware that you were on the edge of Bradford. The basin itself was full of boats but there was little sign of life even on this sunny afternoon. After this point, the canal entered another pleasant rural stretch. Really, this journey from Leeds had been much nicer than I had expected.

I carried on for another four miles or so to the outskirts of Shipley, the next town along. At one point there was an almighty splash in the canal, as if a log or a dog had gone in, but turning for a better view, there was nothing to see. Then it happened again. Three anglers were looking on with interest.

"What was that?" I asked, mystified.

"A fish," said one of them.

"A fish?"

"Aye, a big pike. We get them this big in this canal."

He indicated a size of just short of a yard.

"They can weigh twenty pounds!" he added.

Whatever it was, it was certainly no tiddler, but was this just another angler's tale? I was to find out, eventually, that it was no angler's tale.

I turned for home. The generally fast towpath, the best I had ever had, had beguiled me into staying out too long. I had been able to go much faster and further than I ever had on the South Pennine Ring and by the time I turned round I must have been fourteen canal miles out from the centre of Leeds. The good part about the return journey was the locks. I have never gone so fast on a bike as I did going past these. On previous canals the towpaths had not been good enough, but this time I must have hit thirty or even forty miles an hour. That may not seem a lot to you, because it feels almost like crawling in a car. On a bike, believe me, it does not – in fact you are hanging on for dear life. You know that if you hit a bump and come off, your face will hit the dirt at thirty miles an hour. Now that would make a fairly nasty mess of it, in fact it would push your nose right into your brain. Up to now I had never dared to go so fast.

Half-way back I began to flag and as my breathing got heavier and I felt a distinct pain in my chest. I slowed down and the feeling passed, but how close am I to that heart attack?

*   *   *   *

To get back to Shipley I had to drive through Bradford, and I stopped off to look around. The Leeds & Liverpool skirts round the northern edge of it and does not go into the city. There was once a branch called the Bradford Canal which led up to the city centre. Nicknamed the "River Stink", it was shut down to general relief in 1922 and has not been revived.

Of course no one has a kind word to say about Bradford. It has a Pakistani community of 60,000 people at least, but you know, out of a population of 300,000 (no one is quite sure how many, least of all the Census), that still leaves a lot of white people. The city centre does have some surprisingly grand buildings including the Florentine town hall, St George's Hall (a concert venue) and a nice Teutonic-looking cluster on Hustlergate. The more modern stuff is predictably dreadful, though one concrete monstrosity, the head offices of the Nationwide building society, had vanished since last time I was there. However, whenever you ask an old Bradford hand about it, they always say the same thing: Bradford used to have two department stores, Busbys and Brown & Muffs, they are no longer there and the shops are awful. But it isn't all bad news. Some of the old mills including the magnificent Lister Mills at Manningham are being redeveloped at last, there are many shiny new bank and building society offices around the ring road, and the city is actually growing! It is popular because of its cheap housing – every morning, thousands of commuters take the train to Leeds to work. As a matter of fact, the housing in Bradford – especially on the western or Pennine side – is not only cheaper than Leeds, but nicer as well.

One consequence of Asian immigration is Bradford's reputation as a good place to buy a curry, which is inexpensive, pretty good and practically guaranteed to give you a rich farting experience the following day.

One name which will forever be associated with Bradford is that of Peter Sutcliffe, the Yorkshire Ripper, who was born in nearby Bingley and who was living in Bradford at the time of his arrest. He is known to have attacked 23 women, of whom 13 were murdered outright. The attacks began in 1975 and continued with horrifying frequency until 1981. Many of his victims were prostitutes, but some were not, for example Jayne MacDonald, an exceptionally pretty 16 year-old shop assistant from Leeds, killed in 1977. Her father was said to have died of a broken heart not long afterwards. Another dreadful case was that of Josephine Whitaker, a 19 year-old building society clerk who was murdered on parkland in Halifax, only a few hundred yards from my house, in 1979. I remember driving over to Halifax from Blackpool with my wife one Sunday evening at the beginning of 1981, when the news came over the radio that a man thought to be the Ripper had been arrested. A tremendous wave of relief surged over us. Living through the Ripper's reign of terror is something that few local people are likely to forget.

Bradford has other famous sons, including the artist David Hockney, but he is a Yorkshireman of whom I am not proud. He went to live in California, which I think shows poor taste, and any schoolboy could paint better pictures. Also from here is the former England cricket captain, Brian Close. In the days before cricketers wore helmets, he used to stand ludicrously close to the batsman, a field position known as silly point. The idea was to crowd and intimidate the batman, and it worked often enough, at the expense of a knobbly skull. He was never a great cricketer - Garfield Sobers said of him "Can't bat, can't bowl, and if he stood that close to the wicket in the West Indies, he would get killed." But he was very combative – a typical Yorkshireman – and his sides were very successful.

*   *   *   *

So I arrived at Shipley, a town which offers the odd combination of a BMW dealership and an Aldi supermarket. I parked up and set off near a group of young people including a one-parent family. I sometimes wonder at this modern social arrangement (not permitted when I was a teenager). I mean, there is an obvious sort of biological drive behind it, but it would not seem to benefit anyone – the father, who may be pursued by the Child Support Agency for years ahead, the baby, who has after all only half the optimum number of parents, or the mother, whose prospects with other men are forever blighted. Having said that I must be missing something because it is certainly popular.

I faced the journey ahead with some reluctance. Some days I was raring to go, but other days I was not, especially on cool, overcast, drizzly days like this one, and I had definitely overdone it the previous day. Shall we say the joys of biking are intermittent. Maybe the problem is that I am still not a real biker, not hard and tough like those muscular athletes in the Tour de France but a potato dragged reluctantly from his nice soft couch. Think about that blood pressure! I could die of its consequences! (Well, at least there would be no more brown envelopes to deal with from the Inland Revenue).

I picked up the canal and headed towards Saltaire. The towpath here was the scene of a brutal sexual assault and murder in 1977, one of the most prominent cases in which new technology finally located the killer. The victim was called Mary Gregson (38), a cleaner at a mill who was attacked as she was walking to work. The murderer was not found until a new technique called DNA Low Copy Number was used to obtain a DNA sample from a semen stain on the victim's clothing in the year 2000. The murderer was a van driver called Ian Lowther, who had been 24 at the time of the crime. The police collected a swab from him - he confessed that he had waited over 20 years for that knock on the door. The victim's sister said he didn't look like a murderer, but by then he was a mild and shy 47 year-old grandfather of four. One day he had got drunk and attacked the woman out of the blue. Her husband, mother and father all went to their graves not knowing who the murderer was. She was from Saltaire.

I soon arrived at Saltaire itself, home of the famous model village built in the nineteenth century by the puritanical Titus Salt. A whole complex of building is here – massive stone mills, terraced houses, church, park, institute, school, hospital and square-with-lions. Of course there are no pubs. Titus Salt was a nineteenth century millionaire and he used his money to create monuments to himself in stone. However, millions do not pass happily down the generations. Only 40 years after the building of Salt's Mill, the Salt family had to sell up and get out.

Of course Victorians like Titus Salt were into religion in a big way, but it wasn't always like that. The English are of course just about the most godless people on earth these days, but they were much the same three hundred years ago. Then along came a religious revival inspired by John Wesley and more importantly by Handel and his Messiah. For two hundred years after its first performance in 1742 this was the England's most popular piece of music. You could say it changed the landscape because without it I doubt that churches like Salt's exotic United Reform Church would ever have been built.

*   *   *   *

The next day I planned to visit the famous Five Rise Locks at Bingley, one of the most spectacular sights on any canal in England. Designed by one John Longbotham of Halifax and build by local stonemasons in 1774, the locks carry the Leeds & Liverpool Canal up nearly 60 feet in a cascade 320 feet long. They are one of the "Seven Wonders" of the

British Canal system. The other six include the Burnley embankment, also on the Leeds and Liverpool. Not far away from that is the Barton Swing Aqueduct over the Manchester Ship Canal, built in 1893 on the Bridegwater Canal. Then we have the Pontycysyllte Aqueduct on the Langollen Canal, probably the most famous of all. After that is the Anderton Boat Lift between the River Weaver Navigation (in Cheshire) and the Trent and Mersey Canal, built in 1907. The most unusual "Wonder" is the Foxton Inclined Plane, a form of boat lift in the Leicester section of the Grand Union Canal, opened in 1900. This was built to by-pass a set of 10 locks but was closed as early as 1910 and never reopened. In the south are the Crofton steam beam engines, part of a pumping station near Devizes on the Kennet and Avon Canal. Finally there is the Harecastle Tunnel, north of Stoke on the Trent and Mersey Canal, a mile and a half long. I would be seeing more of these Seven Wonders before the summer was out.

To get to the Five Rise locks I set off from Saltaire and made my way up the leafy canal, arriving soon at the Dowley Gap. Here there is a large aqueduct which carries the canal over the River Aire. From now on, for many miles, the canal would skirt the foot of Ilkley Moor, hallowed land for Yorkshire people. There is nothing special about the moor, there are many more like it, but there is only one *Ilkley Moor Baht 'At*. This is not just a Yorkshire song. Whenever you get a huddle of English people seeking to raise their spirits a tight corner, they will invariably all sing it.

Just along from here I passed a middle-aged couple, giving them the old ting-a-ling.

"What a grand little bell!" exclaimed the man.

So glad you like it! I soon arrived in Bingley where I had some difficulty with an unexpectedly steep set of locks. These turned out to be the Three Rise locks, the little sister of the Five Rise locks. A few hundred yards up the towpath was the main event itself. I think it says something for my progress that I was actually prepared to tackle this on a bike – a few weeks ago, I would have dismounted automatically and walked it. Really, it didn't look very far, only 120 yards or so, but it was horribly steep – each lock is 12 feet deep, very big for a lock. As they are back-to-back, there is no respite between them.

I selected the lowest possible gear, number one out of 24. At first this felt as if I was pedalling thin air, no weight on the pedals at all, but this feeling did not last long. Come on, you can do it! Up I went. I was soon straining at every sinew, I mean, very soon. It was like pushing a boulder uphill. I tried to keep going but at the foot of the top lock my front wheel turned sideways and refused to go on. Damn! Still unfit! So I walked it to the top, where some curious onlookers gazed at this pink and sweaty creature. It's great to have an audience! This short burst of intense exercise knackered me for the rest of the day.

There was a lock-keeper here and I spoke to him after getting my breath back.

"How long does it take to come down the locks?" I asked.

"Twenty or twenty five minutes to come down, but twice that to go up."

"Pretty quick really."

"Oh yes, if you can organize it to come down!"

The lock keeper handed me a leaflet which stated that "all cyclists using the canal must display a British Waterways cycling permit, available free of charge from a local British Waterways office." A permit? Whatever for? Why bother if it's free anyway? And where could I find one of these offices, I hadn't seen one yet? Sod the permit. If they catch me it's nothing that a bit of plastic surgery and a new identity as Juan Ricardo Iglesias from Peru won't fix.

CHAPTER 12

My blood pressure before setting out for the day towards was 171/83 at 12 pm, which is like first the bad news, now the good. Of course I knew I could have got a better reading by taking it at 9 am when I was bright-eyed and bushy-tailed – well at least awake and upright - because it goes up as the day goes on. But why delude myself? I need to know the reality and at 12 pm that was the reality. What would it be like if I was at work? Probably 220/110 by 5 pm. All I know is this – once your blood pressure goes up, you've the devil of a job to get it down again. My doctor doesn't think my case is that serious, but I know different. If I carry on like this I shan't reach 65 and there will be no retirement for me, no sipping Yorkshire Tea on some shady verandah in the Provencal hills.

So on a sunny day I rejoined the Leeds and Liverpool Canal at Riddlesden, the place where the former Chancellor of the Exchequer Dennis Healey (Silly Billy) was brought up. He must have walked on this canal hundreds of times. Because the canal runs along the side of a hill at this point, there is quite a good view looking back across to Keighley. Behind it the moors were clearly visible, the setting for the Bronte novels. I find these interminable and turgid like all nineteenth century classics, and written as far as I can make out for female consumption only. I have never succeeded in finishing one of them. Nevertheless, *Wuthering Heights* is part of the nation's iconography, and a pretty important part at that.

As the views improved, so did the number of moving boats. I entered a shaded passage of bluebell woods where tall oak trees hung over the canal from both sides. Everything was still green and fresh in the country after a long dry spell. The Aire Valley below looked green and fertile, with more tree-clad hills rising on the other side. I thought, you know, you could do a lot worse than this. In fact I have heard good things said about this place and there are moorings (but no facilities) here at Low Wood, next to an old quarry, where boaters have been known to linger for days. The scenery was idyllic but it was noisy with a main road and a railway running through the valley below.

The towpath degenerated to a bumpy, stony track past Low Wood but the scenery was becoming more Dales-like by the minute with sheep in the fields and limestone outcropping higher up. However the small town of Silsden was anything but Dales-like. Situated half-way between its two posh neighbours, Skipton and Ilkley, Silsden is the poor relation at the Christmas party. There is a fairly big aqueduct in the middle of town and there was a group of young people here, late teenagers of both sexes, out in the sun. Their skins were completely white.

I saw some more white flesh a bit further along as my way was blocked by a solid-looking man on a racing bike. He had huge, white, pasty legs below his lycra skin-tight biking shorts (the sort they love in Italy). I couldn't stand to watch this for long and managed to get past. You may think it unusual for me to overtake anybody (it is) but he was having a terrible time on his racing bike with its narrow, low-profile tyres. Those are designed for fast roads, not a bone-crunching towpath like this. My Mongoose is a mountain bike with nice fat tyres and for once I felt as if I had the right equipment. I bet he had one of those horrid racing saddles as well, the sort that bites so hard into delicate areas of flesh. I had one as a teenager. I asked for the one on the Mongoose to be changed to a broader model before I took the bike home. From the look on the face of the guy with the white Queen Anne table legs, it had been a good move. I could hear him after I had gone past.

"Shit! Fucking towpath!"

The next village along was Kildwick, looking old and quite pretty, though opposite more industrial towns, Cross Hills and Glusburn. I must have passed a geological boundary after this because Kildwick was the last town built of sandstone. Bradley, the next village, was built of limestone.

I was now 3 miles south of Skipton and by this time beginning to wonder what exactly had happened to the bane of my life, the canal lock. I hadn't seen one since Bingley. This was clearly quite a different type of canal to the Rochdale or the Huddersfield Narrow. You may recall that the run back uphill from outside Huddersfield to the Standedge Tunnel – 31 locks – had practically killed me. Even if you don't recall it, I do. Anyway I could put up with a lousy towpath like this because the other trans-Pennine canals also have lousy towpaths and lousy locks as well.

At Bradley there is a swing bridge operated by the boat people themselves from an electronic control panel, and it was in use as I passed by. Clearly new, the machinery causes a barrier to close off the roadway and then the bridge swings out of the way to let the canal craft through. There were two middle-aged couples from Ireland on a narrow boat.

"Where have you come from?" I asked.

"We started out in Sowerby Bridge."

"How long has it taken you to get here?"

"Four days."

"Four days?"

"We were held up for one day because some pranksters managed to drain a section of canal we were just going to use, so we had to wait for that to be refilled, and then we arrived at the Five Rise Locks at Bingley just after 6 pm when the locks close."

"Where are you going?"

"Burnley."

It seems that they had hired the boat for a week and would get no further than Burnley, perhaps 70 or 80 canal-miles but with plenty to see along the way. Other boat people I met later seemed to manage 20 miles a day.

There were herons on the canal, and many swans – you don't see them in Failsworth and Ancoats but they like it here in the Dales. Opposite the Snaygill boat yard there were notices warning of aggressive nesting swans but a swan doesn't need to be nesting to be aggressive and one of a gaggle I saw squabbling over bread leaned over and nipped another in the neck.

This section of canal was the busiest I had seen so far with lots of narrow boats going in both directions and some well-used passenger pleasure craft as well, operated by Pennine Boats of Skipton. I saw two of these on the water and there must have been fifty or sixty people on both of them. A lot of them were ladies of a certain age and it did cross my mind that some of them might be from the Rylstone Women's Institute. They might want to take off their clothes to pose for a calendar – Rylstone is quite nearby! The Rylstone ladies satisfy the British penchant for unlikely celebrities in much the same way as Steve Gough, the naked walker, Anne Widdecombe, Johnny Rotten and of course the Tamworth Two, the porcine escapologists.

The town of Skipton itself did not begin to look pretty until the canal opened out into a basin where a spur called Springs Branch goes off towards the town centre, the canal banks attractive with overhanging trees and gardens. It was all very lively – ducks, swans, lots of tourists and boats. Skipton is known as the gateway to the Yorkshire Dales. A lot of its visitors pass through here on their way to Grassington, Malham and other points in the Dales proper. It is an important market town with attractive Georgian and Victorian buildings, good shops, including a Rackhams department store, and a genuine old castle. When I was there hundreds of tourists were wandering about, many of them tucking into fish and chips, which looked quite good.

Setting out on my bike north-westwards from the centre of Skipton I passed a pub/restaurant called the Herriot, and I wondered what the Dales people thought of their famous adopted son who did so much to publicize, I might say glorify, the area. James Herriot would certainly appreciate the idea of a restaurant named after him, because his books are full of descriptions of delicious meals with thick, juicy slabs of farm-cured ham, mouth-watering steak and kidney pudding and apple pie with lashings of fresh cream. But he would never have written his books if he had stayed in Glasgow instead of moving to Yorkshire. And he wasn't the only one. Bill Bryson took a sensible decision for a footloose American, and brought up his family near here as well.

Unlike me, James Herriot was a man who relished his food – even foreign food on a Dutch ship. The foreigners always knock our food, but it suits our bland climate. I mean, you can fanny about all you like with your mixed leaves, extra virgin olive oil and sun-dried tomatoes when you get back from your holidays in Italy, but it won't be long before you are opening a can of baked beans and a bottle of Branston Pickle.

When I was working in Italy one of my colleagues, a young Spanish woman called Barbara, could not understand my attitude toward Italian food. By that I mean the food that is served in Italy, not the food that you can buy in an Italian restaurant in northern Europe.

"Don't you like it?" she asked, incredulously.

"As a matter of fact, no, I don't. I much prefer English food, typical English food."

"Huh! There's no such thing as typical English food!" she snorted. This was not the first time I had heard this attitude from a European, which just goes to show how little they really know. I mean, it's well-known that you can't buy proper Marmite anywhere else, not even in Australia. Steak and kidney pie and jellied eels are unknown even in Germany, and a decent pork pie is unobtainable outside of Britain. Also of course we have dandelion and burdock, chicken tikka massala, rogan josh and chicken satay. I mean to say. Again, just think of the things that Europeans eat that we do not. Snails, frog's legs, quail, pigeon, endives, artichokes, chopped spinach, sauerkraut and lentils (extremely un-English), potato dumplings, polenta or any other maize-flour dish, squid, pumpkins, sheep's brains, and horseflesh. You won't be served any of that lot along the Leeds and Liverpool Canal.

The path virtually disappeared in several sections, being replaced by a well-maintained grassy bank. This looked all right but it was hard going on a bike, because the ground beneath the grass was hard and bumpy. Though progress was far from rapid I felt no envy either for the people in cars or for the walkers, because there is something very satisfying about the pace of a bike. Driving is far too fast if you want really to see anything, walking is too slow, and if you are on a narrow boat, you have to wait for the locks to fill.

The scenery was good in that unspectacular way which is so typical of the Dales – there are few grand sights and no big mountains, but just the same it is very chocolate-box. The canal and the countryside were very quiet, with just the odd boat passing in the water. The crews of the moving boats were surprisingly young. Some of these young men and women wore jaunty sailor's hats, which seemed a bit much for a canal, but then why not if it puts you in the mood? As some of these people were drinking beer, I began to wonder if you can be breathalysed for being drunk in charge of a barge. Is there an equivalent of careless driving? I suppose there must be, you could do a lot of damage if you rammed a lock.

Apparently legislation does exist to cover what you can and cannot do on a narrow boat, particularly in respect of cargo. The authorities became nervous about this when a barge carrying 5 tons of gunpowder on the Regent's Canal exploded with a terrific bang at Macclesfield Bridge in Regent's Park, right in the middle of London, in 1874. The accident killed several crewmen and caused considerable consternation in Parliament where there remains to this day the fear of another gunpowder plot.

The large village of Gargrave hove into view to my left. Here there was a cricket ground. Seeing this reminded me that the great Yorkshire fast bowler Freddie Truman had gone to live in a Dales village on his retirement from the game. In cricket, slow bowling requires finesse and sleight of hand, whereas fast bowling, while demanding accuracy, is basically brute force. Freddie had about as much finesse as a heavy dragoon in a cavalry charge. He gave out that he had weighed thirteen pounds at birth, had been reared in troglodytic conditions down a coal mine, ate broken bottles for breakfast, and was perfectly capable of bowling out the Aussies before tea on the first day with wild, terrifying and brutal beamers aimed at the head. When a young man, Fiery Freddie was the very image of pride, aggression and defiance. He epitomized the Yorkshire spirit of the time, and we loved him for it.

At Gargrave I found something I had not seen for some time – a lock – in fact about eight of them. These were the first locks since the Bingley Five Rise, 17 miles away by now. There was also a coal depot here, the first I had seen. It only occurred to me at this point that if you wanted to keep warm on a canal boat, probably the best way would be to light a coal fire – that must be what the chimneys are for! Here also were signs of active maintenance – a couple of dredgers, a strimmer-man with a face mask and a cheerful lawn mower man moving in a cloud of dust who kindly stopped his machine and said "Oreet" to me.

At the top of Gargrave locks I stopped to pass the time with a boatman who was sitting on a deck chair on the bank beside his boat. He looked about 60 and I noted that he had a motor bike strapped to his barge, which seemed a very good idea, though this chap looked anything but an Easy Rider.

"Are you on holiday?" I asked.

"Holiday? Me? No, I've given up with life on the land, this is my home now."

"OK in summer I guess."

"OK in summer and winter. A lot of the canals close for five months in winter so I moor up in Sowerby Bridge or some such place. Been doing this three years now, you can't beat it. You never know where you are going to be from one day to the next."

"What can you do in winter?"

"Potter about, paint spoons, make candles! But I go and see my family as well."

"Which is your favorite canal?"

"Good question. I think my vote for scenery would be the Llangollen Canal. It heads into the mountains in Wales and there's a famous viaduct on it. The problem is that it's the busiest canal in the country, you can't get a mooring. Best to go in October after the main season is over. I quite like this canal as well, it's nowhere near as crowded as some."

"Any one you don't like?"

"Some canals round cities like Manchester are prone to vandalism and you have to dash through if you can. They put glue in the lock mechanisms, that sort of thing. Idiots. They've done a lot of work on the canal banks around Birmingham, expensive flats and the like, so that's better than you would expect. It's still grim in parts but I avoid the area anyway, I come from there."

"Can you manage a narrow boat on your own? Don't you need someone to go ahead and open the locks?"

"When I'm touring I often have some family with me. Otherwise I try to pair up with another boat, but I can manage on my own."

"How do you open the paddles when you are in your boat in the bottom of a lock?"

"I climb up the ladders on the side."

"I wondered what they were for!"

My Dad once visited these locks and reported an unusual incident. According to his report, two narrow boats had entered one of the locks heading downstream, and the water level was falling quite quickly, when one the boats reared up in the water. A look of panic crossed the face of its boatman, who appeared to be alone. He had tied the boat to the top of the lock and forgotten to untie it. The rope stretched rapidly taught and it didn't seem to be likely to break. The boat people watched powerless and open-mouthed as one end of the narrow boat came right out of the water. The stricken boatman meanwhile grabbed a hammer and hit the rope frantically where it crossed a steel ledge at the edge of his boat. The rope stretched tighter and tighter as the narrow boat reared up at forty degrees and twisted round. Suddenly the rope snapped where the boater had been hitting it and the boat crashed down into the lock, releasing an almighty wash before settling on the water. Everything seemed to be all right and the boater was clearly relieved, with the others shouting encouragement, but it just goes to show, one slip like that and you could sink.

Not far beyond Gargrave, the canal passes over the River Aire below on an aqueduct at a very picturesque spot called Priest Holme. I had passed through Gargrave in a car countless times and never seen this place, which is a good reason for being on a bike. At this point the canal builders must have come to a decision – it is all very well mucking about in the Dales like this but we really have to get into Lancashire! So the canal leaves the Aire Valley and crosses over the divide into the drainage system of the Lancashire Calder, a tributary of the Ribble. It is rather confusing that this Lancashire Calder has exactly the same name as the Yorkshire Calder along which I passed a few chapters ago, but it is a completely different river.

There was a glorious view looking north up the valley of the upper Aire from the aqueduct. A pretty copse spread across one part of the skyline, sheep were bleating and drinking in the river below, a railway viaduct had been built to one side – really if I were a painter I would come just here. This has got to be another of my Top Ten Sights of the North British Canals. To shake me from my reverie a huge train marked "British Gypsum" roared past on the viaduct, no doubt carrying the limestone which the canal was built to transport.

Places like this remind me that there is plenty to see and to do in old England and you do not have to suffer outrageous heat in the process. I read that half a million English people have bought property in Europe, many in France, but is it that good there? France is quite a large country, four times the size of England. It is mainly rural and full of thousands and thousands of small towns and villages, known as "trous" – holes; the French do not like living in these places. There is little work and nothing to do. If you are a French woman of a sexually voracious nature, such as Catherine Millet, whose blatant book *The Sexual Life of Catherine M* merely confirmed what many Anglo-Saxons had long suspected about French women, there is little scope for your activities. What the French like is a smart flat in town.

Therefore, with admirable Gallic logic, they are now in the business of selling off the houses in these villages "en masse" to the gullible English middle classes, who have little discernible interest in extramarital sex and only long for the sun. They in their turn are discovering that there is no work and nothing to do. Provided that they buy into the lifestyle, however, they can be made surprisingly welcome by the French, who will make them *chevaliers de fromage* if only they will learn the language. The French are like the Americans in this respect – in fact probably only in this respect, as in most other respects the Americans think the French are cheese-eating surrender monkeys. Personally I have had enough of France after a couple of weeks of it and want to get back to my valleys, moors, blackened houses and real life in the wind and rain or even, like today, in the sun. But I am just typical. A recent survey of regional names revealed that Yorkshire people are the most reluctant of any in the country to leave their native county, and the reason to me is obvious – this is God's Own County after all.

So I turned round - I knew I would struggle to get back to Skipton on the rough canal bank. On the way back I got a couple of flies in my left eye – so that's why cyclists wear goggles! This eye looked as if it had got a bunch of fives from Mike Tyson when eventually I was able to look at it in the car mirror. I arrived back in

Skipton absolutely knackered. Of course the towpath was crowded and I had to deal with the lamebrain pedestrians. I mean I rang my bell and some would move aside politely, but quite a few others were thrown into confusion and stayed in the way, meaning that I had to stop. Just get out of the way PLEASE! Some of them looked rather alarmed, it must have been that eye of mine.

When got back to my car, after two and a half of hours on the bike, my shoulders, neck, hands, legs and especially bottom all ached so badly that I longed to get off. So much for my original idea that I would spend all day on the bike – when would that day ever come? Never, at this rate. I reloaded the bike across the back seat and slumped exhausted into the driving seat. On the way up to Skipton I had listened to a program about the benefits of exercise on Radio 4. It said that doctors only began to think that exercise is good for you about 50 years ago, but the question is, are they right? It just wears me out!

The Leeds and Liverpool Canal in Lancashire

NORTH   **SOUTH**

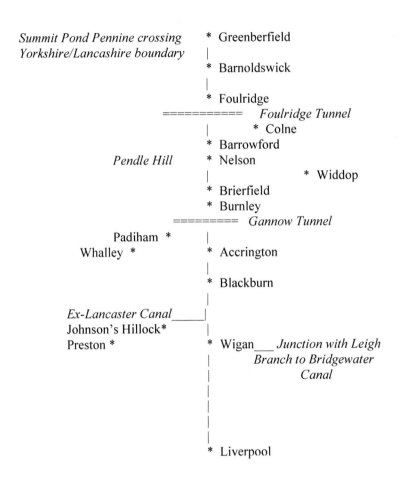

Summit Pond Pennine crossing   * Greenberfield
Yorkshire/Lancashire boundary |
                                        * Barnoldswick
                                        |
                                        * Foulridge
                       =========== *Foulridge Tunnel*
                                        | * Colne
                                        * Barrowford
           Pendle Hill   * Nelson
                                        | * Widdop
                                        * Brierfield
                                        * Burnley
                       ========= *Gannow Tunnel*
           Padiham * |
           Whalley *   * Accrington
                                        |
                                        * Blackburn
                                        |
*Ex-Lancaster Canal*_____|
Johnson's Hillock* |
Preston *   * Wigan___ *Junction with Leigh*
                                        | *Branch to Bridgewater*
                                        | *Canal*
                                        |
                                        |
                                        |
                                        |
                                        * Liverpool

CHAPTER 13

Picking up the canal the next day where I had left it at Priest Holme, I soon arrived at Newton locks. Here I found some leaflets which I perused with interest. It seemed that there was some sort of event organized for canal people in the region every weekend over the summer. Of course I knew nothing about this because I am not a real canal person any more than I am a real biker, I am a fraud and impostor canal person.

Near here was a pretty, square-shaped house – one might almost say hall – with a stone roof called Newton Grange: "For a stay in the countryside". You could do a lot worse – it was the sort of place where Toad of Toad Hall could step out of the door at any moment, smile benignly, then step back inside. There was a herd of black sheep outside it, something I have never seen before. It must have been a special breed because they were all the same colour, black with a white flash on the face. They were presumably unaware of the social stigma of being black sheep, in fact they must be so rare that they look down on the common-or-garden white trash sheep.

A mile or so further on I came across some more sheep, this time on the canal bank itself. I scattered them in all directions with one ting-a-ling of my magic bell. Still, they were impossibly cuddly-looking animals, clean and covered in thick wool. Wild sheep have virtually no wool – just a woolly end to their natural hair – and little resemble these. I have heard people who work with sheep say that they really are stupid animals, but you know, you can't blame the sheep for that. If a human steps in to protect and find pasture for a sheep, then a stupid one can do just as well as a clever one and so domesticated sheep have simply evolved smaller brains.

The engineer for the section of canal I was to ride along today was one Robert Whitworth, son-in law of the builder of the first industrial canal, James Brindley. In general the surveyors fell into two schools, led by James Brindley and Thomas Telford respectively.

Brindley's canals follow the lie of the land as far as possible and take a long route if necessary to avoid going up or down. The Leeds and Liverpool is very much this type of canal. The technique is demonstrated in these meanders here, west of Gargrave, and indeed it is very pleasing to the eye. Telford by contrast cut as straight a line as possible. To do this he used the technique of cut and fill, where spoil from one cutting is used to fill the next valley. This technique is still used in road construction. The difference in the two approaches also reflects the changing times, as the rustic Georgian era moved towards the Big Engineering of the Victorian era.

Heading on to East and West Marton, the canal snakes round the contours endeavoring to find a way down into Lancashire through hummocky country north of Barnoldswick. At East Marton are a couple of pubs/hotels and some moorings, and the Pennine Way crosses the canal here. Also, there was a sign advertising a 57-foot narrow boat for sale for £60,000. The cost of a boat is very variable in that some of them are little more than rusting steel tubs with room only for a galley and maybe a berth, while others are stretch-limo jobs with four sets of windows, gleaming interiors with copper kettles, and roses and castles painted on the outside. Those can cost £75,000 or even over £100,000, though there seem to be plenty of less ambitious boats on sale for under £40,000. You can even buy a timeshare on a narrow boat – I have seen one advertised at £8,600 for four weeks at different times of year. The highest price I have seen, for a perfectly ordinary-looking narrow boat called the Houseboat King, is £295,000! Along with the boat came a British Waterways mooring licence entitling the owner, for £3,500 a year, to live on the Grand Union Canal at Ladbroke Grove in London, with a postal address and the use of a bankside garden.

Just along from here I stopped to chat to an angler.

"Catch anything?"

"Yes," he replied, "a good-sized carp, an hour ago."

"You must know a trick or two because most of the anglers don't seem to catch much."

"Well you see those reeds across by the far bank? That's where the fish hide. You have to cast your line within a foot or two of them or you'll catch nowt all day."

"I'm surprised the fish survive in this muddy water."

"It's not that muddy, there are plenty of fish in this canal. Just the same the mud can be a problem. If you get a landslip into the canal in the winter the water gets saturated with silt. It clogs the gills of the fish and they suffocate and die, hundreds at a time. But water like this is OK."

Passing under a peculiar double bridge near West Marton, one arch built on top of another, the waterway finally crosses the county line into Lancashire at Greenberfield, north of Barnoldswick. Here three locks take it to its Summit Pool at 487 feet. After this point it is downhill all the way. I asked the lock keeper why this canal had ranges of locks and then long stretches with no locks – the next set were at Barrowford, maybe eight or nine miles downstream. He said it was just the lie of the land, but I do not believe that. You cannot say that the lockless 17 miles from Gargrave to Bingley (where there are 8 locks) is completely flat – the engineers constructed the canal in this way for a reason. They could have put in a lock every couple of miles. I believe it was thought more efficient to group the locks to give a good long pound in between. Also canals built this way were easier to administer, where each set of locks would have a lock keeper who could collect tolls.

At the locks I had a kingfisher sighting! The little chap was sitting on a balance bar and his presence was kindly notified to me by the lock keeper. There were also hundreds of seagulls in a newly ploughed field, but which is which? They are all the same colour and general shape and they all seem to have the same cry. There are dozens of different kinds of gull alone – herring, common, black-headed, yellow-legged, ring-billed, Mediterranean, lesser and great black-backed, kittiwake, sooty, Ross's, Sabine's, Pallas's and so on – not to mention terns, of which there are also many species, and which look just the same as gulls to me.

As you look around at Greenberfield, with its manicured lawns and pretty lock keeper's cottage, set in low dale country, you would never guess that you were at the highest point on a 127-mile-long waterway. If this were a canal like the Rochdale you would think you were only half-way up, but there it is. There were quite a lot of boats, and there are facilities marked "shower" and "sanitary station" so clearly many boaters overnight here.

I imagine that the job of a lock keeper at a place like Greenberfield is a much sought-after position. After all, anyone could do it – it would appear to require little in the way of special skills or training. The duties seem light, and the surroundings agreeable. In fact a lot of the British Waterways people do seem a bit jumpy, as if someone were about to say look, is that a real job? Perhaps they are like firemen, not a lot to do much of the time, but essential in an emergency. However there must be many ways in which you could earn a living doing something less useful. You could be a missionary, spending your life in China, only to see your whole life's work disappear in a revolution. You could be a member of the European Parliament. You could be a modern composer of serious music, writing non-tunes, knowing that no one will buy them or pay to listen. You could be an academic, a pure mathematician perhaps, devising algorithms and proofs in ever more abstruse dimensions with no application back in the real world. You could be a colonial administrator, carefully nurturing a society that will one day throw you out and self-destruct. You could sit on government commissions and quangos for the arts, or in the House of Lords. You could be a boffin devising ingenious instruments and experiments to put in a box which crash-lands on arrival on Mars. You could even be a TV archeologist. So much better the gentle life of minding a flight of locks.

Downstream from Greenberfield is the first of a string of unlovely industrial towns, Barnoldswick, where there is a large Rolls-Royce factory. Just here two cyclists whizzed past me. I sometimes think that these bikers make a point of going past me rather fast, as if they were beating me in a race, but I am not involved in a race, and I didn't buy a racing bike. If you want to go fast, you can go in a car. If you concentrate on speed, you miss half of what there is to see. Anyway, I don't do speed, I'm not up to it.

The countryside past Barnoldswick is low fells, a continuation of the Dales with the same fluffy sheep and muscular cows. Just north of Foulridge there are two boundary signs indicating the boundary between the West Riding of Yorkshire and Lancashire – but the map says otherwise, the boundary is north of Greenberfield. It is the same story if you go by road, where you will find a road sign marking the historic boundary of West Yorkshire. Barnoldswick and the area around it grew up as part of Yorkshire but was transferred to the Lancashire borough of Pendle at the 1974 local government reorganization. I knew someone from there who considered this an insult, and he was not alone, because the locals kept tearing up the new boundary signs. I also heard that only quite recently, Granada television (based in Manchester) sent a film crew to Barnoldswick to produce an item for the local TV news. However, no one in Barnoldswick saw it because their TVs are all tuned to Yorkshire TV. From the look of these signs here today I don't think they have got used to the idea yet. I can't say I blame them.

As a matter of fact, Yorkshire itself lost not only Barnoldswick but the whole of the attractive Forest of Bowland to Lancashire back in 1974. But Lancashire itself lost its most attractive area as well – the Furness district of what is now Cumbria. Before 1974, the county of Lancashire actually included Coniston Water and half of Lake Windermere!

So, the broad, beautifully maintained stretch of canal winds on a level to Foulridge, near Colne. Here is the northern portal of the Foulridge Tunnel, at 1640 yards long the biggest engineering feature of the whole canal. In 1912, a cow named Buttercup fell into the canal by the southern portal. Unable to get out, she chose to swim all the way to the other end, where she was revived with brandy by drinkers in the nearby Hole in the Wall pub. Ahead was the tunnel, which is controlled by a traffic light system and is so straight that you can see right through it, though the roof is quite low in places. Unexpectedly difficult rock conditions meant that construction took six years – an average of only 273 yards a year! In places they found it easiest to dig out the whole hill from the top down to the canal level, construct the tunnel and fill it all in again afterwards. Apparently the canal is prone to freezing up in the tunnel. At this high level and with no appreciable current, three inches of ice can form in single night. In the old days ice-breakers were used to provide a passage, apparently a sight worth seeing.

It was a busy little spot with lots of people chatting animatedly as they got into cars – the "Marton Emperor" tourist boat had just disgorged its passengers. Most of these people were white-haired old ladies, with very few men. Where had all the men gone? Dead, of course, most of them, from overwork. Now that is the very reason that I am here today on this canal on a bike. I don't want my wife to become one of these little old ladies, widowed 20 years ago and all alone ever since.

I returned to my car, tired as usual. Though I didn't push myself for speed, this had been a tough ride. I think I am overdoing it, going out every day like this. However at lunchtime the following day I took another blood pressure reading – 160/68. Though the top figure remains high, that is by far the lowest bottom reading I have ever had and no doctor would dream of putting my on pills with a figure like that. Maybe the biking is working after all! Maybe I am slowly opening out those arteries!

CHAPTER 14

Today I head out for east Lancashire, where my wife Christine's parents still live. She is from this area. That's one reason why I know so much about the benighted county. Although she has lived in Yorkshire for 25 years now, I don't think she would for one moment consider herself anything but a Lancashire girl. She's just happy she is living in Yorkshire.

As a matter of fact, it has been a great advantage to me to marry another northerner, because Christine had no desire to live in the south, and visiting her relations is easy. Also, most of her vowels are the same as mine, including the short "a" which distinguishes all northern accents from southern ones. This is the great divide in the English language, at least within England, over which no man can cross and remain the same. One of my schoolfriends did move to London and after a year or two he started calling a bath a barth. This caused hoots of derision back in Halifax of course, but I suppose he was under pressure from his peers in the south. Personally I would rather gouge my eyes out with spoons than do such a thing.

So, on we go. In this part of Lancashire we find Burnley, Nelson, Colne and the Pendle Hill country. When I first arrived in this area in the Seventies I was struck by a number of significant differences between East Lancashire and West Yorkshire. I suppose you can understand it as the populations are completely separated by a range of hills topped with uninhabited moorland. The first was the curiously folksy accent, strong and almost funny to listen to, in which the word order seemed oddly convoluted. For example, instead of saying "Don't you think?" they say "Do you not think?" Also the church and musical tradition which is so strong in West Yorkshire was less evident. Above all the towns looked much poorer – in fact they had every appearance of deep decline.

As I drove over the moors I was soon rewarded with a splendid view of Pendle Hill, an outlier of the Pennines on the far side of Nelson, which dominates the whole area. It is famous for its association with the witches of Pendle. These were real, historic people, the best-known of them one Alice Nutter of Roughlee Hall, who came to a sticky end after their trial at Lancaster Castle in 1612. Incidentally, "Pendle Hill" really means "Hill" in three different languages. "Pen" is a Celtic word for "hill", as in Pen-y-Ghent and Ben Nevis. "-dle" is an Anglo-Saxon suffix that also means "hill". The most interesting name for a hill is Kilimanjaro, which means "I don't know" in Swahili. Early explorer to guide: "What is the name of that striking mountain over there?" Guide: "Kilimanjaro".

I started out again at the southern portal of the Foulridge Tunnel. As far as Barrowford Locks, the countryside was green with low hills, very similar to what I had seen in Airedale in fact, and much too nice for Lancashire. The grassy Barrowford Locks are clearly a focal point on the canal with a bank of half or dozen or more big locks. Here was a lock keeper's cottage, in use by British Waterways. Two of their employees seemed to be filling a lock just for the hell of it, because there was no boat inside. Next to the canal was a reservoir, one of the ones which were built to feed the canal. There were many boats moored at the top end of Barrowford locks and I had seen a number of moving boats on the canal, in fact plenty of activity. I stopped to admire the flower display on one of the narrow boats when an older man stepped off. I recognised him – I was at school with his son, but I hadn't seen him for years. We fell into conversation.

"I bought this boat when I retired," he said. "Me and my wife had had one or two canal holidays and we thought, this is the life for us! So we sold our family home and bought a small terrace with half the money and this boat with the other half. Our plan is to cruise all summer and retire to the house in the winter. But why don't you come inside?"

Curious, I parked up the bike and went in to enjoy a cup of tea and a biscuit. This was evidently not a top-or-the-range narrow boat, in fact it was bordering on the scruffy, but I could see that the couple were proud of it. Inside it had a galley, a wood-burning stove, a bedroom and a sitting room area, though obviously, everything was narrow and elongated. There were old cushions and blankets scattered around. The owner, Derek, a very large man, continued:

"I worked as a manager in a factory. The children grew up and left home, so we made this decision. This is the way forward for the next few years."

"You could do a lot worse," I said. "Better than gin in the mornings in Spain."

I soon passed the M65 motorway – yes, a motorway, built to take the locals to Blackpool (as the M6 takes the Scots there). Going past Nelson it was evident that someone had evidently put a lot of work into the canal. It was clear of rubbish all the way down from Foulridge and there was an excellent towpath. A sign announced the "Pendle Cycleway" and this must be part of it. The verges were well-maintained, landscaped even, with plenty of trees; there were no nettles overhanging the way and even the bindweed was pretty. Such are the joys of my trip that I am beginning to know what bindweed looks like - straggly with nice flowers. Hey nonny no, the birds and the bees, the flowers and the trees!

The canal twisted on under pretty donkey bridges overhung by trees and though there was plenty of evidence of industrial activity, there were fetching glimpses of church spires and views across to Pendle Hill, and best of all, few reasons for the cyclist to dismount; all in all much better than say east Manchester. I came across a middle-aged couple were out picking blackberries and they had filled a couple of containers with this year's bumper crop.

"You seem to be doing well," I observed.

"Aye," said the man, "not bad. She makes a lovely blackberry and apple crumble."

There were lots of canal birds – ducks and white geese in particular. I saw no swans but much better I hadn't seen a single Canada goose on the whole of the Leeds and Liverpool, someone must be shooting the bastards or they would surely be here. The canal birds seem to cluster at certain points, following some system of bankside apartheid with adjacent but non-mingling areas set aside for geese, ducks and pigeons. The geese spat at me a bit as I went past but yah boo shucks to you lot!

I came across a mini-grader on the path which up to now had been excellent. Here it was three times wider but rough and bumpy. Evidently an upgrade is in progress to make a cycleway where two bikes can proceed in parallel. I didn't mind this too much on the way down, but on the return journey the bumpy unfinished sections were so painful that I thought I might do something rather irreversible, such as crush a bollock or two.

At Lomeshaye there was a new-looking B & Q store and a motorway access point, just beyond a new-looking Morrisons supermarket and some new factories. Just next to the B & Q store stands a big old mill which is actually a cotton wool factory. I worked there as a warehouseman back in 1976 whilst looking for a proper job.

One day, the foreman asked for a volunteer to work the night shift for a week. No one came forward. As I was only regarded as temporary, he then asked me directly to do the job. Of course I didn't want to do it, working night runs up against my basic human instincts! So I demurred.

"Well," said the foreman, "we can always find someone else to do your job!"

Charming. So I did it. There were two of us on the job – the other guy did it every week. When it got to three in the morning, with four hours still to go, he said "That's it then, time for some shut-eye," took himself off behind a pile of boxes and went to sleep! I, of course, did the same.

Christine worked at the factory as well. The other women used to talk quite openly about their sex lives. One of them, Elaine, confided:

"I've been married 20 years and I have never had an orgasm in sex with my husband."

"You must have had."

"No, definitely not. He hides behind the bedroom door dressed in his underpants and jumps on me. It doesn't do anything for me."

Quite so, quite so! I finally arrived in the centre of Brierfield, which is just as grim as Nelson and Colne, and immediately noticed a new estate of smallish detached houses. Now back in 1976 new houses were being built in the area, but these were in outlying villages, definitely not in Brierfield and Nelson, where they were pulling houses down. Having taken this to be an area in deep decline I find that there is a motorway and new housing estates, superstores and industrial estates. Clearly things are turning the corner. There are McDonalds outlets everywhere too but I would rather they were not there.

Another thing I noticed was a fish and chip shop called Connelly's Plaice – now that *was* there in 1976 – surely it could not be under the same ownership? Back in those days it had been run by a man called John Connelly, formerly a football player for Burnley. At that time football players were not paid a fortune so he went into the catering trade when he retired from the game. The remarkable thing about it was that he had a beautiful blond wife and daughters to match, and they helped out in the shop. It was like being served fish and chips by Nordic goddesses, they looked far too good for the job.

On the way back I bumped a crashed though the "pathworks", which were a great trial to my sore arsehole, which must be an occupational hazard for cyclists. Though I hadn't been going that long on the day – maybe a couple of hours on the bike - I was suffering and sweating. Clearly I should have had a day off after my tribulations over the last few days – I must be a driven man by now! The sky was clouding over and rain started to fall, and I dreamed up a biker's lament:

Biking's a pain
When you're out in the rain
You can't escape
A knuckles scrape
Your bollocks thump
On a dreadful bump
And your arms and your legs
Are stiff as pegs
Your shoulders slump
You've got the hump
Your shins are scraped
The mud is caked
And your arsehole is sore
You can't take any more

I wearily loaded the bike into the car, watched carefully by four ladies of a certain age, all with dogs, sat on a bench opposite – all right ladies, I'm sweaty and tired, OK? Taking off in the car I drew in at the first garage, bought a Twix – something I have not done for years – and scoffed it down. That must be it – energy shortage!

After that I decided to take in Burnley as a day trip and follow up later with a canal ride. A town of 70,000 inhabitants, it did not look at all prosperous. There were blackened and burnt out mill buildings and there is little to see in the town centre. I only ever found small areas of good-quality housing built for the middle classes in the East Lancashire towns, and I have often wondered why this is. The towns of West Yorkshire such as Huddersfield and Halifax have many, many fine houses – some of them are mansions. One theory I have heard is that the "Power and loom" system was prevalent in Lancashire, whereby small groups of workers would hire part of a larger premises, paying for power and rent. Under this system there were no mill owners and few well-off people.

Not to be put off for long, I resumed on the canal the following day where I had left it previously at Brierfield, a good spot because there is parking provided. I don't much like trying to find a parking place in a town centre, or parking right outside someone's house, they give you funny looks, at least they did in Littleborough. I was keen to see this section of canal because it contains one of the "Seven Wonders" of British canals, the Burnley embankment.

Passing a derelict stone mill on the canalside, I soon found myself in a remarkably pleasant country stretch with view back to cows and sheep grazing on the flanks of Pendle Hill. The path was good and the area had that same landscaped look I had noted higher up. However I was soon back amongst the houses and factories with workmen in overalls enjoying an outdoor lunch in the lovely sunshine. This is more like it! The air was filled not only with the balmy sunshine but also with masses of floating willowherb seeds, the noisome weed propagating itself with vigorous efficiency. A "real" biker whizzed past, muscular legs, helmet, goggles, tight knee-length bike pants, you know the sort of thing. I don't go fast enough to need a helmet though my eyes are flytraps and I often catch one or two. The funny thing about the real bikers is that they invariably give me a broad grin and seem to regard me as one of them. Of course I grin back, I mean, what am I supposed to say: "Actually I am a complete fraud and not fit like you!"

Just the same, it was hard not to feel contented cycling along on an afternoon like this. It cost me nothing to be here, but there are in fact some things that money cannot buy, and indeed some of the things it can buy are more trouble than they are worth. If you are Elvis Presley it can buy you the right to eat yourself to death having made yourself look totally ridiculous first. If you are Robert Maxwell you can just steal the money and buy a gigantic yacht called the Lady Ghislane from which you can drown yourself when you are found out, to be regarded as a crook by all posterity. What money cannot buy is quiet enjoyment, and that is what you get riding a bike on a towpath on a sunny day.

Soon Burnley appeared below me, looking rather a long way down – was I going to have to go all the way down there? No! For I was on the Burnley embankment, three-quarters of a mile long, sixty feet above the town and a massive achievement for its engineer, Robert Whitworth, when it was built. It provides uninterrupted views over the slate rooftops on both sides, on to the moors beyond. However it is rather like the Ribblehead Viaduct in that you can't see it when you are on it. As I looked down on the industrial development below me, it seemed clear why this canal lasted so long as a commercial enterprise. It is broad, it has few locks, it finds a low and scenic passage though the Pennines, and just look at the number of important industrial towns on or near its banks – Leeds, Bradford, the Aire Valley towns, and now Colne, Nelson, and Burnley, with Accrington, Blackburn, Wigan and

Liverpool still to come, not to mention the many smaller but busy settlements.

From the embankment there was a particularly good view of Turf Moor, the home of the football club, which looked a very good ground indeed for a club the size of Burnley. Also there was row upon row of stone terraced houses, packed close together and just what you expect in a place like Burnley. On a glorious day like this, the views of the town afforded by the canal are a considerable improvement on what you get at street level. There was a certain amount of dereliction clearly visible but there was also some fairly large-scale new building going on, and a very smart new bus station. In the middle distance was the distinctive landmark green dome of the Mechanics Institute.

I passed a woman with a couple of fat, foreshortened grey bulldog-type dogs and asked her what they were. "Pugs" came the reply. There must be something wrong with them, their faces are all squashed in. I mean, if you are a dog, the class distinction between pedigrees and mongrels is presumably unknown, and if I were a nice black-and-tan mongrel I would steer clear of ugly pugs.

I dodged under a couple of semi-circular stone bridges built for midgets, then a steel railway bridge. Bridges with girders underneath, I have found, are pigeon territory, because they like to build their nests amongst the girders. There were quite a few people about and of course I had trouble with the usual deaf pedestrians. I rang my bell behind one man walking his dog and he called out:

"Thank you for ringing your bell, young man, I am a bit deaf!"

Not half as deaf as those that can hear, I thought, because no matter how loud I ring the bell, 20% of the walkers do not hear it.

Wait a minute – did he say "young man"? He did! Now it is true that I have never looked my age, and I still have all my hair and I haven't gone grey or lost any prominent teeth or other useful organs, but I just love it when people call me "young man". I know I am getting older internally but actually I don't mind getting older, provided I don't end up looking like someone who might frighten the grandchildren as say Keith Richards or Elizabeth Taylor might. There are distinct advantages in being older – I have more money and can take breaks from work and if I keep at it on the bike, one day I may even be able to stand up straight. Also I have been lucky. Towards the end of his life, George Orwell commented that at fifty, every man has the face he deserves. I have a face I don't deserve.

Soon I came to a place called Weaver's Triangle which had big signs up saying "Conserving and Regenerating this Historic Landmark".

The trouble was that apart from a couple of warehouses on the canal bank, one of which was a restaurant, the other To Let, there didn't seem to be much to conserve. Just along the way I found a narrow boat moored up, from its paintwork a hire boat from Snaygill boatyard outside Skipton. The boatman, bespectacled, middle-aged and middle-class, beamed cheerfully at me as I passed, so I thought I might stop. I asked if it was a hire boat and confirmed that it was.

"How are you finding it?" I asked.

"The boat's fine," he replied. "All mod cons. But there is one problem – I just don't think this industry is very well organized."

"How is that?"

"Well nearly all these hire places are small outfits that operate out of one basin and they want you to take the boat back. That means we shall have to turn round here and go back the way we came, which we don't especially want to do. If we could carry on going forward for a full week we might get as far as Wigan and see a lot more. If things were better organized we could leave the boat there and someone else could hire it for the return. It would be a much better deal for the customer."

Good point. So, I carried on and crossed over the M65 motorway on an aqueduct, soon arriving at Gannow Tunnel. This (I later found out) is 559 yards long and has no towpath. The stones of the tunnel entrance are decorated with hieroglyphics, like Babylonic cuneiform. Coming off the canal I asked the way. "Up the hill (very steep), down again, into the subway, main road, traffic lights, roundabout, ask again...." It sounded complicated, uphill and involving flights of stairs. Nothing for it but to press ahead through an ugly tangle of roads and a motorway junction but I made it back down to the canal, hot, sweaty and bothered. It emerged from the tunnel in Rose Grove, a dingy part of Burnley. There was quite a bit of plastic rubbish in the water and I saw no boats from this point on – something tells me not that many get past Burnley.

Coming out of Burnley and on past the moorings at Hapton, the views started to improve, and in fact I was amazed at just how good the prospect to the north was. There was a big industrial estate in the bottom of the valley of the Lancashire Calder, but beyond that in the middle and far distance, looking towards Whalley, the view resembled an eighteenth-century Arcadian painting by Claude Lorraine. The river cut a gorge through narrowing, plateau-like hills, and the fields below were lined with plump deciduous trees, row after row of them.

After one or two "cycleway" stretches the towpath deteriorated to a rocky, bumpy and bepuddled mess. Why the authorities build these cycleways, six feet wide and a dream to ride on, while leaving the rest of the towpath like this, is a mystery to me. Actually the cyclist only requires a good surface about six inches wide, nine at the most. I would gladly settle for a nine-inch hard surface along the whole canal instead of these cycleways and then muddy mantraps.

A group of three cyclists approached me coming the other way, dressed in all the gear, helmets, goggles, tights, on racing bikes. I always feel a bit out of place because I look like a pedestrian who happens to be on a bike. Properly dressed or not, the middle of the three bikers keeled over on the stinker towpath, right out of the blue, and rolled over the edge and into the canal. Now I know why cyclists wear goggles – so they can see underwater when they fall in the canal! I had been expecting this to happen to me for weeks, but I am so glad it happened to somebody else instead. His friends fished him out. He was about 35, dressed in a yellow T-shirt.

"You fell the wrong way," said one of them.

"I should have given up when I fell off back there!" he said. Evidently this was not the first time.

"It just goes to show, it's not as easy as it looks," I commented.

"Too damned right," he said.

In his shoes I think I would stick to the exercise bike and forget canals, they are nasty, I had known it from day one! But really, it served the silly sod right for trying to ride on a path like this on a racing bike with narrow tyres. He would have stayed on board on my Mongoose.

I moved on across a country stretch to Clayton-le-Moors and Accrington. At the first of these there was a large estate of brand new detached houses. These were built in a sort of ghastly pastiche of a Dutch gabled house with angles taken out of the roof, but a least they were new detached houses. I'm sure that thirty years ago no one would have dreamt of constructing such an estate in Clayton-le-Moors. Accrington itself looked a grim place, but again somewhat moved on from the bad old days of the Seventies when I used to drive through it, with plenty of new factories. I know a woman who taught at a sink comprehensive here for 20 years. In her time at the school, she taught eight children who were subsequently convicted of murder. She left when she was struck in a fight between two of her pupils. Walked straight out to her car and never went back.

On the outskirts of Accrington I passed a jogger, a woman of about 25. She was rather solid and looked in need to of the jog, but she was not at all flushed. She wasn't pretty so much as striking in appearance, with ultra-blond hair – almost white – blue eyes, and a pale complexion. She wore a white T-shirt and skin-tight blue lycra shorts down to the knee. As we crossed, she said "Thanks" as I moved aside. There was nothing remarkable about this encounter, except that 10 minutes later, we crossed again. How had she managed that? I was still heading west, she was still heading east. Did she have an identical twin sister? This time she smiled and said "Hi!". Shortly afterwards I noticed that my willy was poking out of my shorts (I don't wear underpants on these trips). Hells bells! Maybe she had seen this and driven round to have another look!

There was one lovely old ruined warehouse in mellow sandstone by the canal in Accrington, unfortunately not located in a place where anyone would be interested in a restoration. The canal looked semi-stagnant with polystyrene rubbish and traffic cones in it. However I was immediately cheered by the appearance of two narrow boats coming towards me. You really do not see that many moving boats, at least not on the canals I ride along, and they so enliven any waterway.

It was just here that I passed the half-way milestone for the Leeds and Liverpool canal. Surely I must be more than half-way along it by now! As the crow flies, I was, but canals were not dug in straight lines, far from it. Just across the canal was a golf course. It is surprising how often you see a golf course next to a canal. Really I wouldn't have thought it was a happy juxtaposition, how many balls do they lose?

Having passed underneath it twice since leaving Clayton-le-Moors, I came to the M65 again outside Rishton. Here the canal passes over the motorway on a magnificent stone aqueduct – it must be one of the biggest in the country, with a broad tarmac road instead of a towpath. Here I turned round.

I took a blood pressure reading at home in the evening and scored 160/100. This is no improvement at all! Mind you it was 9 pm at night and I was tired, so I shall try again in the morning, when it is always lower.

CHAPTER 15

My wife Christine thought I was planning to miss out too much of Lancashire on this interminable canal. As if I hadn't seen enough of it already! So it was that I paid a call yet another East Lancashire town, Blackburn, a place I had never visited or wanted to visit. Nowadays you get a particularly good view of Blackburn from the new motorway. As it sprawls over mile after mile of low hills with houses and steaming new factories it is difficult to believe that its population is only 105,000.

Starting at the aqueduct outside Rishton where I had left the canal, I set off on my bike in a relatively jaunty mood with a blood pressure reading of 145/80 this morning – not bad, not bad! Enjoying the sunshine and clear blue sky, I observed that the canal water appeared blue (like Venice!). To the south lay a reservoir, one of a number constructed as feeders for the canal. As I made my way into Blackburn I found the towpath was blocked. Suddenly I was thrown into a ghastly urban jungle of roadworks, tatty posters on the walls and an overpowering smell of curry. This was not at all what I wanted on this lovely afternoon but I struggled on past the diversion, eventually picking up the towpath again in the top part of Blackburn at a place called Eanam Wharf, where there is some sort of canal museum.

I noted that there were no moving canal boats whatsoever. However I soon discovered the reason for this – one of the basins at Blackburn Locks had been drained. It was covered in black slime, revealing a distressing mess of supermarket trolleys (3), old tyres (5) and petrol cans (4). Why do people want to push supermarket trolleys into canals? Could some punishment be devised for this, perhaps involving goolies and a chain saw, since the people who do it are clearly unfit to live in any community? I began to speculate on other behaviour worthy of this punishment: the spraying of graffiti, the creation of computer viruses, the emptying of ashtrays by the roadside and in car parks, the installation of speed bumps, the display of internet pop-ups, the playing of music at 100 decibels in cars with the windows left open, the celebration of non-celebrities with London accents, the posting of junk mail and spam, cold-calling by double glazing companies, the tipping back of aeroplane seats without asking the person behind, the spitting out of chewing gum onto pavements, the practice of religious zealotry, double parking, street begging, enthusiasm for Harry Potter books and the Lord of the Rings in adults over the age of 40, the opening of stores on Boxing Day....

Of course none of these things is likely to get anyone prosecuted, but just look at some of the things that CAN get you into trouble, which you might think deserved a nod of appreciation, if not an outright commendation. Members of the public who vandalise speed cameras and teachers who smack naughty children get into hot water. Men and women of the Royal Navy who have sex together on board a ship are equally persecuted. Doctors and teachers who dare to question the existence of conditions which were unknown when I was growing up – myalgic encephalitis (ME), dyslexia, autism – are publicly castigated. The enterprising people who put cooking oil into their diesel tanks to avoid scandalously high fuel taxes, and the "smugglers" who bring back vanloads of cigarettes from the Continent, also to avoid penal UK taxes, are liable to prosecution. And what about the Norfolk farmer, Tony Martin, who shot and killed an intruder at his lonely farmhouse after he had been burgled five times? I am sure in let's say Alabama or Texas, they would have pinned a medal on him.

Well, it's not up to me to sort out the world, so on with the Leeds and Liverpool! There was a gleaming new Asda store below the canal at one point, presumably the source of the trolleys in the canal. When I grew up, a large proportion of the population used to go to church on a Sunday morning, including me. When I go to our local Tescos on a Sunday morning nowadays to do the recycling, I find that the car park is packed. We have a new religion.

I found that much the same applies to Blackburn as to the other East Lancashire towns – there is much dereliction and poor housing, but there is also a revival going on, with lots of new houses, factories and supermarkets as well as the new motorway. The best view of all this is obtained from the canal embankment south of the town centre which, though not on the scale of the one in Burnley, is essentially the same thing, offering prospects to either side. Visible from here were a pair of beautifully manicured bowling greens; red brick municipal buildings in the French Empire style; and Ewood Park football ground, home of Blackburn Rovers, which looked very smart. There was clearly a match in progress on this lovely Saturday afternoon. I could hear the crowd, but they would have gone home disappointed – the score was Blackburn Rovers 1, Liverpool 3.

Heading out of the town I passed miles of detached houses with gardens running down to the canal. It had been pretty quiet on the excellent towpath, the main users being mothers (and some fathers) pushing prams. The anticipated population collapse in other parts of the country does not seem to be happening in the unsophisticated northern towns where mothers – and young mothers at that – are everywhere to be seen pushing prams about.

Beyond Blackburn, the canal enters a quiet country stretch, the peace only punctuated here and there by the roar of motorway traffic. I suppose this part must look pretty in spring because the towpath was lined for miles with hawthorn bushes, but I wasn't in much of a mood to appreciate it. I guess I had just started to overdo things again. I cycled on for another five miles, down as far as Johnson's Hillock, where there are some pretty locks with pools. Along the way there had been plenty of evidence of canal activity, moving boats, boatyards and moorings, including some big ones at Wheelton at the top of the locks. At one point I passed a barge manned by a young and very handsome couple. They both beamed at me and said hello. It seems they were enjoying themselves, very much indeed. I saw them again later at some moorings, the woman stood on the bank, wearing blue jeans, hauling in the boat with a rope around her waist. Tall, well-built and fresh faced, I would very much have liked to have taken her home with me. Can you imagine the conversation?

"Excuse me, you smiled at me very nicely, would you mind leaving that hunky handsome young man and coming away with me, a 53-year old unemployed man with dodgy blood pressure and a wife at home?"

"No, dream on!"

At Johnson's Hillock there were quite a few people about, and also some dogs, including a great dane, coloured white with black spots like a dalmation. This animal apparently went under the name of Danko and his owner had let him loose on the lawns round the locks. It seems he wanted to play with the wildlife. His first option was a group of ducks on the bank. At his first approach the ducks immediately jumped squawking into the water and skittled over to the far bank. Danko seemed puzzled by this behaviour, but opted not to follow them. His next choice was a rabbit which appeared out of a hedge. Oh boy! In seconds he was where the rabbit had been, but of course, the rabbit had hopped back into the brambles. Danko looked round. What is wrong with me? Oh well, the wildlife is no fun, let's try the domesticated animals! There were two other dogs, a small terrier and a dachshund.

The terrier ran off yelping and the dachshund was scooped off the ground by its owner and hurried away. Funnily enough, this dog peered back over her shoulder with interest as if he really did want to play.

"I have to let him loose," said Danko's owner apologetically. She was a blond-haired woman of 40 or so. "It's either that or be dragged through the mud!"

At the foot of the locks was the spur of another canal. I believe that this is what remains of the southern section of the Lancaster Canal, heading off towards Preston. The next few miles of the Leeds and Liverpool, down to Wigan, were actually built as part of the Lancaster Canal and later taken over by the Leeds and Liverpool.

Loading the bike back into the car, suddenly – Argh! My back went. It does this from time to time, though I had had a few years free of it. I managed get back into the car and drive home, but dear me! What a sorry sight I was when I got there, barely able to walk. Too much biking. It cleared up after a few uncomfortable days, but it just goes to show, exercise has its downside.

Resuming once again at Johnson's Hillock and heading south under the M61 motorway, the first sight of note was a big red-brick mill, standing alone in a large car-park. This place has been tarted up and jaunty turrets have been added to each corner of the building. It is called Botany Bay and is some kind of tourist place. One of those ghastly hurdy-gurdy organs was playing in the car park. Apparently this area came to be known as Botany Bay because the residents of nearby Chorley and Preston thought it a long way away from anywhere. You couldn't say that now, it's right on the M61.

Visible from here is the tower on a hill called Rivington Pike. It was here that a park was established by Lord Lever, the famous soap manufacturer from Port Sunlight. Lord Lever was brought up in Bolton and he established this park for the benefit of the local people. It seems he used to do his courting in the area. It's not a park in a formal sense – there are no flower beds, but there are woods and fields. In the bottom is a large reservoir (which was there in Lever's day), and next to it is a ruin, Liverpool Castle. This is a folly – it is a copy of the castle which used to stand by the Mersey, and was built as a ruin from the outset.

Lever built a bungalow at the top of the hill, and an access road to reach it. As he also had other homes, he had to leave this place empty for long periods, and it was burnt down by a suffragette. He swore he would rebuild it, but I don't know if ever he did, as there is nothing there but footings now. But still, it's worth making your way through the old formal gardens to the top of the hill where you can admire the same view that Lever admired. On a clear day I am sure you can see Blackpool tower, but when I went, it was hazy.

Incidentally Lever believed in a fad current in his day – sleeping outside. His bed was covered over, but it was outside, and apparently did get wet in bad weather. Even after his wife died of pneumonia, he persisted in this freakish behaviour. This just goes to show, he may have been good at making money and a pretty good egg all round, but he was still as daft as a bat. In the best Lancastrian tradition.

I carried on southwards for another seven miles or so in the general direction of Wigan. Parts of the towpath were horribly bumpy, and strewn with nasty-looking strimmer debris, but I survived somehow. Wondering if I could make it as far as Wigan, I stopped to ask a middle-aged couple.

"Where is this place?"

This is the trouble with biking – you get to a town and you don't know what it is, there are no signs on canals.

"Adlington," replied the woman.

Great! Never heard of it.

So! "How far is it down to Wigan?" I continued.

A look of utter consternation crossed the faces of the couple, as if Wigan was on the other side of the country.

"Fifteen miles?" said the man, doubtfully.

What rubbish. The next person I asked said it was four miles from the next bridge.

When I got to that bridge I stopped for a break, deciding to leave Wigan with its massive flight of locks to another day. Here I got into conversation with a couple who had stopped their narrow boat to free the propeller of long grass.

"Look at that," said the man, who was about 65 and had a face a good deal redder than mine. He fished out handful after handful of long grass. "A great ball of the stuff!"

"They cut the grass and it chokes the propeller," explained the woman. She was also about 65 and her face was very wrinkly and freckled. "You go slower and slower and eventually you have to stop."

"Where have you come from?" I asked.

"We live on the canal," she said. "We are actually from New Zealand but we have been on the canals here for over 12 months now. We winter on the Shropshire Union – we have relatives close by – then get going again. We've come on this canal all the way from Leeds."

"What do you think of it?" I asked.

"Good, but it has such big locks with heavy gates. It's hard for us to open them and to operate the paddles. It's much easier in the Midlands where the locks are mostly narrow."

"What do you think of England?"

"We love it – especially the canals!"

Maybe they don't have any canals in New Zealand. Actually I suspect that this couple were originally English anyway, they didn't have strong New Zealand accents, the sort where they say "ridhid" instead of "redhead".

"We'll have to decide whether to stay another winter on the canals," she continued. "We still have a house in New Zealand."

Their next target, it seems, was the Lancaster Canal.

CHAPTER 16

I next headed straight for the iconic town of Wigan, which has a tremendous flight of 23 locks descending into the town, in fact just the sort of uphill challenge an up-and-coming cyclist would relish. I wanted to take this one uphill at the start of my ride when I was fresh, so I planned to head back up the Leeds & Liverpool to the point where I had left it a few miles further north.

One reason that Wigan is iconic is that for many years it had the best rugby league club in the country. Rugby league is a northern, proletarian game, part of what defines the north to the south. Especially in smaller towns, it has a much bigger following than soccer. As it is confined to certain parts of the north, there are many derby games. I have no doubt that the citizens of Wigan like nothing better than to see their team give St Helens, Widnes or Warrington a good thrashing, and that passes for a good day out in these parts of Lancashire.

First impressions of Wigan were not brilliant. Gone is the stone of Nelson and Burnley, to be replaced by redbrick terraces and the usual gigantic red brick mills, some of which, again as usual, are derelict with no alternative use yet found. There are just so many of these mills all over the north, they can't all be turned into heritage centres and flats. Those in the less desirable locations are just left, forlorn and unwanted. I approached the town through the rather dismal suburb of Hindley, noting with trepidation a burnt-out mill right next to the entrance to Wigan Pier. Things must still be quite tough in Wigan. Mind you things can't be too bad because housing and transport cost little in places like this, which is why my holiday flights from Manchester to the Mediterranean are always crowded with cleaners and dinner ladies from Rochdale and Wigan.

The waterfront here was pleasant, clean and well-maintained with a glorious towpath of paving blocks which must have been ten feet wide. As my main interest was the flight of locks rather than the "Pier" I took off up this under the shade of some willow trees. The towpath was pretty good for most of the way before it degenerated to an earthen path after the Top Lock, but of course, 23 locks is a lot of locks for a biker to negotiate uphill. I found a waterman near the top and asked him how far I had to go.

"You'll get there on your bike in two minutes", he said.

"How many locks are left to go?" I enquired.

"This is number eight," he said, "so seven."

"Ah." He must have though I am a lot fitter than I am.

I thought it odd that there were so many locks, because some of them are only a few feet deep, and I also asked about this. The waterman said that it was just the way the land lay, a response which made absolutely no sense to me. I finally huffed and puffed my way to the top, then carried on for another three or four miles, past a country park, till I came to a pub called the Crawford Arms where I had stopped on my way southwards. Here I turned round and headed for Wigan Pier. A minute or so earlier I had encountered a small boy of about four years old, also on a bike and riding back in the direction of his parents, and now I met him again.

"What you turn round for?" he enquired.

"Is there anything to see then?" I asked.

"Th'is sum ducks up theer!" he replied earnestly.

The way back down the locks was wonderful on the bike. There was a sign saying that no vehicle was allowed to exceed 5 mph – are you kidding? No biker on earth would go that slowly. It occurred to me on the way down that the bike would make a wonderful getaway vehicle for a criminal. It has no registration plate to be picked up on surveillance cameras, no recognisable make, it is completely inconspicuous and in the right sort of conditions it is certainly fast enough. As a matter of fact the bicycle was used to great effect during the Second World War, by the Japanese in Malaya. Their soldiers could move swiftly and silently along jungle and plantation paths, repeatedly outflanking the retreating British Army. British prestige in the area never recovered, as the Malayans could not understand how their previously invincible masters could be overrun by an army on bicycles. So watch out Wigan, here I come on my war machine!

The prospect of the locks tumbling away downhill was very fine though it must dismay the boat people. It didn't dismay me. I put it into my list of the Top Ten Sights of the North British canals, no question.

I found another water man:

"How long does it take to pass through the locks?" I asked.

"Three hours down and four hours up. To save water we try to pair boats up, so if anyone wants to use the locks they have to ring us first."

This man was busy filling a lock though there was no boat in it, so I decided to enquire after this strange practice.

"Ah," he said, "We sometimes do that to get them ready when we know a boat is coming."

You see – there is an explanation for everything.

I thought that this huge flight of locks must be one of the biggest in the country and it was certainly way ahead of anything I had seen so far, but there are in fact bigger flights. The top score of 30 locks is located at Tardebigge on the Worcester and Birmingham Canal. Now what a biker's challenge that would be! They could put it on the English leg of the Tour de France. Apparently even more impressive from a scenic point of view is the 29-lock flight at Caen Hill near Devizes on the Kennet and Avon Canal, which takes the waterway up from the upper valley of the Bristol Avon to the Vale of Pewsey. So! I decided to go there one day, and one day, I did. It isn't far from the megaliths at Avebury which we were visiting anyway. It's nowhere near as impressive as Wigan. The locks are very small, though there are lots of them, you can't see all the way from the top to the bottom.

I whizzed on down, passing a "Canal Policing" vehicle – I bet you didn't know there were dedicated canal police, did you? At one point I went so fast that the wind blew up my shorts. As I do not wear underwear when out biking I was alarmed to see that my willie was exposed. "Canal police arrest pervert on Promenade!"

Down at the bottom of the flight of locks there is a collection of old warehouses now converted for other uses. One of them is a pub, appropriately called the Orwell after the George Orwell who put Wigan on the map in the 1930s with *The Road to Wigan Pier*. When I grew up Wigan was a joke town before it passed the baton to East Grinstead, Neasden and then Milton Keynes, and the butt of the humour was this Pier, because how can an inland town have a pier? It seems that coal wagons from the pits used to drive up to the canal over the River Douglas on a raised gantry. The whole basin used occasionally to flood leaving only this gantry visible above the waters which some wag called Wigan Pier. There is nothing to see now, just the loading quay, so hey! It's a fraud! There is no pier at Wigan Pier.

George Orwell also noticed the absence of the pier. Despite the unprepossessing air of the town today, however, it is very clear that things have moved on a long way from Orwell's days: "the houses are poky and ugly, and insanitary and comfortless...they are distributed in filthy slums round belching foundries and stinking canals and slag-heaps that deluge them with sulphurous smoke." This type of housing was for the lucky ones – the unlucky people had to live in "caravans". Orwell writes: "Along the banks of Wigan's miry canal are patches of waste ground on which caravans have been dumped...The majority are old single-decker buses which have been taken off their wheels and propped up..."

Orwell was an Old Etonian (though not a rich one) who had been working in a bookshop in leafy Hampstead before setting out for the "industrial areas". Though he was accustomed to squalor and poverty in the poor areas of Paris and London, he comes across very much as an innocent southerner horrified at what he sees from the Potteries northwards. You can tell he was a true southerner because he once ate a plate of jellied eels his wife had left out for the cat. I think even an impoverished and half-starved Wiganner would still have left them for the cat. This dish is unknown in the north but we did used to like our dripping and tripe – in fact Orwell lodged over a tripe shop.

Only half of *The Road to Wigan Pier* is about the northern industrial areas such as Wigan. The rest of it is his attempt to identify a solution to the desperate conditions of 1936. More than anything, he fears Fascism, which had already taken over in Germany and Italy. His solution was Socialism, but his big problem was the image of the Socialists themselves – creeping Jesus types, vegetarians, teetotallers, fruit-juice drinkers, aspirin eaters, nudists, yoga practitioners, sandal-wearers, sex-maniacs, Quakers, birth-controllers, nature cure quacks, pacifists, feminists, beard-wearers etc. However Orwell righty prophesied that machines such as cars and aeroplanes would become more or less foolproof and user-friendly. He feared however that mankind's finer attributes such as loyalty and courage would become so useless in this machine-run world as to be "no more valuable than the animal faculty of moving the ears".

I thought I might stop off at the Orwell for a pot of tea after my haul up and down those locks. At the bar I found a canal man of about my age who said he had brought his boat up from Cheshire.

"How do you find the canal?" I asked.

"Oh, fine, pretty much as it always was, not like some of them," he observed.

"How do you mean?"

"Well some of these canals nowadays, the are so twee and gentrified. I started on the boats 30 years ago. We were a different crowd then, there were no £70,000 narrow boats and weekend boaters with naval caps. We were a more bohemian bunch."

"So don't you like these restorations then?" I asked.

"What I like is that you generally have enough water to get about. In the old days there wasn't much dredging done and as often as not you were more or less churning through mud. But look at the popular canals like the Grand Union and the Oxford. They're more like a form of moveable vintage car rally nowadays, not that some boats ever move far from Braunston. There's a lot of class distinction. I wouldn't be seen dead in a hire boat, they are the bottom of the pile."

It seemed as if he was part of this class distinction thing, but honestly – there's no pleasing some people! British Waterways contrive to spend all these millions on canal restorations and improvements and he still isn't happy.

At Wigan as at Saltaire one is confronted by a brand new form of employment, the heritage industry. This is an attempt to make use of the assets – the buildings, the people, the infrastructure including the canals – left behind by the march of time, technology and the global economy. You cannot help but applaud this and Wigan Pier does seem to get a lot of visitors. At the large red brick Trencherfield Mill overlooking the Pier complex, you find "Welcome to the Wigan Pier Experience!" This contains a 2500HP steam engine with a 26 ½ft diameter flywheel, not the sort of thing you would like to get your fingers caught in. It would be like getting a light bite from a hippopotamus or a good gumming from a shark. The wheel is used to drive the hundreds of individual spinning machines in the mill at a terrific level of decibels. It is just the sort of thing to appeal to Fred Dibnah and also it is suitable for deaf pedestrians.

One tourist sight no longer available in Wigan is a mill chimney built at Wallgate to the incredible height of 435 feet. It collapsed into the canal in 1846. Now that must have been a sight worth seeing, from a suitable distance of course. I don't think even Fred Dibnah could have run away fast enough from 435 feet of tumbling masonry.

I had heard that Wigan town centre was surprisingly good, following the implementation of a planning decision in the 1920s requiring the construction of black and white timber fronts to new buildings. So I strolled up into the town, and it was all true. It was amazingly pleasant and prosperous-looking, and the black and white timber fronts were indeed there. There was an arcade, modern I think, but blending in nicely, a good church, and a number of decent buildings squashed into a limited area. There was also a large, new Debenhams store. It was all so much better than say Rochdale or Blackburn. I thought Wigan was a town of no more than 100,000 people, but for a town centre like this it must be twice that size.

CHAPTER 17

Altogether there are 35 miles of the Leeds and Liverpool Canal between Wigan and Liverpool, a long route as the canal swings northwards towards Southport to follow the contour. A branch line takes the Leeds and Liverpool up to the Ribble estuary and so on to the Lancaster Canal at Preston. The main line arrives in Liverpool proper at Aintree racecourse – remember the Canal Turn in the Grand National? The last 8 miles of the existing canal is little used by boaters and was at one time fenced off completely after several local children drowned in it.

Half a mile beyond the foot of Wigan locks is the junction with another section of the Leeds and Liverpool Canal, the Leigh Branch. This heads off back eastwards to the town of Leigh, where it joins up with the Bridgewater Canal on its way over from Manchester. This branch is important to canal users as it enables them to cut back to Manchester and the various routes back over or to the south of the Pennines, enabling round trips from one of the basins along the way. I too would be taking this branch on my Central Pennine Ring, turning in the direction of home at last.

Although I wasn't going to complete the journey to Liverpool along the canal, there was nothing to stop me making the journey by car, so I continued on the great city. This was hardly the first time I had been here – I lived in the place for a year in 1972 and 1973 when I was a postgraduate student at the university, and I must say that of all the unlikely places to emerge on the tourist trail in recent years, Liverpool must be one of the most unexpected. Back in 1972 the city presented a most unprepossessing air, being in an advanced state of decay. The commercial and shopping centers in the middle of the city looked prosperous enough, but some of the suburbs were simply frightening, and indeed there were riots in Toxteth in the 1980s – you may remember Michael Heseltine getting involved. It was not recommended to walk through Toxteth alone, at any time of day. Upper Parliament Street, near here, was cobbled and all the property along it had been demolished. Down on the Mersey, the docks were virtually derelict.

Some of the other towns on Merseyside were just as badly affected by decay – Bootle and Birkenhead, for example. The problem was that the main sources of employment, the port and shipbuilding, had simply gone elsewhere. Merseyside had to find something else to do, and understandably, this took time.

Another problem was that the wealthy people had deserted the city, fleeing across the Wirral to West Kirkby or up the coast to Crosby and Formby. They had obviously been there at one time – you could see that, for example, from the large houses round Sefton Park and on Princes Street, which in the Seventies were sad and dilapidated and divided into poor flats. For anyone with a taste for decaying grandeur, Liverpool was the place. This even applied to Birkenhead. There is a tube tunnel under the Mersey from James Street in Liverpool, and the first stop on the other side of the river is Hamilton Square. This should have been a perfect Georgian Square with a garden in the middle; it was just so run down, but charming all the same.

It cannot be denied that despite the obvious dilapidation, Liverpool still had a certain grandeur, unlike, say, Bootle. There were big, impressive buildings with cornices, parapets and columns in the area around St George's Hall and the Walker Art Gallery, while the massive, stubby shape of the Anglican cathedral – at that time still unfinished – loomed over the city centre. There was a breezy and pleasant sea front on the Mersey where the Liver and Cunard buildings stand. I found I could go down to the Pier Head, one of the truly iconic places in England, and have a good blow and if I really felt like it, there was always the ferry across the Mersey. I enjoyed visits to the two cathedrals and to the Walker Gallery itself, which contains some wonderful Victorian moral paintings.

However I noted after a time that the people of Liverpool had a fair opinion of themselves and that they were not particularly friendly. Also, there was one slightly disconcerting habit: strangers would be addressed as John, which happens to be my name. So I would be walking down the street and someone would stop me – "Have you got the time, there, John?"

I would say – "How do you know my name???"

They would say – "That's what I call everybody!"

The university campus was situated not far out of the city centre, a collection of buildings of different ages, one quite grand with a clock tower, others modern, including a tower block. Also it had its own pub, the Augustus John. The campus was in the middle of a seemingly illimitable area of desolation and decay, and there were no leafy suburbs for miles.

Going back today, the most notable thing is the vast improvement in the Georgian housing around the Anglican cathedral, which all looks very smart. Upper Parliament Street has filled up with modern houses, and the area has been landscaped with little hillocks. The whole of the central area of the city has a different atmosphere. There are huge new buildings going up on the waterfront. Of course the Albert Dock has been redeveloped and now houses a museum and the Tate Modern. The Anglican cathedral was finally finished in 1978 and looks much better without the crane. If you ever go here, go at lunchtime. They serve an excellent roast dinner in the canteen for only five or six pounds!

It's the same story across the Mersey in Birkenhead, where Hamilton Square is now fully renovated and filled up with solicitor's and accountants offices and the like. Also on this side is Port Sunlight, the well-known model village developed by Lord Lever. I went here too, to look around and visit the Lady Lever Art Gallery. When you walk into this place, the first thing you see is a French white marble female nude clutching a snake (Salammbo), a most blatantly pornographic statue. Well Lord Lever was obviously unafraid to buy what he liked, but it doesn't quite chime in with the popular image of the Victorians, does it? In fact, Lever was a grocer from Bolton who moved into the soap business. Like many such people, he was member of the Cromwellian United Reform Church, though apparently not so vicious a prude as Titus Salt. But his gallery in Port Sunlight is the finest provincial gallery I have ever seen. It contains a lot of very expensive-looking furniture as well as paintings and statues, and you can't help thinking, when you look at this collection, that there must be an awful lot of money in soap!

*   *   *   *

So I returned to Wigan to head back the six or so miles to Leigh, having been kept at home for a day or two by heavy rain and an equally heavy cold. The previous day I had felt ill and feverish, but I thought I was sufficiently recovered. The weather forecast threatened more rain, but it turned out to be a pleasant, sunny afternoon. So I crossed over the main line of the Leeds and Liverpool and set off out of Wigan on an excellent setted towpath.

Immediately after the town, there is a dramatic change of scenery. The countryside is dominated by large lakes or "flashes" either side of the canal, caused by mining subsidence. Back in the eighteenth and nineteenth centuries, this area was central to the economy of the whole north-west, shipping out coal on purpose-built canals in all directions. Today it looks as if it has barely recovered from its centuries of exploitation. Though some scars have healed, much of it has an air of desolation. There isn't even much in the way of agriculture along parts of this stretch of canal, just weeds. There are slag heaps (used for that most irritating of sports, moto-cross) and quite a number of bridge footings, the bridges themselves, presumably for railways, long gone.

Having said that, the largest of the flashes (one outside Wigan and one outside Leigh) have been landscaped with trees. They were dotted with the white sails of dinghies, moving quickly in the breeze, and the prospect across them was fair, suitable for nice houses in fact. (The sort of nice house that ceases to be nice when you wake up in the morning 20 feet underground.) The waterfowl and seagulls were also making the most of this wetlands environment. Hey, it's the Lancashire Broads! (The Norfolk Broads are also man-made, dug out for peat.) If only George Orwell could see this, he would be amazed. Housing subsidence is one of the themes of his book.

As it was a Sunday there were plenty of people about on the canal banks. A lot of them were plebby-looking, tattooed men and women with dyed blond hair in outrageous light pink clothes with flesh and bra straps poking out. One burly man, naked to the waist with a large, white pot belly ("Would you mind putting your shirt back on please?") was carrying a large plastic bag full of bread, which he threw to the ducks. "All right, lad," he said to me as I passed, nodding. I would say he was younger than me but if he wants to call me "lad", really I don't mind.

The going got tougher, and the towpath was barred with difficult metal barriers every half-mile or so. These persisted all the way into Manchester and I would like to take the tedious idiot responsible and crack his shins on the damned things till he screams for mercy. Passing an interesting structure called Plank Lane lift bridge, I began to think I was never going to get to Leigh, but eventually the mills of the town hove into view. If you like mills, you will like Leigh, because from the point of view of the towpath, they absolutely dominate the place. The final complex was particularly impressive, on the far bank and built like a palace, separate buildings many storeys high with tall towers and variegated brickwork.

The Leeds and Liverpool merged seamlessly with the Bridgwater Canal in Leigh – there is not even an exit lock. I turned round here, to resume another day. When I got back to my car and looked at myself in the mirror, I doubted the wisdom of coming out on the day. My face was covered in sweat and bore an unhealthy pallor, and my hair, also sweaty, stuck out at wild angles in the manner of Struewelpeter or Wurzzle Gummidge. I hadn't thought much of some of the locals on the towpath but they must have found the sight of me positively alarming.

This then was my goodbye to the Leeds and Liverpool, so what to conclude? Unlike most canals, it never closed down. By the 1960s serious maintenance problems had built up including mining subsidence on the Leigh Branch, and British Waterways threatened to close the canal. However a huge rally of canal enthusiasts at Blackburn in 1965 convinced them that it did have a future. So this is a very important point – because this canal moved more or less straight from commercial waterway to tourist route, it did not require the huge amount of restoration that other canals did. Certainly British Waterways have maintenance to carry out, and indeed they employ about a hundred people on this canal. Even so the rebuilding costs in terms of new bridges, tunnels and locks and canal walls must have been a fraction of those on the South Pennine Ring, and look – it is full of boats! Tourists! It goes through the Yorkshire Dales, for God's sake. It has "winner" written all over it.

Having said that, it's a hell of a long way round.

The Bridgewater Canal – Northern section

WEST

| *Leeds and Liverpool Canal*
*Leigh
|
| *Bridgewater Canal*
*Boothstown
|
*Worsley
|
++ Barton Swing Bridge
*Eccles
|
*Trafford Park Industrial Estate
|_____Junction with southern branch of Bridgewater
|
*Salford Quays
|
*Castlefields, central Manchester
| *Rochdale Canal*
|
|_____ *Junction with Ashton Canal*

EAST

CHAPTER 18

As I got up in the morning , I noted rather grimly that is was now the second of September. Christine went back to work at school this morning and if I had the choice, I would be going back too, but there is no work to go to. There has been no word from Honeywell and barely a tickle from anywhere else. It is beginning to look as if I shall have to find something else to do - the biking season is getting on. Still, at least I would have time to finish my Central Pennine Ring. Today I planned to do the last stage of it on the Bridgewater Canal. This is Britain's oldest industrial canal, its first section having been completed by the famous engineer James Brindley in 1763, at the instigation of the eponymous Duke of Bridgewater. This was a 10-mile link between the coal mines at Worsley and Manchester. Together with the invention of the steam engine, this canal launched factory development in South Lancashire and the Industrial Revolution with it.

Beyond the basin at Castlefield in central Manchester, the canal snakes round the south-west corner of the city centre, running parallel with the terminus of the Manchester Ship Canal, just at the start of the area known as Salford Quays (formerly Salford Docks). From here it heads out to the Trafford Park Industrial Estate in south-west Manchester, where it splits into two. The northern branch crosses the later Manchester Ship Canal on the Barton Swing Aqueduct and goes out to Worsley and then on to Leigh, six miles west of Worsley. The southern branch extends to the River Mersey at Runcorn. The total length of the canal is 43 miles. Commercial traffic on the canal continued through to 1974 by which time tourist traffic had become significant, so this canal has never closed.

The other important canal in this area is like no other in England, the Manchester Ship Canal. Completed in 1894, it stretches 36 miles from Salford Quays to Eastham on the Mersey estuary, near Birkenhead. It is Britain's most ambitious man-made waterway and with truly massive bridges and locks. Sadly I don't think there is a single crane left in Salford Quays nowadays and the Ship Canal, or at least its upper reach, no longer carries commercial traffic. It seems remarkable that the Bridgewater Canal, built 150 years earlier, is still going strong while this monster lies almost empty and unwanted.

*   *   *   *

I set off once more in Leigh. Leaving the town behind, it seemed a long way across unattractive country to Worsley, though I was diverted by the many swans, the largest I had ever seen. I passed some pithead winding gear, rusty but still standing, then re-touched civilization at a point called Boothstown, previously unknown to me. Here the canal basin was overlooked by very smart modern Executive Homes (the sort of place I would never buy in a million years), and a large modern pub of a type I particularly dislike, called Miller's. The towpath was poor, alternately muddy and stony. When you are on a bike, a good towpath makes all the difference. Also I must have crossed 16 steel barriers between Leigh and Worsley, placed quite unnecessarily under every bridge. What is the level of intelligence of the person responsible for this? Approaching that of President George W. Bush, one assumes. However at least there weren't any locks and I picked up a second wind near Worsely where the towpath improved.

Before I got there I met a man in his thirties with a suspicious orange suntan and a very large and muscular black and tan dog, looking anxiously back the way I had come.

"Does that lady have a dog?" he asked, indicating a grey-haired woman I had passed on the towpath.

"I don't think so."

"I daren't let him off if there are any other dogs around, you see."

"What kind of dog is it?" I asked. (I am not very good at dogs.)

"A Doberman."

Who would want to own a dog that is so dangerous that it cannot be trusted with other dogs? Someone with a lot of enemies. I made myself scarce while the brute was still on a lead, it looked extremely fast and ready to consume flesh, canine or human.

Approaching Worsley there is a massive – and I mean massive – double motorway bridge, a junction of the M60 Manchester orbital motorway over the canal. This has been here a good few years now, but the cost must have been astronomical. Huge concrete stanchions support the steel structure of the bridge. It is really quite impressive from below, but noisy, very noisy.

Worsley announced itself in advance by the orange colouration of the canal water, caused by iron-rich seepage from the old coal workings in Worsley itself. The original construction of the canal included 46 miles of underground tunnels draining the coal mines themselves and the water comes out from these with a deep orange colour. However, it is hard to imagine a place less like a pit village than Worsley, for it is lovely. The canal passes through a leafy park dotted with distinctive houses, many of them carrying black and white timberwork or stucco and each and every one of them a delight, even the modern ones. Best of all were the Packet House, home to the old passenger services on the canal, and the Bridgewater Hotel. The Duke of Bridgewater is to Worsley as Shakespeare is to Stratford, everything is named after him. A picturesque iron footbridge framed the canal. Really, I only live 30 miles away and I never knew it was here! I must bring Christine! Another one for the Top Ten Sights.

Worsley marks the start of the Manchester conurbation proper. From here the Bridgewater heads on into Eccles, an industrial suburb of Salford and pretty poor viewing for a tired cyclist, but never mind, a sight lay ahead, the Barton Swing Aqueduct, another of the Seven Wonders of the English canals! This was built in 1893 to replace James Brindley's original aqueduct over the River Irwell, which had itself been replaced by the Manchester Ship Canal.

This part of the canal is overlooked by tower blocks and I was surprised to find a dozen or so boats moored up here. Surprised, because this is not the sort of place I would like to leave my car for more than 15 minutes, never mind a narrow boat. I soon came to the Ship Canal, huge and silent. In the middle of it is an island and on this is a control tower, and a turntable which supports the aqueduct. This was a battleship grey steel lattice structure with some traffic on it, heading off into Trafford Park. I have seen photos of the aqueduct painted a jaunty red, white and black to I guess the grey is just temporary, but it certainly looked drab.

The aqueduct is 235 feet long. I suppose that must mean that the Ship Canal is 235 feet wide or thereabouts at this point – if it was a river, that would be a very big river. To me the aqueduct now looked fixed in position, as if there is no longer any need to swing open to admit tall ships on the Ship Canal. When it was built, it was considered a marvel of engineering, which just goes to show that engineering has come a long way since 1893. I am only sore about it because it was built after the introduction of powered canal craft so there was no towpath and I couldn't go on it. However the aqueduct and the surrounding area are just too dingy for me to put this place in my Top Ten Sights of the North British Canals.

Rejoining the canal, I found myself in the vast Trafford Park Estate, home of the Kelloggs Corn Flakes factory. It is mean, old and ugly, though the Trafford Shopping Mall has been built in one corner of it now (new and ugly). After passing dozens of broken-down factories and the odd new one I finally came upon the junction with the southern branch of the Bridgewater. Soon the canal veered eastwards, passing right by the red and grey stands of the Old Trafford football ground, home of course to Manchester United F.C. and a cathedral to a modern religion. When I worked at Kelloggs I found that half the real Mancunians were in fact Manchester City supporters, a breed which has evolved a highly developed gallows humour, required to sustain the misfortune of having been brought up supporting City.

Past the football ground I arrived at a footbridge which announced itself Throstle Nest Bridge, where I came up for air. I emerged opposite Exchange Quay, the biggest and newest office complex in Manchester, impressive with its plate-glass palaces. Some fairly spectacular new buildings have been erected in Salford Quays in the last few years. The most famous is the Lowry (Centre), straight ahead of me now on the banks of the Ship Canal. Naturally it contains quite a few paintings by Lowry. These demonstrate that he knew how to draw and paint before he invented his famous matchstick men, but he was certainly an odd old bird. He should have been like Augustus John, Lucien Freud and countless others in the tradition, who painted their nudes and had sex with them into the bargain (with or without consent). Much more fun than matchstick men for an artist with talent. But you have to look at it from Lowry's point of view. He was from the Lancashire working class and he wouldn't have wanted to do anything that would have upset his mother.

Right opposite the Lowry stands the new Imperial War Museum. The building is spectacular enough, if you like modern architecture, though to me it looks like a reject from a project to design a hat from lumps of metal. The architect was Daniel Liebeskind ("the shards of a fractured globe", according to him). Salford Quays is a good place for it, it looks as if it has been flattened by a nuclear bomb.

I came upon a narrow boat moored up by the canal where a man of forty or so was pacing up and down the towpath with a huge black dog.

"What kind of dog is that?" I enquired.

"A Great Dane," he replied. Of course!

"You take him with you on a narrow boat then?"

"Oh yes, he runs along the bank most of the time. Here, Lennox, here boy!"

"Lennox?"

"He's big and he's black, isn't he? But he wouldn't harm a fly."

"Hmm!" Lennox approached me for an eyeball to eyeball confrontation, slobbering at the mouth. I gave him a friendly nod and he gave me a pretty mean stare. I decided to keep talking.

"It isn't too scenic here is it? Yet there are plenty of boats."

"Oh yes, it's part of the Cheshire Ring, you see. Nobody spends a lot of time here but it's much nicer further along."

The southern arm of the Bridgewater Canal is important in the canal world because it forms a major section in the ring of canals around the old county of Cheshire. Lennox was losing interest.

"Have you tried the Rochdale canal since they reopened it?" I asked.

"Not yet, but I plan to fit it in some time this year."

It was a poorish run into Manchester and I began to feel that I was knocking on the door of a mighty city at the tradesman's entrance. Then there were suddenly signs of improvements with lots of smart new blocks of flats and offices. I finally arrived at the restored canal basin at Castlefield, where I had been at the end of the Rochdale Canal. Across the basin was the exit lock of the Rochdale Canal, framed under a lovely old stone bridge. Castlefield came as a welcome lift. My afternoon's ride had been rather disappointing because the canal takes a low level and there isn't much to see from the towpath itself. However if you want to spend a wet afternoon traipsing through dreary suburbs and industrial estates, this section of the Bridgewater is definitely the one for you.

I had at last achieved my second objective, the Central Pennine Ring from Sowerby Bridge to Skipton and back to Castlefield. I wasn't going to repeat the run up the Rochdale Canal back to Sowerby Bridge, obviously. The ring had been a massive undertaking for me, generally much easier going than the South Pennine ring but much, much further. And do you know what? I was beginning to feel fit!

CHAPTER 19

I needed another canal target. Having had a look at Leeds and Manchester, the next obvious place was Sheffield, but how was it connected up to the canal network? How would a boatman get there from, say, Sowerby Bridge? So I fetched out the maps and found that the journey is possible. From Sowerby Bridge the route heads eastwards on canals and rivers. Past Castleford and seven miles short of Goole, the waterway turns right onto the New Junction Canal, a late canal built in 1905 which runs dead straight down to the River Don Navigation north of Doncaster. It then passes on this through Doncaster and Rotherham as far as Tinsley, four miles short of Sheffield, finally running into the city centre on the Sheffield and Tinsley Canal.

Some of these waterways are large-scale, similar to the Aire and Calder Navigation and the Manchester Ship Canal, and now suffering a similar fate. The locks on the New Junction Canal and the River Don Navigation were extended to 230 feet by 20 feet as late as 1983 in the hope of attracting commercial traffic in 700-ton boats, and many new wharves and staithes were created. However commercial traffic is now virtually non-existent and the new infrastructure and the big boats are rotting away. I wonder whose idea that was?

I set off one lovely Saturday afternoon aiming for the last eastward run on the Aire and Calder Navigation and the right turn into the New Junction Canal. Not for the first time on this same run of canals, however, I found myself lured into a trap. I started out south of Selby in the shadow of the giant Eggborough power station with its eight cooling towers, by my calculations about three miles from the canal junction. With its better-known twin sister just up the M62 at Ferrybridge, Eggborough generates a significant proportion of the country's electricity, and as there is nothing round it, no one much minds it being here. By this point Yorkshire and indeed eastern England has flattened out completely and the only hills are landscaped slagheaps.

Now, Eggborough, that is some name! It reminds me of the time England, according to *1066 and All That*, was ruled by an egg – Egbert, actually King of Wessex. Of course, Eggborough would not have been in Wessex but Northumbria, the kingdom lying north of the Humber. This was ruled for centuries from nearby York, capital of the north. In those days Lancashire was little more than a rainswept, sodden marsh and Cumbria was part of what became Scotland.

Although there was a boat club where I joined the canal, the waterway and indeed the banks of it were absolutely deserted, and on such a good day. There was no towpath, just a grassy bank, which looked bikable if tough going. Well that wasn't the half of it - after a mile or so I was biking through a field. Less than half an hour after starting, as the grass and weeds rose in height to nine inches, I could take no more and got off and pushed. I was covered in sweat, thoroughly hot and bothered and frankly glad there was no one about to see me. In fact I do sweat rather easily, I think because of my raised blood pressure – my body is running on hot before I start. However I pushed on, but the canal stretched away with no sign of the junction. On and on I ploughed, driven man! It was simply hellish. Eventually I gave up and turned round, pushing the bike wearily back.

So the following day I made my way to Sheffield the easy way, on the motorway, starting out on foot in the city centre. George Orwell had been here before me, relating his experiences in *The Road to Wigan Pier*: "(Wigan) was a world from which vegetation had been banished; nothing existed except smoke, shale, ice, mud, ashes and foul water. But even Wigan was beautiful compared with Sheffield. Sheffield, I suppose, could justly claim to be called the ugliest town in the Old World....It has a population of half a million and it contains fewer decent buildings than the average East Anglian village of five hundred. And the stench! If at rare moments you stop smelling sulphur it is because you have started smelling gas. Even the shallow river that runs through the town is usually bright yellow with some chemical or other....An interminable vista of factory chimneys, chimney beyond chimney, fading away into a dim blackish haze."

Well, when you enter Sheffield today you are still left in no doubt that this is a vast, industrial city. As I drove into the city I could see that all the crumbling old red brick factories have been replaced by a shiny set of new ones on industrial estates. The city has no pretensions to be an office park, though it does have two big universities. The skyline is dominated by gigantic blocks of flats, a leftover from Sheffield's days as capital of the Socialist Republic of South Yorkshire.

I would say that the Yorkshire personality reaches an extreme form in this region. After all it is the original home of Fred Truman, Arthur Scargill, Michael Parkinson, Geoffrey Boycott, David Blunkett and William Hague. You may think that Lancashire people are slightly dotty, in the manner of say Fred Dibnah, George Formby or Ken Dodd, but at least, deep down, they want to be loved. So many Yorkshiremen, at least until they reach middle age, don't seem to care whether they are loved or not.

The explorer Sir Ralph Fiennes caused an uproar in the county when he announced that he would be prepared to consider anyone for his next expedition except a Yorkshireman, he didn't want to take any more of them. The Mayor of Barnsley commented dismissively and I don't think many in the county took Sir Ralph seriously, but of course, the rest of the country nodded in agreement. The fact is that the sort of Yorkshireman you would not want on a polar expedition does exist – the sulker. My dad used to sulk for three days at a time, never speaking a word and emanating hatred, and my grandfather could keep at it for a week. I used to sulk too, but I married a girl from Lancashire, where they do not understand such behaviour, and she stopped me doing it.

Sheffield is also a major centre for that other famous Yorkshire characteristic, plain speaking. I used to work here and it shocked even me, a tender lily from West Yorkshire. There was a woman there called Sandra. "I love Spain," she used to say, "apart from the Spaniards. Greasy little men!"

Before going out to the canal, I wandered round the city centre. This is no beauty spot but it looks like a big city centre, with perfectly normal people walking up and down the streets, as if there was nothing wrong with Sheffield at all. There is a cathedral, but this is only a parish church with a kitsch extention added in the Sixties (and hopefully removed any time soon). The town hall was impressive (usually a bad sign for the rest of the place) and there is a new building with a botanical garden inside it and a few exhibits including a gleaming Ferrari. I never was one for sports cars, they are for the boys.

I found the canal at Tinsley, where it runs next to the River Don, parking my car with some trepidation in the massage parlour area ("Bamboo Massage Parlour for Oriental Pleasure"). There had been heavy rain and the prospects for staying dry looked middling at best. In fact it felt like the first day of autumn. There was a nip in the air and I noticed piles of brown leaves blown off the trees by the towpath, and here was another sure sign – a big thicket of Michaelmass daises.

I set off under the M1 heading for the Meadowhall shopping mall. Now Sheffield is of course known as steel city and though some of the steel industry has moved out, there seems to be a lot of it left. Over to my right behind Meadowhall lay Sheffield Forgemasters in a building that looked exactly like a steel mill to me, and a modern one at that. Along the canal bank were many other heavy metal industrial works. I passed a flight of ten or eleven low locks, heading up, arriving pretty soon opposite the Sheffield Arena, an indoor concert venue that seats 15,000. There was some kind of event going on there and cars were parked everywhere. In 1991 Sheffield hosted the previously unknown World Student Games and it used this event to leverage funds for the redevelopment of one of its old industrial sites, just as Manchester was to do in 2002 with the Commonwealth Games. Beside the Arena I could see the Don Valley athletics stadium, and somewhere nearby there is also a swimming pool complex called Ponds Forge. Connecting these and also Meadowhall to the city centre there is an electric train service, clearly new or newish, which ran very frequently. Also this part of the canal had been landscaped and provided with moorings and an elegant high footbridge, and really it looked from here as if they were getting somewhere in Sheffield.

The going was simply dreadful, as bad as I had ever known, because the towpath was one discontinuous, slippery, muddy puddle most of the way into Sheffield, narrowing alarmingly under some of the bridges. After the excitement of the Arena the scenery soon deteriorated to broken-down mills and demolition sites, as bad as I had seen anywhere. This was unreconstructed Sheffield and it continued like this all the way to Victoria Basin where the canal terminates. There were absolutely no residential or office developments by the canal – not a bit like Leeds or Manchester. This stretch of the canal appears in the opening scenes of *The Full Monty*, which is set in the city.

I inched along, gliding slowly through the puddles, but half-way along another cyclist barged past me at full speed. He had no mudguards and no bell, but unlike me he was dressed in proper riding gear. He whizzed along oblivious to the mud and puddles. "Why can't I do that?" I thought. However when I saw the cyclist again at the basin, he looked as if he had been dipped in chocolate. It doesn't matter what you wear, you still have to get it clean afterwards.

When I arrived at Victoria Basin there was a complete change. This is where the money had been spent, big time. There were new office blocks and hotels, beautifully restored warehouses and carefully laid-out cobbles. Really, it looked excellent. Beyond lay a tangle of roads and a garish-looking shopping centre and clearly the centre of town was nearby. There were one or two shops under the arches of a viaduct, but otherwise no tourist facilities, no café or museum. I suppose they have to be realistic in Sheffield, they are not going to get many tourists.

Cycling back the rain poured down and soon I was cold, spattered in mud and wondering why on earth I was there. At one of the stinker bridges, Bacon Lane Bridge, I nearly fell in the canal, which was practically overflowing, ripping the arm of my jacket on the bridge wall. Still I had found, as ever, that there is no such thing as a dull day on a bike on a canal.

The Peak Forest Canal

NORTH

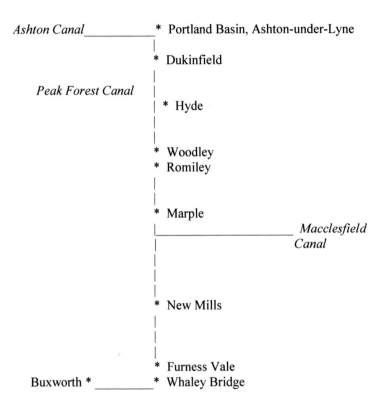

*Ashton Canal*_____* Portland Basin, Ashton-under-Lyne

    * Dukinfield

Peak Forest Canal

    * Hyde

    * Woodley
    * Romiley

    * Marple
    |_____ *Macclesfield*
                                   Canal

    * New Mills

    * Furness Vale
Buxworth *_____* Whaley Bridge

SOUTH

CHAPTER 20

I had identified the Cheshire Ring as a possible target in my early planning. This ring is a far more important in canal terms than anywhere I had been so far. It is a run of canals, 97 miles long, roughly round the old county of Cheshire. I had already done three short links of it in the Manchester area – the Ashton Canal, the last nine locks of the Rochdale Canal, and the first part of the Bridgewater Canal. I liked the idea best of the attractively-named Peak Forest Canal. This waterway had engaged my curiosity at Portland Basin in Ashton where it terminates under an old stone arched footbridge.

The Peak Forest Canal is 14 miles long, running from Whaley Bridge in Derbyshire, where an arm also services the nearby Buxworth Basins, down to Ashton. At Marple the canal descends a flight of sixteen locks, lowering the level by 214 feet before crossing the River Goyt on an aqueduct. That is a tremendously steep drop – the Five-Rise locks at Bingley lower the level by only 60 feet, by comparison. Each of the locks was constructed with a rise of thirteen feet, nearly twice the usual depth. These locks were clearly a formidable challenge for the engineers and they were going to be a big problem for me and my bike. The engineer for the canal was Benjamin Outram, also engineer on the Huddersfield Narrow Canal.

So it was back to Portland basin in Ashton-under-Lyne, a place I had visited on my South Pennine Ring. From here I planned an ambitious ride, eight miles down to the main event, the aqueduct and locks at Marple. Parking up in Portland Basin I observed that what used to be waste ground next to the Heritage Centre was now a block of "luxury" apartments – things have moved fast in Ashton! But can you have luxury apartments in a place like Ashton? Here they cannot have location, location and location because for all its virtues, Ashton is not a luxury location.

The Peak Forest Canal leaves the basin and moves straight onto an aqueduct over the River Tame. All in all it was a pretty good start because I then entered a parkland with lawns and tall trees, with the

River Tame flowing broad, fast and clean to one side. I could see at once that this was a narrow canal as there was a passage only seven feet wide under the bridge where I started. However the going soon got worse. The towpath, though good in patches, was generally bumpy, bepuddled and nettle-infested – just like the last time I was in Ashton, in fact. I had got used to a better standard. Imagine, you are riding on a strip two feet wide with nettles leaning into it three or four feet high on either side. The canal is only two feet away. One false step and you're in, mate! It amazes me that I have kept out of it.

Under the noisy M67 and past some equally noisy factories, the view generally improved with some country stretches and a lot of woods. Over to my left, but scarcely visible, lay the town of Hyde. That is where Dr Harold Shipman had his practice. You might recall that despite his 215 murders, Shipman was actually caught because he tried to forge the will of one of his victims. The relatives cried foul and the police were onto him. It was in fact a criminal, get-rich-quick scheme. He should have known better, and stuck to my way – get rich slow. The thing about Shipman is that he could have been stopped. He was convicted of forging an NHS prescription and the unlawful possession of the drug pethidine in 1976 and suspended, but he returned to practise in 1977. Is it a good idea to give a man with a conviction like that unlimited access to lethal dosages of drugs? His motives remain unclear. Though the youngest was only 41, most of his victims were old people living alone. Maybe he thought he was doing them a favour. He was certainly the world's least-likely looking mass murderer, and he denied any wrongdoing to the last, but we know different, don't we?

Beyond Hyde the canal is dug into the side of a hill as it crosses over the divide between the Tame and the Goyt rivers. There were moving boats on it, one every seven or eight minutes on average. Presently I came upon a tunnel, about 170 yards long, but with a towpath! Halleluja. This was very dark and spooky and I had to dismount. Soon there was another tunnel and this had no towpath – blast! Why build one tunnel with a towpath and not the other? Perhaps because this second tunnel, Hyde Bank, is longer – over 300 yards. But perhaps it is that this canal must have cost a fortune to build and that was a towpath too far. So I came off the canal where a track brought me up by a picturesque farm and one or two smart houses. Clearly I had crossed the border from Manchester into what used to be the much more leafy Cheshire.

In hilly country along the canal, I observed that the towpath was rather busy with walkers, bikers and anglers, including one female angler, the first I had seen. The sight of this solitary female anger seemed somehow an affront to common sense, like the idea that the entire mass of the universe was concentrated into something the size of a pin head at the Big Bang, or the strange conception that the former Spice Girls, Kylie Minogue and Charlie Dimmock represent the epitome of feminine beauty. Isn't angling something that men do to get away from their womenfolk?

Passing a last group of angers, I came abruptly to the Marple Aqueduct. This is one of the great sights of the English canal system. You must in fact get a good view of it from the parallel railway viaduct, which runs at a higher level and so has ten or eleven arches, the aqueduct having only three. On this glorious sunny day there were woods and fields over to my left, framed between the elegant arches of the railway viaduct, where the sun picked out variegated yellows and greys in the stone. The views across it were a very photographer's dream. To my right lay the wooded valley of the River Goyt, the river flowing directly below, a long, long way down. The aqueduct itself was a seven-foot wide band of water with a towpath at either side, though the far side had no wall! I wouldn't want to cycle on that side. No matter, this place is certainly one of my Top Ten Sights of the North British Canals.

There is a memorial stone to one Dr Cyril Boucher at the end of the aqueduct. It seems he was one of the prime movers in getting the canal reopened in 1974. I wondered where the name Boucher came from, I had not seen it before and it sounded French. Apparently it is an earlier version of Butcher. I find it rather touching, the way the English hang on to odd names – if you were christened Nutter, Snodgrass, Pratt, Jawkins, anything involving bottom, Trollope, Balls, Boggis or Crapper, wouldn't you be tempted to use your mother's maiden name instead? (Too bad if your mother was called Peabody.) If you were an African the problem of honouring the family name could be even worse - would you really want to hang on to a name like Sir Abubakar Tafawa Balewa (Prime Minister of Nigeria in the 1960s and much lampooned by Michael Bentine), Archbishop Desmond Tutu or the Reverend Canaan Banana?

Past the plaque and ahead of me now loomed the locks, even the first one looking horribly deep. You may not think that riding up a slope past a lock amounts to much, but you probably haven't tried it. Remember, you are not on a road. There is no smooth tarmac surface, but one made of rough stones, often with lines of cobbles laid transversely across it at intervals. If it was tarmac it would be easy, but the wheels frequently slip, and dive between the sharp stones. Believe me, the north face of the Eiger is only slightly more daunting than Marple locks on a bike.

The locks are very scenic, with a pool at the foot of each one, overhung by trees. They rise mercilessly upwards, one after another. I did stop once or twice – just to make notes, you understand. At one point I inadvertently rode into someone's front garden to find a woman cutting the grass - "Sorry! What! Ho!" – act the idiot, like Bertie Wooster, then they humour you to make you go away quietly. I finally reached the top and I think it is an achievement that I was not all that tired after this feat. At the very top of the locks is located the junction with the Macclesfield Canal, so everything really comes together at this one place – the intersection, the locks and the aqueduct. There were a lot of boats moored around here. The Macclesfield Canal looked tantalizing, setting off under a beautiful turnover bridge.

I turned round here and set off back to my car. Of course the downhill swoop through the locks at Marple was a breeze. Just past the aqueduct an angler blocked my way with his telescopic pole and I asked him how he was getting on. He looked fed up.

"Waste of time," he said, "too many boats!"

Up until this point it had not occurred to me that the interests of the boatmen and the anglers are far from coincident. The anglers must hate the boats, because they destroy the careful setup of a cast and disturb the fish. A conversation with a boatman further back on the canal confirmed this.

"Oh aye," he said, "the anglers don't like anybody. They don't like bikes and they don't like boats. You say hello to them and they look the other way. There's big money in it, you know. They have competitions at the weekends, you'll see these groups of anglers and they're deadly serious."

"I thought it was just a way of passing an afternoon for the unemployed!"

"Not for some of them," he said. "Have you seen those giant poles they use?"

"Certainly, they block the towpath often enough."

"Carbon fibre jobs, seventeen and a half meters long. A top-of-the-range job can set you back five thousand quid."

"They still don't seem to work."

"Not on the canal maybe, but they work on the carp ponds all right."

Cycling down the quieter part of my way home, I moved into the silent woods, the dappled sunshine filtering through a mysterious glade below me on my left, and I thought, you know, you could do a lot worse than the Peak Forest Canal. However the feeling did not last. Very tired and struggling to negotiate a troublesome cobbled turnover bridge where the towpath changed sides, I put the bike into low gear and suddenly found myself peddling thin air. The chain had come off! This caused me some consternation but I needn't have worried, it was easy to put back on, at the price of oily fingertips. I arrived back at the basin sweaty, spattered in mud and covered in nettle stings. There must be something about Ashton, it was exactly like that last time I came here.

As I still had plenty of time, if not a lot of energy, I decided to motor on to the canal terminus at Whaley Bridge. Soon the moors of the High Peak loamed ahead of me. Just outside Whaley Bridge I got out and walked into town on the towpath. There must have been 150 if not 200 narrow boats between here and the town, I would say more than I had seen anywhere in my travels. So although it lies at the end of a cul-de-sac, Whaley Bridge is a major canal centre for the north of England. The canal ended in a tiny triangular basin, just about big enough to turn a narrow boat around. Here there was just one warehouse. The town itself seemed quite an attractive spot with boards up advertising the charms of old pubs, the Navigation and the Goyt.

Just before reaching the town I had noted the spur to Buxworth, once a hive of activity in the limestone industry with three basins which used to be packed with wharves and cranes. On a bridge over the branch canal was an ominous sign which said "Bugsworth Basin Closed". As I had come all this way and didn't plan to come again, I decided to explore anyway. After less than two miles I arrived at Buxworth to find that the basins were in fact a building site. Clearly they had been restored, having once been completely derelict. A notice announced that the basins had been opened in 1998 but closed the following year because of heavy water loss. It would cost a cool £1 million to sort this out and evidently they were on with the job in a very big way. You could see the potential of the place, though, no doubt about it, a lot of people would want to come here when it was finished. There were boards up announcing that it was an ancient monument. I thought this was a bit much for something that was only 200 years old.

*   *   *   *

The following day I had to make an unwelcome trip back to the bike shop. When I opened the back of the car, there was the bike all right – but no front wheel. I had left it propped up against the rear bumper of the car when reloading the bike the previous day. I wasn't going back to look for it, it was too far and it probably wouldn't be there anyway. That's the second time I have fallen for that trick and it would cost me another £50! Last time it was my glasses.

When I arrived at the bike shop, to my surprise I found that the bike man was no longer there. That seemed a shame because I had developed a great respect for this man, he knew everything about bikes and had a very pleasant manner.

"What happened to the other man?" I asked the new owner.

"Sold out to me a month back now," he said.

"I wonder why he did that?"

"He's 35 and has worked in bike shops since he left school at 15. He'd had enough, wanted to broaden his horizons. He's training to be a primary school teacher – a year's foundation course and then four years for a degree."

"He must have a very understanding wife."

"He must. But he's taking part-time work. Anyway, what can I do for you?"

I explained about the wheel and he soon fixed me up with a new wheel, tyre and inner tube.

"What sort of tyre do you want?" he asked. "I haven't any of those you have on now, except for second hand ones where people have upgraded to better tyres."

Hmm. Mine must be ultra-cheapo.

"Have you anything that offers any protection from thorns?"

"Certainly! These here have a Kevlar strip inside them. They make bullet-proof vests out of that. It will cost you twice as much (£15) but it will halve the number of punctures you get."

You live and learn. I took it, like a shot. There is nothing I dread more on my bike than another puncture.

CHAPTER 21

The next stage of the Cheshire Ring is the Macclesfield Canal. Thomas Telford was the engineer and the influence of his cut-and-fill techniques is clear as you go along the canal. The Macclesfield Canal is 27 miles long and has only one flight of locks, the top half of it running at a very high level for a canal – 518 feet. Like the Peak Forest, it was built as a narrow canal. It's a funny thing about canals – the smaller ones have survived better than the big ones. After falling into disrepair it was brought back into use with the rest of the Cheshire Ring in 1974.

I set off down the Macclesfield Canal from its junction with the Peak Forest Canal above Marple locks. I whizzed down the steep slope at the bridge over the canal and was almost immediately cursing at some idiot who had placed impassable steel barriers just a few hundred yards downstream, where I had to cross a road. I had to lift my bike over an adjacent wall to proceed. I mean just whose towpaths are these? My bike the Mongoose has many virtues but it is no lightweight and this job had me risking injury from the cogwheels. This made me so mad that I almost forgot to notice the gigantic red brick Goyt Mill on the bank side. If there is one thing that my long canal journey has shown me, it is that the southern image of the north as a place full of mills and factories is not misjudged. They are everywhere, even here in a leafy suburb like Marple, even in the Yorkshire Dales, they are there, be they old, new, restored or derelict, they are definitely there! I mean you would expect nothing else in Rochdale or Oldham, but here in Marple?

By this stage, rural country of the type I found along this canal bores me - I would much rather be somewhere with more character, say Todmorden or Burnley. Things perked up when I reached Bollington, about three miles north of Macclesfield. Here on the canal bank was a wonderful old mill, built of light stone and draped in ivy, known as Clarence Mill. It is just the sort of place envisaged by Elizabeth Gaskell when she wrote her novel *North and South*, recently televised. Its proprietor would have been a Mr Thornton as portrayed by Richard

Armitage in the TV series. The impact of this program was remarkable. Until it was shown I was not aware that southern middle-class women swooned in their millions over gritty northerners. The effect was scarcely visible when I was at Oxford, for example (ah, Mr Thornton may have been gritty, but he was also rich!) Still I take my hat off to Mr Thornton/Armitage and also to those southern ladies who have shown such good taste at last.

I pressed on to Macclesfield, formerly famous for its silk parachutes and knickers. Here were some rather unattractive moorings, overlooked by a red brick mill called Publicity Works Mill. This was once used for milling flour for Hovis but is now "luxury apartments" – of course. I wondered how much these apartments cost – I bet £180,000 for two bedrooms, quite possible more than that. Who is buying these places?

I moved on to Bosley locks, a few miles to the south of Macclesfield. Although there are twelve of them, heading downhill here, they were no more fearsome than a few flights of stairs for a veteran of the dreaded Marple locks. Moving on under a disused railway I found myself on a large embankment over the River Dane with a vista across to an elegant railway viaduct. There was a repeat of this at Congleton, a mile or two further south. Both offered excellent views and it did strike me that here was a type of canal I had not seen before. The Macclesfield may only be a small canal, but the engineering behind it is on a much greater scale than on say the trans-Pennine canals. There are big embankments, aqueducts and cuttings all the way along it. The country through which it passes is by no means flat but the canal makes no attempt to follow the contour.

After passing through Congleton I made for home. It had dawned on me that I had come out without a pair of underpants. Congleton must be 60 miles from home and, you know, 60 miles is rather a long way away from home to be without underpants.

I have heard the Macclesfield Canal described as the highest and one of the most beautiful waterways in England. Maybe, maybe, but both the Rochdale and the Huddersfield Narrow Canals go higher, parts of them are more beautiful, and they are certainly more interesting!

*　　　　*　　　　*　　　　*

The next leg of the Cheshire Ring is the Trent and Mersey, one of Britain's oldest canals, completed in 1777. The canal starts at Preston Brook outside Runcorn, where it connects with the southern arm of the

Bridgewater. It is 92 miles long and goes all the way to Shardlow in Derbyshire on the navigable River Trent. There are many locks on the canal, including more than 30 on "Heartbreak Hill", the run up from Middlewich to the junction with the Macclesfield Canal.

There was time this year to look at one or two highlights of the Trent and Mersey, and my first choice was Heartbreak Hill. So I picked up the canal near Alsager, about three miles before the intersection with the Macclesfield Canal. At Heartbreak Hill I hoped to find a good, tough flight of locks, but I was to be disappointed. The thirty-plus locks I had read about are strung out over a number of miles. This last run only had ten or a dozen, and as the towpath was excellent, I barely broke sweat. Whoever called this Heartbreak Hill hasn't been up the Narrow Canal from Huddersfield with its 42 locks.

I noted that the locks and the bridges on the canal were built of blackened red brick and looked old, over 200 years old in fact. The water was orange-coloured, presumably because of seepage from iron-rich sediments, as at Worsley on the Bridgewater. Before long I saw a town perched high on a hilltop, and I thought to myself, what a funny place to build a town! It is over a thousand feet high, amid all these lush Cheshire plains. I asked a woman on the bank what it was called. "Mow Cop" came the reply. If it was a funny place to build a town, it was also a funny name to give it!

I turned round at the junction with the Macclesfield Canal. Back behind Alsager are some canalside villages and I rather fancied taking a look because I know someone who lived in one of them, and accountant and Oracle consultant called Wilf. In fact I knew his address, and I knew it was right by the canal. So I moved on and successfully located his house, then called it a day. He had moved on.

* * * *

I decided to make another call on the Trent and Mersey, away from its Cheshire Ring stretch, where it runs into the River Trent at Shardlow on the border between Leicestershire and Derbyshire. I had read that this was an unspoiled Georgian town, but I was to be disappointed. There are a number of old, red-brick canal buildings – warehouses and the like, some converted for other uses. But the overall effect is not especially pleasing to the eye. Close to the M1 motorway, the prospect is blighted by the eight cooling towers of the Ratcliffe power station. I was conscious that here I was standing at the soggy bottom of England.

Although many miles inland, it wouldn't take much of a rise in sea level for the spring tides to flood this place.

*   *   *   *

My next stop along the Cheshire Ring was at Preston Brook outside Runcorn. I aimed to find the junction between the Trent & Mersey and Bridgewater Canals here, then head off into Runcorn down the last five miles of the Bridgewater. The reason I wanted to go down this canal – strictly speaking off the Cheshire Ring – was to find out what happened at the end of it. On my map the canal appears to terminate in the middle of the town, rather than on the Manchester Ship Canal, which is the logical place for it to end. The intersection with the Trent & Mersey was right in front of me as I parked up, so I set off into Runcorn. It wasn't until the last mile or so that the views became interesting. A vast panorama opened out to Widnes across the River Mersey, with a big modern bridge to connect Runcorn to Widnes. Most striking of all was the mammoth Fiddlers Ferry power station, which dominates the landscape for miles around.

The canal terminated against a bridge in the middle of Runcorn. The arches of the bridge had been filled in, and I asked three old anglers whose fat collie was blocking the path about it.

"Is that the end of it then? No more water?"

"Aye, that's it," said one of them in a notable Scouse accent. "There used to be ten locks taking it from here down to the ship canal, but they've built over it now. There was some plan to put 'em back, but it'll never happen. It would cost a bloody fortune."

On the way back I began to flag as I struggled through the mud on the stinker towpath. On days like this I wonder whether biking is adding years onto my life or taking them off! Things improved as I carried on along the Bridgewater through Warrington. Until 1974 this was just another Lancashire mill town, complete with rugby league team, canal, factory chimneys and gasometer. Then it was transferred to Cheshire (better postal address) and it has expanded vastly over the past few years. One of my colleagues at Kelloggs lived there, Roger, an accounts clerk. Although a native of Salford, he liked Warrington. Why?

"Because everything is new – the schools, the hospitals, the roads, the houses, the doctors' surgeries, you name it."

I would have thought that was a reason for not liking it myself. However it turned out there was another reason.

"And you don't get many perverts there like you do in Manchester."

Roger clearly didn't think Manchester's claim to the liveliest gay scene outside San Francisco was anything to brag about.

"Look at that Boy George," he said. "Says he prefers a cup of tea to sex. Who's he trying to kid? Why does he dress like that then?"

"He's certainly colourful."

"That's what I hate about them," replied Roger. "It's the way they flaunt it."

I passed on under the M6 to Lymm, the sort of place that gives Cheshire its reputation as the Surrey of the North. Plenty of rich people live here (the only person I ever met who came from here was a judge). I always think of Cheshire as Judith Chalmers territory. So many of the women look like her – big mouth, good teeth, blond and posh hairdo, big smile, gym subscription. Many of these women have no need to work and you can see them swanning around Wilmslow and Prestbury in their BMWs or SUVs, driving to the dress shops. There is money in Cheshire because it is not either (a) Manchester or (b) Liverpool. When I was at Oxford I knew a girl from Wilmslow. She wasn't that good looking but in those days we Oxford men were desperate, there were five men for every woman, and I fancied her a bit. That was until I saw her picture plastered all over the Daily Mail. She had gone to a party in London dressed entirely in banana leaves. Large amounts of naked flesh were clearly visible and I thought to myself, you know, I don't think that girl is really quite my type!

Through Lymm I pushed on another five miles or so to the outskirts of Altrincham. I am less and less keen on rural sections like this – it would be nice to press fast forward and get to the next town, but there is no fast forward button on a bike. However this particular stretch of canal was interesting in one respect, in that it was almost entirely original. The bridges, aqueducts and embankments were exactly as they would have been when they were first built. There were no concrete monstrosities. None of the bridges looked as if it would support more than a couple of tons weight – why should it? There were no vehicles weighing that much back in 1770. The drawback of these very old bridges, however, is that they are very low, and the towpath has sharp bends going into and out of them. You have to be very careful on a bike and I admit to being terrified coming off one aqueduct when I just missed a pedestrian and nearly went in – whoa! I think the pedestrian thought I was an ace biker but in fact I was practically out of control. It's a good job I don't have a fast bike or I would be mincemeat by now.

Thank goodness for the Mongoose. Remember, this bike cost me just £229. I could have spent four times that amount. But I wanted a bike I could ride on muddy and bumpy canals, not a fashion statement. It was fit for the purpose for which I bought it and I am beginning to see it a wonderful investment. However, not everyone would agree with me. I spoke to another biker about this on the way home.

"What kind of bike is that?" he asked.

"A Mongoose, cost me 229 quid," I replied.

He gave me a pitying look.

"I bet it weighs a ton," he said.

"As a matter of fact it is rather heavy!"

"If you had paid five or six hundred, you would have got a light bike. Bikes are all about weight. On a lighter bike you would get much further in a day and it would be easier to get into your car."

My Yorkshire parsimony had let me down.

The Bridgewater Canal – Southern section

EAST

```
*Castlefields, central Manchester
|
|_____Junction with northern section of
|         Bridgewater
*Trafford Park Industrial Estate
|
*Sale
|
|
*Altrincham
|
|
*Lymm
|
|*Warrington
|
|_____Junction with Trent & Mersey Canal
*Preston Brook
|
|
*Runcorn
```

WEST

CHAPTER 22

I resumed on the Bridgewater for the final stretch of the Cheshire Ring, just outside Altrincham and heading into Manchester, having first checked out the weather forecast first – OK for today, but not good beyond the weekend. However by then I might not care. I had a phone call this morning from the Honeywell factory in Scotland! At last! They want me to go there for three months! What a good time to ring, now the summer is over! Of course I shall take my bike with me and set about the canals between the Forth and Clyde. Am I ready to go back? My blood pressure this morning: 144/88.

Altrincham and Sale, once part of Cheshire (now Greater Manchester) are middle-class dormitory towns for Manchester. I don't know which is considered the better address, but on the towpath, Sale looked better than Altrincham, though there were some very expensive-looking new canalside blocks of flats going up in Altrincham. You can tell this is an up-market area, because Sale is the home of the main rugby union club in the region. A member of their current team comes from my home town, Halifax. In fact I dated his mother for twelve months when I was 18, but she married a man who was much older, much richer and much balder than me. She would not have made a suitable wife for me, however. She liked driving Jaguars too much.

The canal ran dead straight right through Sale, shimmering blue to reflect the sky. In the water I passed a rowing eight, with the obligatory female cox, a rather pretty girl. That did not surprise me because after all, with eight beefy rowers for company, there must be a lot of competition for the job. Soon I came across another boat, a ladies four. I never knew that women went in for rowing! This lot didn't look at all beefy, presentable and blond in fact, why do they want to do something so totally masculine and hunky as rowing? It is well known that no more strenuous form of exercise exists or is ever likely to be devised. I have read in the newspapers that modern woman wants to be physically strong, but as a man, I would advise modern woman that this will do nothing to increase her attractiveness to me.

Just outside Sale centre, a canal wedding was taking place. The wedding party had taken charge of three narrow boats. This is the first time that I had seen anyone steering a narrow boat wearing a collar and tie, and drinking beer from a can. Some of the party were swaying wildly. In Sale town centre itself, the pubs were overflowing with people. Three drunks assailed me, making motor-bike noises. I ignore this sort of thing, just as long as they stick to making noises. Otherwise I would punch their heads in (yeah!).

The Mersey valley separates old Cheshire from Manchester proper and I headed across this relatively open area, crossing the Mersey on an aqueduct. Immediately I arrived in Manchester, in the Stretford area, there was a deterioration in the scenery. I mean, does Manchester have any good areas? I haven't found one yet. In the water was a loose narrow boat, completely unattended. When the owner goes to find this at his moorings, he is in for a shock. But how had this happened? I suspect vandalism – somebody deliberately untied the boat. The Kelloggs offices are just up the road from here and occasionally at lunchtime we would nip out to the Arndale Centre in Stretford. My friend Wilf from Alsager way used to call it the White Trash Centre. I think he was referring to the one-parent families which are much in evidence there, the broken-looking men, the skinheads, hoodies and the many people who appear to be of Irish immigrant origin with a nasty taste in shell suits.

The dreary housing and factory sites continued right up to the junction with the northern arm of the Bridgewater at the corner of the Trafford Park Industrial Estate. I had done the rest of it before on the South Pennine Ring so this was the end of the Cheshire Ring for me. The Bridgewater itself terminates at Castlefield a mile or two further on.

*   *   *   *

Have you ever wondered if you are going crazy? Becoming obsessed? Why did I find myself diverting 30 miles from my chosen route and 30 miles back again to look at a chemical plant in Cheshire? Because the Anderton Boat Lift is there, and that is one of the "Seven Wonders" of the canal world!

Near Northwich the Trent and Mersey runs parallel to the River Weaver, which was converted to a Navigation early in the eighteenth century. To avoid the long way round via the Bridgewater and Runcorn it was decided in 1870s to build a boat lift which would carry canal traffic down 50 feet from the Trent and Mersey to the Weaver Navigation below. At a cost of £7m, this boat lift was restored to working order in 2002, and a visitor centre has been built.

When I arrived at the site I was taken aback by the number of narrow boats in the adjoining canal basins – more than I had seen anywhere else. I was getting close to the Midlands now, and the Midlands, I was learning, is where the real action is on the English canal system. Unfortunately road works to improve access to the site were under way and the visitor centre was closed. Nevertheless, the site was spectacular enough with the far bank absolutely dominated by a gigantic chemical plant. The boat lift, first operating in 1875, has two "caissons" or steel canal sections. The boat lift we see day replaced the 1875 version in 1907. It is a black-painted steel tubular structure, the sort of thing you might expect to see at a pit head – kind of Arthur Scargill meets Lloyds of London. The Weaver swirled below.

The Anderton Boat Lift is known as the "cathedral of the canals" and while it is interesting enough in its way, all I can say is that whoever dreamt that up can't have spent much time in York and Ely. And do you know what? They have a better one in Scotland!

The Union Canal, Scotland

NORTH   SOUTH

```
                        *  Edinburgh
                        *  Ratho
                        |
Union Canal             |
                        |
                        *  Linlithgow
                        |
                        |
                        |
                        *  Redding
                        *  Falkirk
                        *  Camelon
                        ++ Falkirk Wheel
                        ++
                        |
Forth and Clyde Canal   |
```

CHAPTER 23

Today is D-day. Tomorrow I have to be in Scotland. I have to decide whether to head north now, and start on the canals, or get up early tomorrow and leave the canals for some unspecified later date. Although the weather forecast for Scotland is poor, I think I shall risk going today. Why? I took my blood pressure this morning at 9 am (the most favorable time) and it came up at 144/78. Also, Christine says my posture has improved, I am standing up straight – ah, thank the locks for that! When I look in the mirror I see that my eyeballs are clearer than they have been for years. After a long summer of riding the bike almost every day, the benefits are beginning to show. I am leaving for Scotland today.

So it was that I found myself in Scotland, home of the deep-fried Mars bar, at a place called Newhouse, near Motherwell, about 12 miles to the east of Glasgow. I had a contract with Honeywell as an Oracle consultant for three month's work. I knew I was in Scotland all right when I arrived in the canteen at Honeywell on the first day. One item on the menu for lunch was "haggis, neeps and tatties".

Until first arriving at Newhouse I had always thought that Scotland was roughly divided into three parts – the Southern Uplands, the Central Lowlands, and the Highlands and Islands. I very soon discovered that there is a far more important distinction. That is the one between the east of Scotland, centred on the splendid city of Edinburgh, and the west, centred on the rather less splendid city of Glasgow. Here are two very different worlds. One is urbane, European, cosmopolitan and possessing architectural wonders such as the neo-classical New Town. The other is gritty, tough and sprawling but oddly sympathetic, speaking a language which is only partially comprehensible to outsiders. I found myself on the western side of this divide.

My first impression was that I was certainly not amongst the English, because the physical appearance of the Scots reflects their history. Here are dark-haired, blue or brown-eyed, thick-eyebrowed people, some tall and well-built, many diminutive. These are the descendants of a race that dominated the Atlantic coasts from Spain to Scotland in the period 1300-600BC – the Hibernians. Then we have the ginger-haired, freckled, green-eyed type, not as many as in Ireland, but still a lot more than in England. After that are the Scandinavians, very many of these in the Glasgow area. Like Agnetha of Abba these people have a characteristic turned-up nose and are often blond-haired. Finally there are the Anglo-Saxons. The area as far as the Firth of Forth was part of the Anglian kingdoms of Northumberland and Berenicia for five hundred years, and a form of English has been spoken in Scotland for as long as it has in England. So if you want to know why Edinburgh is such a fine place, well, perhaps it was built by the English Scots!

I was taken aback by the poverty of the environment. The industrial estate at Newhouse where the Honeywell factory is located is glum enough and appears to double as a dumping ground for rubbish. Most of the roads in the area are bumpy and potholed. Around Newhouse lie any number of grim towns and villages – Holytown, Airdie, Bellshill, Chapelhall, Coatbridge, Motherwell and Cumbernauld. The whole area would serve as a nightmare challenge to a landscape painter. This district is known as Monklands and its MP until his death in 1994 was John Smith, Leader of the Opposition and Prime Minister-in-Waiting. As he was only 55 when he died of a heart attack, his is the very fate that I am trying to avoid with my bike.

Occasionally I needed to do a bit of shopping after work and would drop into the Kwik Save in Chapelhall. I always felt overdressed for this place in a collar and tie, amongst the one-parent families, broken men smelling of alcohol, and troublesome children in scruffy trainers. I suppose Kwik Saves are like this everywhere, it isn't just Chapelhall. Even more depressing are the small shops in Holytown. Here a conspicuous product on sale is Buckfast Abbey Tonic Wine, thought by many in Scotland to be an instrument of an English conspiracy to bring Scotland to its knees. It is the cheapest form of alcohol available, occupying in Scotland the role once taken by British Sherry in England, and still very much a force to be reckoned with. I suppose if the English have given the Scots Buckfast Abbey Tonic Wine, they have given us whiskey, which you might agree isn't a bad swap. (Or maybe not – last words of Dylan Thomas – "I've had 18 straight whiskies – I think that's a record!")

*   *   *   *

There are two lowland canals in Scotland. First is the Forth and Clyde between the Clyde near Clydebank west of Glasgow and the Forth at

Grangemouth. Then we have the Union Canal between Edinburgh and Falkirk, where it joins the Forth and Clyde. The Union Canal does not reach the sea at its eastern end, terminating in central Edinburgh. This waterway link through central Scotland was broken when the basin connecting the two canals was built over. Now it has been revived with the construction of the Falkirk Wheel, midway between Glasgow and Edinburgh, reconnecting the two canals. This is the spectacular centrepiece of the £84.5 million 'Millennium Link', the UK's largest canal restoration project. I think you'll agree that £84.5 million IS rather a lot to spend on canals. More about the Falkirk Wheel later, because I was going to start my exploration in Edinburgh on the Union Canal.

Work began on the Edinburgh end of the Union Canal in 1818. There were problems with the workforce, including riots, excessive drinking and fights between Highlanders and Irishmen. (Their descendants have kept up the tradition.) However, some remarkable engineering was involved in the construction. There were three spectacular aqueducts to build over the river Almond, the river Avon (the longest and tallest in Scotland) and the Waters of Leith in Edinburgh. Then there was the canal itself, only five feet deep for most of its course, and built to run along on a contour for its whole length. There is not a single lock on its 31 miles (bliss!) until it connects to the Forth & Clyde Canal at Falkirk. Here a flight of 11 locks was built, which lowered the canal 110 feet over a distance of just over a mile. The canal also boasts Scotland's longest (and until recently only) canal tunnel, on the outskirts of Falkirk. This was built when the local landowner refused to allow the new canal to cross his land.

Two of the workers on the Union canal were William Burke and William Hare, who came from Ulster. After the completion of the canal they set themselves up as body snatchers, digging up corpses to sell to the medical profession. It was much more profitable than digging the canal, as a surgeon would pay up to £10 for a good body. Before long they decided to save digging time by snatching live people in Edinburgh's Old Town – so much easier, a nice clean fresh body and no dirty fingernails. They suffocated their victims by covering the mouth and nose as this method of murder left no evidence of foul play. According to a contemporary account, number one was an old woman from Gilmerton who they found intoxicated and further stupefied with drink. Two was a peddlar from England who had the bad fortune to lodge with them. Three was an old man, Joe the Miller. Four and five were a woman called Mary Haldane and her daughter. Six and seven were an old Irishwoman and her grandson. Number eight was a cinder-gatherer; nine, an old woman taken out of the hands of police officers; ten, one Mary Patterson; eleven, a woman from the country; twelve, a girl called McDougal. Number thirteen was a Mrs. Osler or Hosler, a washerwoman; fourteen, "Daft Jamie"; fifteen, a girl murdered by Hare alone; sixteen a woman called Campbell or Docherty.

After they had murdered their sixteenth victim, Burke and Hare were caught, another Irishman finding the body of their last victim under a bed, covered in straw. There was little direct evidence and the prosecution only obtained the conviction of Burke by persuading Hare to turn King's witness in return for immunity from prosecution. This was a great deal for Hare, would he get it today? The trial caused a sensation at the time. However there was much dissatisfaction (quite rightly) because the job had only been half-done, in that Hare had got away scot-free (he survived until 1859).

Burke went to the gallows in 1829, cheered off by a crowd of over 40,000 people and no doubt wondering what would become of his own body. In fact it was cut down and given by the Town Council to one Professor Munro for dissection. The head was sawn off the body to illustrate a lecture about the human brain. Such was demand, however, that it was arranged that the body would become a public exhibition. The reassembled Burke lay on the black marble table of the Professor's dissecting-room: naked, horrible, and exposed to the gaze of a stream of necro-tourists who filed passed at the rate of sixty people per minute.

Like all canals, the Union had its own victims, one of the most notable being George Kemp, the architect of the wonderful Scott Monument on Princes Street in Edinburgh. He was an unknown draughtsman and former country joiner when his design won the competition for the building. However he drowned in the Union Canal before his monument was completed in 1844.

*   *   *   *

I set off to Scotland to take a look at the Union Canal for myself, passing through a temperature warp as I moved northwards. The long, extended summer we had enjoyed in England was here replaced by a chilly wind. I made my way to Edinburgh, a city which is despised for its pretentions in western Scotland but which is still streets ahead of any regional capital in England. The site on which Edinburgh is located is spectacular, with its plugs and hills. Approached from the west, it resembles Tenerife with clothes on – a volcanic landscape.

I parked up at a place called Ratho, about nine canal miles from the centre of Edinburgh, and set off eastwards to find the end of the canal. Ratho has a canal basin and it did look a pleasant spot with some nice old houses and an old hall. There were four big tourist boats in the water, and beyond that a dozen or more narrow boats moored up with a few other canal craft. In terms of the number of private boats, this was the busiest spot on the canal (as I was to discover, on any canal in the Scottish Lowlands).

As I set off I reflected that I must be crazy to do this instead of curling up with a good book in the warm hotel room. In the sky there was the V-shape of a flotilla of birds departing for the winter, and there were yellow and red leaves on the trees and on the ground. Autumn had arrived in earnest, but there was that beautifully clear light which you only seem to find in northern areas. I pulled on my kagool feeling certain I would soon be drenched – there had been heavy showers all the way over from Newhouse where I was staying.

Ahead of me in the distance loomed Edinburgh castle, on top of a hill. It looked gaunt and medieval, like something you might expect to find in Transylvania rather than in Scotland. After three miles or so I arrived at the Edinburgh bypass, which I crossed on a new aqueduct. Passing through the Wester Hailes council estate, I noted that lot of the pedestrians had pale faces and looked like Rod Stewart. Along the way I came to a long aqueduct which had a narrow, cobbled towpath sloping into the water on both sides. This was the Slateford aqueduct over the Waters of Leith (what a pretty name for a river!). With eight arches it was built on a much larger scale than say the aqueduct at Marple on the Peak Forest Canal, which has only three arches. There were clear views over to the hills on the northern side of the Firth of Forth, with aircraft landing at Edinburgh Airport in front of them. I am always surprised at how busy Edinburgh and Glasgow airports are, given that each city has its own. It would seem more logical to have one airport mid-way between Edinburgh and Glasgow, but it hasn't worked out that way. This reminds me of the reason that Glasgow has three major football grounds – Ibrox (Rangers), Parkhead (Celtic) and Hampden Park (Scotland). The only reason that Hampden Park exists is that it is not the home of either Rangers or Celtic.

Moving along the canal I passed the transition from the modern suburbs, where I could have been anywhere in Scotland, to the old ones, where I could only have been in Edinburgh. I arrived at the most attractive section at Harrison Park, across which there were views to handsome Georgian stone terraced houses, the sort of thing for which the city is famous. It occurred to me (not for the first time) that they did things so much better 200 years ago. There were four narrow boats and a number of small launches in the canal at Harrison Park, as well as some racing boats. One of the narrow boats bore the name "Capercaillie Cruises" and I did wonder what kind of Scottish thing a capercaillie was – a vegetable, a type of deer, a spice or a large game bird perhaps? (The last!)

The canal terminates in a grotty basin at the Leamington Boat Lift. There were no boats here, just a line of old bangers parked up next to walls covered in graffiti. Beyond this point it is no longer possible to follow the canal, which is drained and continues a little further. There are plans for creating an impressive development around the terminus of the restored canal to replace the brewery and the run down old buildings that are here now. Although it was getting on I biked around the streets trying vainly to find the very end of the canal, when I turned a corner and bumped pretty well straight into the new buildings of the Scottish Parliament, at the foot of the Royal Mile. This institution was popular at first, but it isn't now. The only thing it has done is to spend £430 million on these buildings, and what have they got? They look like the head offices of a building society in Spain. For an Englishman like me, asking the locals questions about this is not sensible. It's like asking an Australian about his convict ancestors or a Frenchman about Waterloo.

I made my way back as quickly as possible as it had become cold and my eyes and nose were streaming. I had managed to avoid getting wet but that night there was a frost, the first of the season. When I reached my hotel I revived myself with warm sweet tea. There is a French girl at Honeywell and she thinks it hilarious that the British give this substance to victims of shock such as people who have had limbs severed by industrial machinery or helicopter blades, but I love it, brewed in the Yorkshire fashion, strong and sweet.

CHAPTER 24

I set off from my hotel one evening with the intention of picking up the Union Canal again at Ratho, where I had started last time. I would see how far I could get in the couple of hours of daylight maximum I had left. Luckily it was a clear evening, cool and crisp, in fact ideal for biking – you don't want it hot, wet or downright cold. I was finding that if it isn't too wet or windy, autumn biking has certain advantages – for a start the weeds grow much less vigorously. Prominent to the south were the Pentland Hills, trackless, bare and volcanic-looking. You can't explore these hills by road because there are no roads, literally none.

So I didn't have to stop later, I had a few puffs on a cigar before getting on the bike. It is hard not to feel persecuted if you are a smoker these days. The medical books all scream at me to stop, but they fail to point out the advantages of smoking. There is strong statistical evidence that the evil habit offers considerable protection against brain decay. At a time when senility is becoming a serious and expensive problem for our society, that is hardly insignificant. In fact my Uncle Donald smoked 30 cigarettes a day all his adult life until he was 88. He died two years later, so I think stopping smoking probably killed him. At any rate, mentally he was as bright as a button right to the end – he did the *Daily Telegraph* cryptic crossword the day he died.

Getting going, I soon arrived at the aqueduct over the River Almond, which looked just like the one over the Waters of Leith in Edinburgh. The view was lovely – first to the river in its gorge below, then into the distance. The river bed, 75 feet below the aqueduct, is most unusual, being formed of flat stone, criss-crossed with joints. Moving along past some moorings, I came to a wooded section with trees overhanging the canal on both sides. This was gloomy even now and would be decidedly dark later. The track was excellent and I soon picked up speed, moving along quickly in high ratio.

I passed the M8 motorway under a brand new bridge. The construction of this bridge must have entailed a serious disruption to traffic with months of delays, all for a canal whose entire population of boats seemed to be moored up at Ratho. A mile and a half away to my right stretched one of the architectural wonders of Scotland, the Kirkliston rail viaduct over the River Almond, 36 arches long, a dreamlike, fairyland structure. More striking from the towpath, however, was the enormous slag heap which towers over the town of Broxburn, straight ahead. This looked for all the world like a red and menacing volcano, devoid of vegetation as if recently erupted. The closer I got to this thing, the more monumental it looked. Cut into fantastic shapes by erosion, it must be 200 feet high at least. Known locally as a shale bing, it represents the remains of mining for oil shale. If ever it became unstable Broxburn would be engulfed, like Abervan. Beyond Broxburn there were several more, not quite as large.

Beyond Broxburn is Niddry castle, built of grey stone in the fifteenth century. Tall and narrow, it is obviously restored as it is the only mediaeval castle I have seen with a slate roof and Velux windows. Set amongst green lawns, the aspects are blighted by the distinctly unmediaeval shale bing which overlooks it. Noting that there were rabbits everywhere, not a good sign as they come out at twilight, I came to the small town of Winchburgh. By this time I was six or seven miles from my starting point in Ratho, rather a long way even on a Scottish towpath, so I turned round and headed back in the gathering gloom, pushing on at record speed. The open sections were fine but it got scary where there were woods on either bank, as I had expected. Faster, faster – I had never gone this fast on a bike. In a dark wooded section I startled a rabbit which seemed to make quite a noise crashing through the undergrowth – in fact at first I thought it must be something bigger, let's say a triceratops. There was no artificial light whatsoever and eventually I just had to slow down and take things carefully. After a long straight stretch – where the hell is Ratho? – the bright lights of the Bridge Inn at the canal basin finally came into view. I made it back to the car and put the bike away with great relief, making a note not to be so ambitious again.

As I was getting into the car an airliner flew directly overhead on its way into Edinburgh airport, large, impressive and glowing with lights. Less than two hundred years ago they were still digging canals like this one and now these planes are everywhere. What will it be like two hundred years from now?

I resumed at Winchburgh on another evening, heading west for Linlithgow. Passing along a long wooded cutting another great slagheap hove into view. After this point the view became very scenic - the monstrosity was behind me. Visible from the towpath were the tops of the Forth rail and road bridges, and a huge full moon hanging just over the horizon – could it be the harvest moon? I passed a pair of joggers, a man and a woman, puffing and blowing a bit, while I glided along in high ratio. Yes, I thought, this biking beats jogging any day.

Further along the bank I arrived at Linlithgow, a historic town with interesting turrets, towers and gabled stone fronts. Its palace is depicted on every tourist brochure of Scotland. It was partially burnt down during the 1745/6 Jacobite rebellion and was never rebuilt, so that today it is a ruin. This is not actually obvious because all the external walls are still standing. In fact, the palace would make a good restoration project, if rather an overdue one. After all they restored Windsor Castle quickly enough following the fire in 1992, didn't they? (Ah, but that is in England!)

Just along the way I saw a swan, floating along with its neck and head fully submerged in the water, a familiar sight by now. How on earth these gleaming white birds, the aristocracy of the canals, manage always to look so immaculate is a mystery to me, and what is it that so attracts them in the murky water? You find some weird things in water, some of them requiring no oxygen and living off sulphides. Things like pink filaments in pools in Yellowstone National Park which are genetically unrelated to any other plant on earth, and tube worms twelve feet long thousands of feet down in the Pacific growing next to vents of superheated water. There must be something like that hiding away in the Union Canal that tastes good to swans.

A couple of miles further along I arrived at the Avon aqueduct, which looked just like the other two aqueducts I had already crossed on this canal, with a cobbled towpath on either side, though it is longer, spanning 12 arches. Altogether the aqueduct is 810 feet long and 86 feet high. There is only one longer aqueduct in Britain, Telford's Pontcysyllte on the Llangollen Canal, one of the Seven Wonders of the English canal system. The setting was lovely. The river ran over a weir in the Avon Gorge a long way below, surrounded by trees in autumn hues and impossibly green grass. In the middle distance a big, picturesque viaduct carried the main line railway from Glasgow to Edinburgh, and hills rose beyond this. The Avon is one of Scotland's unknown rivers – unknown in England, that is – but it has a very pretty gorge.

I picked up speed and shifted into high ratio, something which is not much use on the South Pennine ring but which was coming in handy in Scotland where there are wide towpaths and few locks. I heard the comforting scrunch of the tyres on the gravel of the path, and reflected that there is something just right about the level of exercise I get from a bike. Things like rowing machines, jogging and squash are just too violent, too much of a shock to the system, for a man in his fifties, and therefore likely to do more harm than good. Walking is just not enough – you could go for a stroll round the park for half an hour a day and I don't think it would make a bit of difference. But biking is just right.

Before long I passed a large factory complex, stood alone in the middle of this rural area, and I thought, what a funny place to build a factory! This is the property of the American computer company Sun Microsystems. How did they get planning permission to put it in the leafy Avon Valley when there are industrial estates galore down at Livingstone and Bathgate only a few miles away? Perhaps it is that when Sun Microsystems comes knocking at the door and says it wants a factory in a nice place (i.e. not Livingstone or Bathgate), the local authorities say "How about outside Linlithgow, that's a nice place! You can put your factory in the green belt a couple of miles outside, no one will see it!"

I pressed on as far as the outskirts of Falkirk, then turned round – it was getting dark again. Believe me, you do not want to ride a bike by a canal after dark. I got back just ahead of the rain as night closed in.

One evening, months later and wondering just what I could revisit in the evening, from all the places in central Scotland, my first choice was the Avon aqueduct. So I went back, on foot. It was not my intention to go on foot, it was just that when I arrived I found I had a puncture. I observed that a wooden walkway with steps had been constructed down to the river below, so down I went. The river, quite a size, swirls past in a bend, with woods on either side. The aqueduct soars over it, really looking much too big for a mere canal. It is so solid, so beautifully constructed with tapering sandstone pillars. This spot is a wonderful secret and there is no road to it, no car park, no signposts, and no people. At any rate, the Avon aqueduct definitely merits a place in my Top Ten Sights of the North British Canals.

I returned to the Union Canal at Falkirk, a few miles west of Linlithgow, one evening after work. Here is the canal's only tunnel, 690 yards long. To my surprise I found that it had a towpath, so I set off eastwards through it in the general direction of Edinburgh. This tunnel features a traffic light and even internal lighting! Now they could use that in the Standedge and Scout Tunnels on the Huddersfield Narrow Canal. At one point water poured from the roof into the canal, with the force of a couple of bath taps, but otherwise the tunnel was quite wide and relatively commodious. It is quite high – the roof must be twelve or thirteen feet above the surface of the water. It must have been built that way to accommodate ships with masts, because other tunnels such as the Standedge are nothing like this height. I passed a man coming the other way with an open umbrella. I thought that was going a bit far until splat! I got a good soaking right near the end of the tunnel.

Passing under a bridge, I observed a housing estate on the hillside consisting entirely of grey cement-rendered buildings. Why is property so ugly in this part of Scotland? In many estates they don't even plant any trees to soften the stark houses. I passed a man walking an Alsatian, which he pulled it to one side: "Hello there! Nae bather!"

Not far along the far bank I came upon a Young Offenders Institute, a huge place. The perimeter along the canal bank must have been 600 yards long. The site contains a whole complex of buildings, some very large, some new, some old, and all surrounded by a 20-foot high grey steel fence topped by barbed wire and overlooked by spotlights. If I were a young offender, I would not like the look of this place.

A mile or so later I turned round. Ever aware of the thorn threat, I really did not want to be caught out by a puncture so far from safety after a long day at work. I sped along on the good track, anxious to get back. The Young Offenders Institute looked grim and menacing. Then I had to go back into the tunnel. Splat! - caught me again as I went in. The other end looked a long way away and by now it was properly dark. The lights in the tunnel seemed to throw out the ghosts of its builders at points along the path - my heart jumped twice at the illusion. I wondered how many men had died blasting this thing out. It was seriously spooky, not the sort of place where you would want to bump into say Hannibal Lecter, the Hound of the Baskervilles or even Peter Mandelson, the Prince of Darkness. I was tired, these evening stints are tough, but I got through in the end.

The canal leaves the tunnel in a pleasant wooded area with lawns. I came back here the following night, finding it populated by distinctly untimid rabbits and noisy crows. Rocky outcrops glistened beneath colourful trees, reds, yellows and greens at this time of year. Moving along the canal there were good views across the spires of Falkirk to the Firth of Forth. Whatever man may do to this place, it certainly impresses me. The fiery lights from the huge oil refinery and power station at Grangemouth created an impression of a science fiction city on a distant planet, populated by beings requiring strange metallic structures to support their existence, cooling towers, chimneys, storage tanks and steaming condensers. Across the Forth, flashing blue lights shone out from the massive tower of the Longannet power station. Mountains loomed to the north.

After a couple of miles the canal swung north in a new stretch up to the Falkirk Wheel. I soon arrived at a couple of new, deep locks, then another tunnel, also new and known as the Rocastle tunnel. This takes the Union Canal through the Antonine Wall, believe it or not. The wall was built by the Roman Emperor Anthony to keep the Picts out of the Empire. The tunnel is 200 yards long and above it runs the main line railway between Edinburgh and Glasgow. Through the tunnel the last short stretch of the canal leading to the Wheel was visible, with an arch over the last few yards, but I could not get there – there was a gate at the tunnel and that was locked. Never mind, it was my intention to return to the Wheel itself as a separate visit. Everything round here looked smart, new and expensive.

Riding back in the gathering gloom a young man suddenly lunged at me uttering incomprehensible Glaswegian. Oh God, I thought, a nutter – these Scots can be so troublesome when they forget their medication! Then I realized he had said "I'll get oot ya road!" and had simulated a dive. I suppose he was being friendly but he gave me a shock. Spare me these antics at the end of a long day like this one - up at 6.30 am, at work all day and then this excursion.

Cycling back, having now ridden along the whole length of the Union Canal, it struck me that it is the princess of the Scottish canals – after all, it does go to Edinburgh, Linlithgow and the Falkirk Wheel and it does have three magnificent aqueducts. The Forth and Clyde Canal did not seem so fair a prospect, much of it winding through the towns of the lower Clyde.

*   *   *   *

So now it was time to look at the new Falkirk Wheel, which connects the Forth & Clyde and Union canals. Replacing a flight of eleven locks, the Wheel is 115 feet high. It cost £17 million to build and it can transfer up to eight boats at a time, water and all, up and down between the canals. While one arm goes up with four boats, the other, also carrying up to four boats, descends. The apparatus of the Wheel is two huge pairs of prongs, each of which carries a steel section of canal (a "gondola"), so that when one goes up, the other comes down. It uses almost no energy – about enough to boil two electric kettles. The reason is that the gondola going up is exactly balanced by the gondola going down. It doesn't matter if there is no boat coming down because of the Archimedes Principle. The boats displace their own weight in water so the two gondolas weigh the same, with or without boats.

I drove up from England one Monday and parked up at the Falkirk Wheel, arriving at the Visitor Centre at 4.15 pm, just in time to catch the last tourist boat of the day. Everything here is shiny and new. The site itself is set in a grassy amphitheatre with a concrete aqueduct bringing the Union Canal from the exit of the Rocastle tunnel up the Wheel. The "wheel" itself appeared surreal. There is not a word in the language to describe this thing – it looks like a gigantic kitchen utensil designed for slicing bulk quantities of vegetables. It is the only structure of its kind in the world. Just the same it definitely goes into my Top Ten Sights of the North British canals, though I did have one rebellious thought about it – wouldn't it have been cheaper and easier simply to build a few more locks?

The tourist boat ride takes 45 minutes and costs £8. It was a rainy autumn day, but there were nevertheless 85 people on my boat, many of them children, because for some reason the Scots choose to have a public holiday at this time. Our "captain" was called Donald, a short, fat man, bald with bright blue eyes and the Slavic or Scandinavian nose you see so often in Scotland. He kept up a cheery banter:

"Why do you suppose that me and my crew Ian have life jackets and you don't? Because it cost a lot to train me and Ian, but we can always get some more passengers!"

The operation of the lift was utterly silent and I didn't actually realise we were moving until I looked over the side and saw Grangemouth in the distance. We moved along the aqueduct and into the tunnel. In the basin at the far end there were the two high locks which have been built to access the Union Canal, but we did a sharp turn and went back. We re-emerged from the tunnel to rainswept grey skies with good views over the Firth of Forth. On a sunny day this must all look quite splendid, but of course, there aren't many sunny days in this part of the world. Also clearly visible was the Longannet power station across the Forth.

I asked Donald how many private boats used the Wheel.

"There were only 50 through in the first year, but we've had three times that number this year. Next year we've a block booking from Capercaillie Cruises which will bump that up some more."

However as I had seen a total of less than 20 narrow boats the whole Union Canal (none moving) I must have looked pretty skeptical.

"In my opinion, within a year or two traffic's likely to increase to a point where capacity will be stretched. A priority system will need to be established between the private boats on the one hand and our tourist Wheel-only boats on the other," said Donald. "We might have to start charging."

"So don't you charge now?" I asked.

"No, it's absolutely free. This is not England," he said darkly.

Of course the Scottish people like to play up the differences between themselves and the English. They will proudly tell you about their legal and education systems which are apparently superior to their equivalents in England (something which is not hard to credit). However the supermarkets are virtually identical to those in England, except that they sell the loathsome Scotch pies, and the TV is also mostly the same, screening the same soap operas as in England. There is a certain amount of TV broadcast in Gaelic every week, subsidized by the European Union. This bemuses most of the Scots because they have long abandoned this language in favour of English. The cars, the road signs, most of the newspaper titles, even the weather are all very similar to what you will find south of the border, at least until you reach the gale-swept Hebrides. The policemen look the same.

Yet there are some differences. Scottish scenery is very different, with mountains, dark rocks and fast-flowing rivers never far away, and it is also noticeably darker in winter. Above all the people look different. They act differently too – despite the Glaswegian reputation, I find them gentler than the English – less ruthless – more Irish.

Some of the Scots are inclined to muse gloomily about their affairs. One of my colleagues at Honeywell, Jimmy McGann, never liked to look on the bright side.

"Look at that," he said to me, brandishing a newspaper. "The population of Scotland has fallen below five million. People are leavin', there's nae jobs! We used to make cars and trucks here. That's all gan noo. We had a giant steel factory at Ravenscraig. You should see it noo. Hiroshima. Nothin' left, just grass."

"You are going back ten or fifteen years, aren't you?"

"Aye, all the old industries are gan or goin'," said Jimmy. "Coal minin' gan, shipbuildin' gan, oil goin', even feshin' is goin'. In my home toon at Cullen every family sent someone out feshin' and noo look at it."

"Well, it would have worked better if they had left a few fish in the sea."

"The worst thing is these new factories in Silicon Glen. Here today and gan tomorrow. We've lost 9,000 jobs there."

"That is a lot!"

"Aye, we dedna leek it much, but that's no' the end of it. Boots is closin' its factory in Airdrie and that's another 1000 jobs gan. D'ye ken, Airdrie's no' the sort of place that can just brush aside that kind of a loss. Then look at the Hebrides. Nae work there, the young ones leave, never to return, what they gonny do?"

"Well, the way they bang on in that Parliament of yours about Scotland this and Scotland that, it's enough to put anybody off!"

The Forth and Clyde Canal

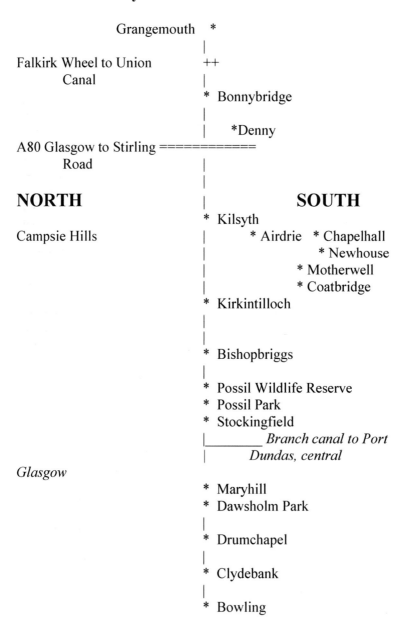

```
                    Grangemouth    *
                                   |
Falkirk Wheel to Union             ++
       Canal                       |
                                   *  Bonnybridge
                                   |
                                   |   *Denny
A80 Glasgow to Stirling ============
        Road                       |
                                   |
NORTH                              |            SOUTH
                                   *  Kilsyth
Campsie Hills                      |     * Airdrie   * Chapelhall
                                   |                    * Newhouse
                                   |                 * Motherwell
                                   |                 * Coatbridge
                                   *  Kirkintilloch
                                   |
                                   |
                                   *  Bishopbriggs
                                   |
                                   *  Possil Wildlife Reserve
                                   *  Possil Park
                                   *  Stockingfield
                                   |_____ Branch canal to Port
                                   |          Dundas, central
Glasgow
                                   *  Maryhill
                                   *  Dawsholm Park
                                   |
                                   *  Drumchapel
                                   |
                                   *  Clydebank
                                   |
                                   *  Bowling
```

CHAPTER 25

After all this time, I have finally learnt some more about blood pressure from the internet. It does seem to me that my lower readings ("diastolic") are quite normal, but the upper readings ("systolic") are high. Apparently this is a recognized condition, know as isolated systolic hypertension or ISH. Now that may sound bad, but it could be worse! The diastolic reading represents the level when the blood is not under pressure from a heartbeat, and for many years this was regarded as the only reading of real importance by the medical profession. As I said before, if that goes over 100, you are in trouble. The systolic level measures the pressure when the blood is being forced through the arteries by a heartbeat. Now as we get older, our arteries harden, and this makes the reading go up. It is really part of the aging process, and it is very difficult to do anything about it, as structural changes to the arteries cannot be reversed!

Half the population over the age of 60 has the condition, defined as a systolic level over 140 and a diastolic level below 90. My problem is that the systolic level is usually a lot more than 140 and apparently this does predispose me to heart attacks and strokes. Also, although this condition is common in countries like England, it is not found in other societies such as in the Orient or amongst primitive groups. So it is really down to diet and lack of exercise, the very position I am attempting to correct right now! Realistically my aim has to be to get down to the 140 level. I am never going to make it to the sunny uplands of 120. Still I am working on it right here in Scotland.

It may be away from home but at least my job in Scotland allowed me the scope to go and see restored canals that I think very few English people will ever see. It was time for me to start my next one. The Forth and Clyde Canal extends across central Scotland from Grangemouth in the east, on the Firth of Forth, to the village of Bowling on the north bank of the River Clyde in the west. It is 35 miles long, with 39 big locks, and there is also a short branch running into Port Dundas in central Glasgow. In its planning stages in the 1760s there was much argument between the Edinburgh men and the Glasgow men (does nothing change?) about the route. Eventually a line was chosen well to the north of the modern direct route taken by the M8 motorway. During the construction of the canal the wages were low, the workers were a tough lot and discipline was hard to maintain given the ready availability of cheap whiskey. (Of course it's not like that nowadays – the workers are still a tough lot but the whiskey is expensive.) Theft of tools and equipment was common but the job did get done after 22 years. After years of dereliction, it was reopened in 2001.

I started on the Forth and Clyde Canal after my trip on the Falkirk Wheel, heading off on my bike for its eastern terminus, a distance of five or six miles. There were showers (some heavy) and it seemed risky to set off, but what! Fair-weather cycling is for wimps! At first it seemed a decent stretch of canal with a fast cycleway. Before setting out on this stretch, I had finally invested in something that was long overdue – a pair of goggles. Well it was wonderful - I had no problem at all with midges and flies. The little bastards just bounced off!

The scenery started to deteriorate as I passed a large, darkened school before heading through an industrial estate. The locks came thick and fast, some restored, some brand new. To my right at Bankside were two new 4-storey blocks of flats, overlooking the canal. This was the only new canalside development I had noticed since leaving the Falkirk Wheel, so this is not like Leeds or Manchester. After a long straight stretch the canal turns and terminates in a dismal basin, opposite a sewerage works. It tips into the River Carron right in front of the M9 bridge. There were quite a few motor boats in the terminal basin, but no narrow boats, and who can blame them – from what I had seen any canal man would be advised to turn off onto the Union Canal at the Wheel and leave this stretch alone.

I now had to face the 15 locks uphill on the way home, into a headwind and with rain driving in my face, but never mind! I finally made it back, wondering once again why I was doing all this. Everybody else who had been at the Falkirk Wheel had got into their dry, comfortable cars and driven off! Mine was the only car left in the car park.

Falkirk itself is an old market town. As it lies at a strategic crossroads in the Scottish lowlands on the road to Stirling and the Highlands, one or two notable battles were fought here. At the end of the thirteenth century, William Wallace raised the standard of rebellion against the English king Edward I. He beat an English army at Stirling (1297), but Edward came after him with another army. Edward attacked and utterly defeated Wallace at Falkirk in 1298. Wallace escaped but in 1305 he was captured, taken to London and executed. A Hollywood approximation of this story is told in the film *Braveheart*, starring the Australian Mel Gibson. This film is nothing better than a flagrant piece of Pom-bashing but it got the Scots going all right.

Anyway, since those times Falkirk has been a peaceful and prosperous place, so I returned there early one evening to continue westwards in the direction of Glasgow on the Forth and Clyde with little fear of meeting wild Highlanders. The canal was broad and clean, lying in a gently undulating countryside of green fields. I could almost have been in England, but no, there is usually something to indicate that this is Scotland, and sure enough in the distance, a jagged line of hills framed the horizon.

This stretch of canal runs parallel to what remains of the Antonine Wall. Now that would be the daddy of all restoration projects! What a noble aim, to restore this wall to its original condition! Never mind about fifty years of stagnation and neglect, here we are talking about nearly two thousand years. There really was a wall here, or rather a large embankment, and the remains of forts are scattered along it. In fact the best place for a restoration might be at the Falkirk Wheel, it would add another dimension to the Visitor Centre. Mind you they would have to do something about the Glasgow to Edinburgh railway, you can't have a Roman wall with high-speed trains running on top of it.

I arrived at the town of Bonnybridge after a long clear run, but I didn't stop, having heard that the town has a reputation as the UFO-sighting hotspot of Scotland. However it has been observed that alien abductions, thankfully temporary, peak amongst the consumers of Buckfast Abbey Tonic Wine. Beyond Bonnybridge the scenery became rather more dramatic. When I arrived at lock 17 I found a pretty stone lock keeper's cottage, Underwood Lockhouse. This is now called Passage to India and smelled distinctly of bhuna and biriani, and I thought, what a funny place to set up an Indian restaurant! Here in the only glen in the Scottish lowlands.

I pressed on. The canal reflected the blues and greys of the sky and the green of the trees in a mirror surface disturbed only by the occasional pair of gleaming white swans. Hills rose to either side. I reached lock 20, the final lock on the eastern side. From now on the canal would run on a level all the way to Glasgow, maybe 15 miles away. The canal, broadening in bays to maybe 60 yards wide, resembled some African river flowing through bosky hills. It was a fair prospect, in fact the best reach of the Forth and Clyde.

At one point a swan and a duck appeared to be having a conversation. I imagine it went something like this:

Swan: "Get off my patch, Donald."

Duck: "This is my patch, Giraffe-bird. You move on."

Swan: "Don't speak to me like that, laddie. Might is right."

Duck: "I've got a lot of mates, you know, whitey!"

Swan: "Where are they, then?"

Duck: "Look, there's a wheel-man on the bank! Let's go and ask him for some bread, who cares whose patch it is?"

Swan: "Yes yes! Just let me arch my wings and make myself look pretty!"

In order to get back before dark I turned round and set off back to my car, eight miles away by now on this fast towpath. Soon I came across a cyclist mending a puncture. He was one of the very few people I had seen on the canal, taking his dog for a walk on his bike. I stopped to commiserate. His head was down, attending to his tyre.

"Unlucky to get a puncture at this time of year," I observed. I had learned that the thorn season is the high summer.

"Aye, it's a root pippin da," he replied.

"Well yes," I said, mystified.

"Ah hen the lookie missen fofar," he continued.

"I see." Hmm!

"Hamilton reek awar dunoon," he said darkly.

"Right! Must be off, it's getting dark!"

On these evening stints, the return journey is slower than the outward run as I begin to flag and I just made it back as night fell, profoundly grateful as always to reload the bike and get back in the car.

Back on the canal at the same point the next night, I noted some very expensive-looking new houses on the lip of the Antonine Wall which must have a good view over the valley. According to my map, they are in a village called Dullatur. Over the Wall and out of sight lies Cumbernauld, which has a reputation as the roughest, toughest and also coldest new town in Scotland. Its modernist town centre is widely considered to be the ugliest place in Britain. I have been there. Given that the planners started with a clean sheet only about 40 years ago, I simply don't know how they managed it. It is awful.

Just along from here the southern bank rose to a steep and scenic summit. Here there were information boards by the towpath, noting that generations of steamers called the Fairy Queen I, II and III used to bring the toiling masses from Port Dundas in Glasgow to this very spot to get them out of the city for a spell. This place must have seemed wonderful to the city dwellers, it is as near as you can get to the Highlands without actually going there. Another board here remarked on the presence of mallard, goldeneye and tufted ducks. Mallards are ubiquitous but I had never seen a tufted duck. However I did see one goldeneye, which looked just like a bathtub duck with a big round head. Really you could not invent a more convincing toy duck, but it was no toy.

The canal skirted Kilsyth, a small town located on the rising hills. Though it is an ancient town its townscape looked mostly modern, bleak, concrete and treeless in the Scottish Lowlands style. Just outside the town, there was a large quarry just off the canal. Although obviously man-made, its sheer rock faces made a handsome feature, obviously popular as climbers in hard hats crawled all over it. It seems it is called Auchinstarry quarry, just the sort of name a place like this should have.

Beyond this point the canal, up to now spotlessly clean, did have some plastic rubbish and old tyres in it for a short stretch. On the far bank was a high, man-made mound, scattered with smooth, blackened stones – the remains of a Roman fort. People with names like Maximus Libidinus and Ludicrus Livy once lived there.

Suddenly I saw something white floating in the water – what is this? A dead swan, its plumage still brilliantly white, its wings spread out but its head under water. There was not a mark on it, as if it had drowned. This was a distressing sight, it couldn't have been dead long. A little further on the canal was another swan, floating still on the water with its head tucked under its wing. I have never seen a swan in this position and I can only assume it was grieving for its mate.

I passed a rather wild-looking man with a push-chair contraption who seemed to want to stop me, then asked for the time. On the way back I passed him again, catching him putting a bottle of whiskey into his pocket. I suppose it is only Scottish tramps who drink whiskey. George Orwell, who knew a lot about tramps, once observed that there was scarcely one alive without some sexual aberration. They frequently expose themselves. I suppose sex is a party everyone wants to join, and tramps must get few opportunities.

I suppose whiskey drinking is ingrained in Scottish culture. When I was at Oxford, one of my tutors was a fearsome old Scot called MacDonald. He was said to harbour a grudge against anyone with the name of Campbell, harking back to the massacre of Glencoe in 1692 – Celtic prejudices die very hard. But MacDonald drank a bottle of whiskey every afternoon.

I headed on towards Kirkintilloch, a pretty-sounding place away from the main Strathclyde conurbation. It occurred to me that the canal, in taking this long sweep to the north, had been built in the wrong place. It should have crossed more or less straight over from Grangemouth, because that is where the towns are. For all that, the Forth and Clyde gives the modern tourist a better view than he would have had in Chapelhall and Coatbridge. Soon I arrived at Kirkintilloch, where bright lights shone out from the night school overlooking the canal. Behind this was an ominously large new police station.

I rode on out westwards to a pub called the Stables. From this point on the canal bank suddenly became much busier with joggers, bikers and walkers, and there were even two moving narrow boats, my first in Scotland! Passing a rather smart-looking golf club I approached the town of Bishopbriggs. Beyond the town the scenery becomes bleak and grey. Though there are no buildings, lines of pylons and tower blocks are visible in the near distance – Glasgow ahead.

CHAPTER 26

I first went to Glasgow back in 1970. Alighting at the railway station, I was taken aback by the huge, brown and red buildings, covered in grime. Glasgow has undergone a transformation since then. When I went back to there to install a computer system in 1990, work was in hand in readiness for Glasgow's turn as European City of Culture, and parts of it looked a lot better. I found the western suburbs around the University and Art Gallery and Museum, stretching out as far as Kelvinside, very handsome indeed. Oddly enough this is now the student area, and the eastern end of it, Woodlands, is the home of the Asian community. I can't think of any other city on earth which gives its finest suburbs to students and immigrants, but that's Glasgow for you.

For all its aspirations, you have to remember that Glasgow is still Glasgow. It is never going to be another Edinburgh, or even another Liverpool. Some drastic steps have been taken to modernise the city. For example the main east-west motorway, the M8, slashes brutally straight past the city centre, crossing the Clyde on the Kingston Bridge. Other cities do have urban motorways, but they are nothing like this. In Leeds, for example, the motorway ducks under the city at the critical moment and doesn't bother anyone.

I drove into the city one evening and accidentally missed my way, soon hitting some pretty rough stuff. There were cars parked everywhere and it soon became evident that there must be a sporting event on somewhere. As I passed through an area positively radiating menace, people started to appear in green and white hooped jerseys, lots of them Rab C Nesbitt and Billy Connolly lookalikes. Pretty soon I came to Parkhead and the football ground of Glasgow Celtic. If you want a long life, do not try wearing a Rangers scarf in places like this. It would be tantamount to suicide. By now there were people and policemen all over the road. Inching past, I moved on towards the city centre passing a building marked "Gorbals Social Centre". After what seemed like hours of driving though this shattered and now largely empty land I finally found the motorway and got away as fast as I could.

Glasgow is also notorious for its poor diet, famously based on chips and deep-fried Mars bars. You might risk one of the Scotch pies, though at 45 pence a time, I wouldn't try it. They are always bragging about smart restaurants in Glasgow nowadays but of course everyone knows that the Glasgow is the heart attack capital of the world.

*   *   *   *

The weather forecast was extremely unpromising when I left home to return to Scotland – gales and heavy showers, and warnings for shipping in Rockall, Hebrides and Cromarty. So I found myself splashing through the communist suburbs north of Glasgow city centre, an area known as Possill Park. I'll bet you have never heard it because they like to keep quiet about it. If you were parachuted in and didn't know where you were, your first guess would be in the suburbs of some ghastly city in Eastern Europe such as Minsk or Chernobyl.

I found the Forth and Clyde and kitted up for the ride with some trepidation. The cold rain lashed down and the gale blew in my face. Still I wasn't going to give up, it was 5.20 and this was my only opportunity to get out on the canal so far away from my base all week. Any other day and it would be practically dark by the time I had fought my way through the traffic. Soon my hands were freezing and my pen refused to write on my wet notebook. What was the point in this? I could never have imagined even a few months ago that I would be doing anything like it. It would have been so easy to say sod it, I'll just go to the hotel. However I was determined to finish the canal and I was rapidly running out of daylight.

There were quite a few other cyclists on this part of the canal, so these were obviously normal conditions for this hardy breed. The cycle track was excellent, as usual in Scotland. I have come to the conclusion that these cycleways have been made so well to encourage people to use the canals. Even the most optimistic canal enthusiast must have realised that there was never going to be much actual boat traffic. In fact I had seen more narrow boats moored up in Sowerby Bridge on a winter's day than I had seen right along these two Scottish Canals.

At first my view was a depressing mixture of grey tower blocks and electricity pylons, but things soon greened up. It is surprising how often you can ride along a canal in the middle of a city and yet find yourself in semi-rural surroundings. I suppose that urban development until recently sought to avoid the semi-derelict canals. So there is plenty of room for new housing and, in Glasgow at least, this space is being used at several points. The canal itself was very clean and full of coots, not normally the commonest canal bird. The banks were well maintained but weedy as ever, with many Michaelmass daisies in flower.

I had only gone a mile or so when the canal was joined by another canal, in fact the branch that leads down to Port Dundas near the centre of Glasgow. Continuing straight on, I came to the first lock on the downhill run at Maryhill. Up to now I had been riding along the summit pound, stretching miles back almost to Bonnybridge. Here squat tower blocks sit on low hills, grim like Gormenghast, some with windows boarded with galvanised sheets. Nevertheless the downhill flight of five big locks presented a noble prospect, with grassy banks and a good flow of clean water. At the foot of the locks is an aqueduct over the river Kelvin, a big, impressive structure. So this area presents the same combination as is found on the Peak Forest Canal at Marple – a canal junction and a flight of locks down to a big aqueduct.

Soon I came to a smart new development of flats called Northern Waters, and a very swish fitness centre with tennis courts. Clearly I was in a much better residential area by now. Before long, with the hills ahead of me, I entered an ordinary kind of suburbia, could have been anywhere really, so I turned round and headed back, because I wanted to explore the branch canal leading into Glasgow. I turned off down this on the way home, where a sign indicated "Spiers Wharf 2.5 miles". On the map at least, this did not look like promising territory. In fact I half expected to be mugged along the way. However, the area of Maryhill through which the branch canal passes proved a good deal better than the area around the locks. There were many handsome terraces of old tenements, and some of the modern blocks of flats looked smart enough. However at one point there is an old harbour, like a lagoon off the canal, and here I lost the towpath. I came away from the canal to explore the other side of it and passed a group of Albanians wearing tea-cosy headgear on the pavement but they left me alone.

I found the path again close to a football ground, Firhill Park, home of Partick Thistle. I understand that this club gets quite a bit of support from people who do not happen to be religiously bigoted and are not prepared to risk it in the intimidating environments where the grounds of both Rangers and Celtic are sited. The canal kept up high and views opened out over Glasgow. The skyline was fascinating, especially the group of buildings formed by the tower of Glasgow University, the former Trinity College and a prominent white church. In my opinion the Victorian Gothic university, designed by the Englishman Gilbert Scott in 1865, is the best building in the city. It has two grassed-over quadrangles and was clearly modelled on an Oxbridge college, but it is on a different scale, massive, ornate, muscular and very handsome.

I shortly arrived at a basin, the headquarters of British Waterways in Scotland. Just beyond was what I had come to see – Spiers Wharf, an impressive restored warehouse and office block. Built of a light red sandstone and six or seven stories high, this stretches along the canal side for maybe four hundred yards. It is in fact several buildings, erected at different times – one block had 1866 on the front - but all the buildings present a common front. It appears to be in use as offices and flats, there being almost no retail development. The canal is broad at this point, and lined with old stones. It terminates right here, which must in fact be close to the M8 motorway, though I didn't see that. Driving past heading east on the M8 later, however, I found I had an excellent view of Spiers Wharf!

On the way back I started getting pretty cold, especially my hands, and felt a little sorry for myself, but another biker came the other way dressed in shorts! He must be perishing! Clearly a man of iron, not like me. Anyway it had been worth getting wet for the big locks at Maryhill, the aqueduct and Spiers Wharf. I arrived back at my starting point muddier than I had ever been since I gave up rugby at the age of 18. So what, I won't melt in the mud and rain!

I resumed one evening on the main line of the canal where I had broken off previously. Driving out through fairly rough territory along the Clyde to get there, I marvelled at the fantastic red sandstone tenement buildings. A pity that so many of them seem to have been demolished – they line the Dumbarton road like a set of dentures with a lot of the teeth knocked out.

From this point on the canal has a suburban air, passing through housing estates of various grades in the manner of a linear park. On the south bank I came to the suburb of Yoker, at the back of the Clyde, where I has previously worked installing a computer system back in 1990. I had found this a grim spot, just what you would expect, but the locals were friendly, as they generally are in such places. The manager was a former lorry driver. I spent quite a bit of time with the accountant, and even picked up a bit of Glaswegian, learning, for example, that "stay" means "live", and "doon Sooth" means "England".

So the question "Where do you stay doon sooth?" translates as "Whereabouts do you live in England?" Again, all day long I would here the phrase "Nae bather", "It's no trouble", as it were. Then there was the mysterious expression "That's you", as if to say, "That's you sorted out".

I found that whenever I went to see the manager, the accountant went with me, unasked. I soon found out the reason for this.

"Inverary halang yigonny bear nata thes fickn dockin taim?"

"How long are you going to be here?" interjected the accountant, smiling reassuringly.

"Dyaken hoolah ducka thesa trossochs lotsacoast enema?"

"Do you know how much this going to cost?"

So it went on. I understood some of it, but not much.

Today Yoker looked better from the towpath than it had from the industrial estate where I had once worked. However every girl or woman I saw on this stretch of canal had dyed blond hair – I could have been in Russia.

On the northern bank lay the notorious suburb of Drumchapel. The people who used to live in central Glasgow districts such as the Gorbals have largely been moved to the outskirts of the city where they sit glowering in the tower blocks of Drumchapel and Easterhouse. Also living here is a recent immigrant population of Kurds and Albanians. As these people are keen to work and want their children to go to school and learn English (well a form of it), their presence is widely reckoned to have upgraded Easterhouse! One of my Honeywell colleagues, Patrick, used to live in Glasgow.

"I've only been to Drumchapel once, and Easterhouse once," he said. "Both times to recover a stolen car!"

Ahead of me was a large crowd of teenagers malingering on the towpath. Now if I had to choose, Drumchapel would not come first as a place to encounter a gang like that. Not second either, or third, but I ploughed doggedly onwards. Although it was wet, these people were stood around wearing T-shirts.

"I like your bell," said one of them.

"It is good, yes," I replied.

"Can I have it?"

"No."

"Hi-ho, Silver!" said another bright spark.

I ignored this.

Another lad began to bark, like a dog, exactly like a dog. He must have been six feet tall, gangly, spotty and hatchet-faced, but he was definitely barking. Ignore. A couple of them blew raspberries. Ignore. Another chimed up "Rudolf, the red-nosed reindeer..." I presume this was a reference to my red face, not red nose, but I didn't stop to correct the lad.

Coming clear, I stood on the pedals to speed away.

"Yah boo shucks!" I called back.

I then put into practice one of the things I have learnt in my travels. Bikes are faster than people.

Soon I arrived at the outskirts of Clydebank. The canal cut right through the middle of the town, the whole area being laid out with paving setts, black railings and new concrete banks on the canal. I had begun to wonder exactly where the £84.5 million had been spent on this canal because apart from the Falkirk Wheel there isn't much evidence of heavy expenditure, but all this must have cost a bit. It reminded me of Stalybridge town centre on the Huddersfield Narrow Canal, everything shiny and modern – for now.

I was now five or six miles from the terminus of the canal at Bowling, so I pressed on. Once clear of Clydebank there is a stark deterioration in the scenery, with electricity pylons overhead, grey sheds off on one side, and low grey tower blocks across the canal. I guess the designers of these must have gone out to Sverdlovsk, Archangel or Vladivostok for instruction because this scenery looks just like the old Soviet Union. Soon I came to the Erskine Bridge, which spans the Clyde and looks very much like the Humber Bridge, towering above me on slender concrete pillars. Beyond the bridge the scenery improved as the escarpment of the Kilpatrick Hills loomed ahead. On a grey but rainless day, the autumn tints in the leaves were striking, with some trees a flaming yellow colour. There are reasons for the brilliant autumn colours this year – plenty of lovely autumn sunshine, enough rain to sustain the leaves, and little wind, to keep them on the trees.

I noted that my front tyre was a bit flat, but I was lucky enough to pass another cyclist at a barrier and he had a pump. I was in for a Glaswegian conversation.

"Would you mind if I borrowed your pump for a minute? My front tyre's a bit flat."

"Och aye, nae bather!"

He handed me the pump.

"I just want pump it up a bit, I don't think it's a puncture."

"Nae bather! I've a wee spanner as wayell. You can have that if you want, tighten up a bit, nae bather!"

"No, it's all right, I've done it now."

I gave him back his pump.

"Thanks very much."

"Nae bather! That's you now!"

I came to a lock – aha! – 37 – only two more to go! There were one or two restored footbridges over the river, known as bascule bridges. These are boarded with wood and flanked with iron railings. There are turning mechanisms at either side to allow the bridges to be raised, splitting in the middle, so that boats can pass. Two or three cyclists whizzed past me whist I was taking notes, going faster than I would ever go. None of these fast cyclists seem to have bells so they have to call out before they overtake – I wonder why, I love my little bell, it is so simple yet so effective. No one minds you ringing a bell, it's not like hooting a horn.

At last I had a view of the Clyde, at this point a couple of hundred yards wide. The Clyde Valley is very scenic at many points. A memorable view of it can be obtained from the hill road from Kilmarnock to Glasgow. One is taken aback by the sudden appearance of this huge metropolis – housing a quarter of the population of Scotland, a million and a quarter people – in this otherwise dramatic valley. Who put it there? Was it such a good idea? I mean, if you could take this area out of Scotland and float it off somewhere else, let's say Ireland, you would be left with rather a good Scandinavian country.

Suddenly I arrived at the twin basins at Bowling – the end of the Forth and Clyde. The outer basin was crammed with yachts overwintering. By the exit lock there were good views out over the Clyde, which widens into an arm of the sea at this point. Downstream from here islands and peninsulas begin to jut out into a windswept sea in an especially exciting way.

So what is the outlook for the Forth and Clyde Canal? Its prospects seem poor. I have cycled along the whole of it but I do not remember seeing more than a handful of privately owned and occupied boats. The canal is really a harbour for seagoing craft at either end and a take-off point for short trips at the Falkirk Wheel in the middle, but it doesn't go to Edinburgh and Linlithgow like the Union Canal and the bankside scenery is poor at either end.

The Scots are very proud of their Millennium canal restoration project and the Falkirk Wheel, not least because it has a future and is not seen as a white elephant. I have read that the Millennium Project as a whole is supposed to create 4,000 permanent jobs, directly or indirectly. It is difficult to see how. One problem which seems obvious to me is that these Scottish canals do not join up to any other canals, so that it is not possible for a tourist in a narrow boat to make a circular trip, and that is the one thing that a tourist in a narrow boat wants to do. I imagine that the main users of the Scottish lowland canals will be boat tourists and indeed the Edinburgh Canal Centre at Ratho does advertise a one-way trip which it somehow manages to spread over four days. That must involve some very long lunch stops and a fair amount of the old haggis, neeps and tatties, prime Scottish Angus beef and Arbroath smokies.

In point of fact very few canals were ever built in Scotland. There was one, the Monklands, connecting Chapelhall about twelve miles east of Glasgow with Port Dundas within Glasgow itself. This may not have been as large and impressive as the Forth and Clyde, or as technically innovative as the Union, but it was actually the only really successful Scottish canal in a financial sense. Most of it is now gone, filled in beneath the M8 motorway. Apart from that there is the Crinan canal, built across the Kintyre peninsula to cut out a 160-mile sea voyage round the Mull of Kintyre, and the Caledonian Canal, a ship-sized waterway along the Great Glen in the Highlands. This was financed by the government and was mainly created for military and strategic purposes, to avoid the long and perilous journey round the north of Scotland. (As it has no towpath it would always be a no-no for me!) So the extensive network of accessible canals needed to support a modern Scottish boat-based tourist industry is simply not there, and never was there in the first place.

On a separate trip, I took Christine to look at the Caledonian Canal. Loch Ness itself is a central part of the waterway. We drove along the northern edge of the lake, stopping of at the suitably gothic ruined Urquhart Castle and its many Japanese tourists. At Fort Augustus at the southern end of the lake, we found a boat moving northwards down a staircase of very big locks into Loch Lomond. It was far and away the largest boat – well, ship – I have ever seen on any canal. It must have been purpose-built as there were literally inches to spare on either side of the lock walls. Still a cruise up the Caledonian Canal must be a popular holiday option, if you like cruises, which I don't – they run contrary to my Yorkshire nature! We pottered around at the sea lock at Inverness as well, but there wasn't much to see there. Better to spend time at the Georgian Fort George, just round the corner on the Moray Firth.

The Lancaster Canal

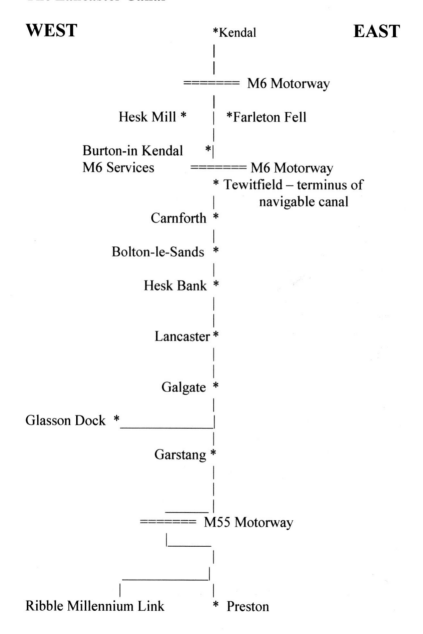

WEST   *Kendal   **EAST**
                              |
                              |
                  ======= M6 Motorway
                              |
          Hesk Mill * | *Farleton Fell
                              |
     Burton-in Kendal   *|
     M6 Services   ======= M6 Motorway
                          * Tewitfield – terminus of
                          | navigable canal
               Carnforth *
                          |
      Bolton-le-Sands *
                          |
            Hesk Bank *
                          |
                          |
            Lancaster *
                          |
                          |
              Galgate *
                          |
  Glasson Dock *_____|
                          |
              Garstang *
                          |
                          |
              _____|
          ======= M55 Motorway
              |_____
                  |
        _____|
        | |
Ribble Millennium Link   * Preston

CHAPTER 27

My sojourn in Scotland lasted much longer than expected. Although I had gone for six months, I was there for a total of twenty. I had already cycled down all the accessible Scottish canals, but there was another canal for me to visit on the way there - the Lancaster Canal. It would involve little deviation from my route north, and it was an excellent candidate for an exercise route if I set out early. After the opening of the cycling season in April I was able to get going on this. In fact, I needed to get back on the bike, because I found that biking is a summer thing. It's unpleasant in winter and I never went out once after October. For one thing, the towpaths just become extended puddles.

What is more, I had found out more details about my condition, which as I have mentioned is called isolated hypertension, when the upper reading is high but the lower reading is normal. I bought a little book on the subject of blood pressure written by a man from Birmingham University, one Professor Beevers. He confirmed some suspicions which I already had. One is that there is a direct statistical link between high blood pressure and life expectancy. It is really very simple. The higher your blood pressure is, the shorter your life will be. Hmm! The professor also said that it is very difficult to get high pressure back down to normal levels without resorting to drugs. Well yes. And there were some alarming graphs in the back of the book which showed that my chances of having a heart attack over the next ten years are in the "red" area – the danger zone. Just to cheer me up some more, the prof said that isolated hypertension is very rare in people under 60 (!) and that it is just as dangerous as general hypertension.

So I began to devise my own life expectancy system, based upon what I have read.

Do you regard yourself as successful in life?
Definitely not   10
OK   5

Very much so   0

What was the sum of your parents' ages when they died?
Below 100   10
Below 140   5
Above 140   0

How much do you drink?
Bottle of whisky a day   10
4 pints or more a day   5
Less than that   0

How much do you smoke?
Over 20 a day   10
4 to 20 a day   5
4 or less a day   0

Do you exercise:
Rarely   10
Irregularly   5
Regularly   0

Are you 3 stones or more overweight or underweight?
Yes   5
No   0

Are you happily married?
Definitely not   6
OK   3
Very much so   0

    If you score 30 or more your life expectancy is 60 or under. If you score around 18 you can expect 70. If you score 12 or less, then 80+. So I got the bike back out.

    The Lancaster Canal was built in two sections, north and south of Preston. The first 41-mile section north of Preston runs on a level all the way – the longest long pound of any canal in England. Its crown is a big stone arched aqueduct over the River Lune north of Lancaster. A branch was also built down to the sea at Glasson Dock on the Lune estuary, which needed 6 locks. The canal was later extended to Kendal, 16 miles north of the previous terminus at Tewitfield. This involved the construction of a flight of 8 locks at Tewitfield, the only locks on the mainline northern section. These "Northern Reaches" of the canal between Tewitfield and Kendal still exist but are not navigable, so Tewitfield is now the end of the line for the English canal system. However restoration work is in hand and there are plans to spend a further £30 million to finish the job. There was once also a southern section of the canal which ran from a few miles south of Preston down to Wigan. As most of it has now disappeared under the M61, there will be no revival for that one!

The Lancaster Canal was not finally connected to the national network until as late as 2002 when the Ribble Link was completed. This consists of four miles of new canal and nine locks, costing £5.8 million. This wasn't a restoration project – no link had previously existed! Boats can now come up the Ribble estuary from the Leeds and Liverpool Canal and pass up this link into the Lancaster Canal. Boaters tell me that you have to get the timing right, however – there are only 17 tides a year which a narrow boat can use to cross the Ribble.

The Lancaster Canal has a reputation as one of the fairest waterways in England. In his book *The Inland Waterways of England*, L.T.C. Rolt quotes one John Fox, who travelled on this canal in 1839 and described it as the most delightful journey of his entire life. His packet boat was pulled by two horses running at a canter which were changed every four miles, so that an overall speed of 9 mph was maintained. Fox relates that the experience was "Like a journey in a dream or in an Eastern tale".

I made my own start on the canal in Preston, where it gets off to an unpromising beginning half a mile out of the town centre. I found a man sat on a bench, about to open a can of Carlsberg Special, drink of choice for today's alcoholics. Unsure whether I had found the actual start of the canal, I asked him if this was it.

"Yes, this is it," he said. "The urinary tract of Preston."

I thought this was supposed to be the fairest waterway in England!

Preston is one of the few very old settlements in Lancashire, having for centuries acted as an important staging post on the road to Scotland. There was a big battle here in the Civil War in 1648, when Cromwell's English army heading north met a Scottish army heading south, with predictable results. However Preston reinvented itself as a cotton town in the nineteenth century, and from the towpath at least, it looked like Wigan or Blackburn. Nowadays it has a very large university, and it has recently produced the most exciting English cricketer for a generation – Andrew Flintoff, whose father is a plumber in the town. I award Flintoff the title of Honorary Yorkshireman.

After a couple of miles I came to the junction with the Ribble Link. I decided to take this, thinking everything here would be smart and modern, but it didn't quite work out that way. The new canal winds through soggy fields, its banks piled high with dredged mud. I came across three dredgers in as many miles, and one lock was a building site. This canal must be costing a fortune to maintain. Eventually my way was blocked by a construction site where a mass of mud had been churned up by the diggers and I had to turn round.

Back on the main line and heading north, I noted a sign saying that I was in the area controlled by the Westinghouse British Nuclear Fuels Planning Authority. It politely suggested that if a siren were to go off, I should get out fast. You bet I will! Immediately after this point, a massive industrial complex appeared off to my left. One tall building had "Oxide Fuels" in big letters on the outside. I mean, what kind of oxide is that exactly? Presumably the sort that, if it happens to explode, leaves a big hole in the ground where Preston used to be.

I was buzzed by a Eurofighter presumably on a test flight from nearby Warton, and managed to disturb a couple of herons, but generally moved along nicely until I came to an extremely smart narrow boat, moored up. I stopped for a chat as the owners were on deck chairs on the bank. Their boat was registered on the Kennet and Avon Canal so clearly, they had come a long way. The man was about 60, bronzed and tatooed with a full head of grey hair. He spoke with a West Country accent.

"Is that where you have come from, the Kennet and Avon?" I asked.

"Originally, yes, but we set out this year from Nuneaton on the Coventry Canal."

"Do you have any favorites?" I asked.

"Every canal has something to recommend it," he replied, "even in unlikely places. We've recently been on the Caldon Canal between Stoke and Leek and that was very nice. Lovely valley. Then we were on the Macclesfield Canal as far as Congleton and that was good too."

"What about this one?"

"Also good," he said, "but the problem is the M6 motorway. So noisy, it makes you want to blow it up!"

When John Fox described his delightful journey on the Lancaster Canal, you have to remember that they didn't have the M6 in 1839, and they didn't have British Nuclear Fuels or Eurofighters either.

"Did you get across the link OK?"

"No problem, you don't need a pilot."

"I hear that the Severn estuary is another matter."

"It is. I knew someone whose engine conked out in the middle of that. He had to abandon his boat and then pay £3000 to the salvage merchants in Cardiff to get it back!"

He told me that he worked for 20 years in the Royal Navy. One of his ships was the HMS Fearless, which had a crew of 550 men. A narrow boat on the Lancaster Canal seemed tame after that, but the couple were great enthusiasts.

"Have you tried the Pennine canals?" I asked. "There aren't many boats on them."

"No, but there will be."

"There are a lot of locks."

"We like the locks! You can stop and get out, there is usually another boat and you can have a chat, you can walk on to the next lock. In fact this canal is boring for us – 41 miles and no locks."

I doubt he would like the locks on the Huddersfield Narrow Canal as much as THAT, and in any case, those locks only hold one boat.

I asked about one point on which I remained curious.

"Can you be had up for being drunk in charge of a boat?"

"At the moment, no. There is talk of introducing the same laws as for road traffic, but nothing has happened yet. In any case these boats are expensive things. The owners look after them and so do the hirers. You don't find people drinking and driving on canals, except..."

"Yes?"

His eyes narrowed: "...for hen parties. We stay well clear of them."

*   *   *   *

I set off again on a viciously cold day in April. Near an isolated pub called the Hand and Dagger I hit a very sticky patch of bank. Just here a boater gave me a cheery hello. I grinned back but I thought to myself, it's all right for you, mate! Here am I in the freezing wind trying to ride a bike through three inches of oozing mud. All you have to do is call your wife and you can go inside and warm yourself by the wood stove!

I rode on northwards through the rural Fylde with a heavy heart - this canal was really not so interesting after all. I actually prefer the grimy towns and the threatening cities to this Arcadian parkland. Really there was nothing wrong with the view, it's just that the canal was so EMPTY. There was the odd boat in the water but there were absolutely no towpath users, no anglers, no dog walkers, bikers, mothers pushing prams, hikers. It was more fun in Accrington. There was a biting cold wind, it was spitting with rain and my hands had turned blue. Why am I doing this? I turned round. I got within a mile of my car when the drizzle turned into a shower. I did have a kagool with me but being so close I didn't put it on. Maybe I should have because by the time I got back, I was drenched. A man sat in a pickup truck watched dispassionately as I struggled off the towpath onto the road. As I was stacking my bike in the car, he drove past and stopped.

"That was a bit unfair, wasn't it?" he observed.

A few miles to the north I came upon the branch down to Glasson Dock, which I took. There was no towpath as such, just a grassy bank - these are always tough. Riding into a strong headwind, the going was murderous - I had to stand on the pedals to make much progress. Pretty soon I was up against one of the toughest bike rides I had ever had. After six locks I assumed I was nearly there but no, the canal stretched straight ahead across marshland and there was another agonising mile to go. This was simply no fun at all. Not, say, in the way that shoving a lighted jumping jack down Gordon Brown's underpants would be fun. Finally I pitched up at a large basin containing yachts, trawlers and other sea-going craft. At the back of the main basin a short track led to a view over the Lune estuary. The river flowed between broad sandy banks, with low green hills across the other side. Off to the right was a sandy bay. I wouldn't be surprised if this wasn't a favored spot for amateur artists.

I set off again in open country just south of Lancaster itself, in low but rising hills which resembled the lower parts of the nearby Yorkshire Dales. This was a different world from the Lancashire of the mill towns, and far prettier. Immediately north of Lancaster I came to the Lune aqueduct. Although they are not built on the scale of the Victorian railway viaducts, these aqueducts are still considerable structures. This one is six spans in length and is built of a mellow and weathered yellow sandstone, carrying an ornate balustrade. Unfortunately the view from it is marred by large-scale industrial development below it. The higher views were better, to Lancaster Castle and a white classical building with a green dome, the Ashton Memorial. This was built by a local manufacturer in memory of his wife, in the manner of the Taj Mahal, and it is a monumental folly which dominates Lancaster. Ashton owned a lino factory in the days when every floor was covered in the stuff.

When the aqueduct was built, the engineer John Rennie insisted on using a special type of mortar from Italy for its underwater sections, called pozzalano (is it mortar or a pizza?). This had to be shipped from Leghorn during the Napoleonic Wars, running the gauntlet of French privateers. The ship got through, but just imagine the chagrin of the privateers if they had risked life and limb to capture a cargo of sand and cement!

Just beyond the aqueduct, a first! I came across a group of three excited anglers, one of whom had actually caught a fish, and it was some fish! It was long and brown with big jaws and it looked extremely fed up, insofar as a fish can look fed up. Its eyes were sort of glazed over but then, if you live in a canal, broad daylight must be absolutely blinding.

"What is it?" I asked.

"A pike."

"How heavy is it?"

"We just weighed it – fifteen pounds!"

"Is this canal big enough to support a predator that size?"

"Course it is, there's 51 miles of water here, we've fished them out twice this size before."

Just the same the angler looked pretty pleased. One of his friends took a photo of him holding the fish; then they put it back in the water where it immediately disappeared.

"You have to put them straight back in," said the angler. "I know they eat other fish but they're pretty delicate really. You don't get many anywhere near this size because the ducks eat the fry."

You see! It may be just canal water to you and me, but to an enterprising duck or a swan, it is nothing less than a living soup.

"What do you use for bait?" I asked.

"Sprats," said the angler, "Here, look."

He fetched out a packet of sprats, each about three or four inches long, wrapped in plastic.

"Just the sort of thing a pike would go for," I observed.

Just beyond the next bend I saw a duck and a swan in the water, and I imagined a conversation between them.

Swan: "The water is full of fry just round the corner, ducky. Pike fry. Good to eat."

Duck: "Very decent of you to mention it, Vestas. Not like you at all in fact."

Swan: "Well there's more than enough for both of us, ducky. Really I've had as many as I want."

Duck: "Mmmm! Pike fry! I'll be off then!"

Swan: "There is just one thing, ducky."

Duck: "What?"

Swan: "There's a fifteen-pound pike with them and he'll bite your head off if you stick it under water."

Just here on the far bank was a strange, large bird, like a cross between a turkey and a swan, mainly white with black markings and a red head and neck. The nearest I could find in my bird book was the ptarmigan which I thought inhabited the Arctic tundra, so either I was wrong or the bird had had gone soft and headed south like a retired Englishman.

Before long a beautiful panoramic view opened out over Morecambe Bay. Over the vast acreage of sands and river channels, the sea shone away to the west while across the bay lay Silverdale, with the hills of the Lake District rising behind it. Large flocks of seagulls occupied various stretches of sand. The weather was beautiful, a crisp sort of day with big, blue skies and thin scattered cloud and really this did look a picture. I once knew a young woman who came from here, a schoolteacher in her twenties. She had come to work in Halifax. How she loathed it, only longing to get back to Silverdale, which she did at every opportunity. I don't think that was such a reflection on Halifax, which isn't a bad town at all, so much as an appreciation of this place. Another one for my Top Ten Sights of the North British canals.

The scenery across Morecambe Bay is deceptively tempting and my Ordnance Survey map carries warnings in red for people attempting to hike across the sands. The bay is funnel-shaped and the incoming tide is forced into an ever narrower space, rising rapidly and flowing faster than a man can run. Only three months before my visit, on a dark night in February, 23 unwary Chinese illegal immigrants out gathering cockles were swept away and drowned right here. The locals maintain that the huge increase in the number of shellfish which lured the Chinese has been caused by the unnatural warmth of the water in Morecambe Bay, which is heated up by the nuclear power station at Heysham on the shores of the bay!

I arrived at a place called Hest Bank, a small but evidently popular tourist town. The sea shore could have been no more than a quarter of a mile away from the canal. Passing on and arriving at the centre of Carnforth I espied the canal basin with many boats in it. Most of them were motor launches, as they had been at Galgate and Garstang lower down, no doubt here to take advantage of a safe harbour conveniently close to Glasson Dock and a rip-roaring ride on the Irish Sea. I had seen these boats chugging down the canal, carefully observing the speed limit.

I continued doggedly northwards, determined to reach the end of the navigable canal at Tewitfield four miles further north. It was well worth it - I have rarely ridden on a more lovely stretch of canal. Set in low hills with pretty copses, dry limestone walls and hedges, the canal edges northwards. In the distance lay a higher hill called Farleton Fell, an outlier of the Yorkshire Dales, featuring steeply dipping bare limestone rocks and covered in yellow gorse blossom. North of Carnforth and passing under a bridge, suddenly Whoosh! I was buzzed by a Eurofighter flying out of nowhere at about fifty feet, emitting a terrific roar. I nearly jumped straight out of my skin and into the canal. Finally I reached Tewitfield where the canal ends against an embankment. The M6 runs right by the basin which must make for a noisy night if you are staying there. However there is a convenient pub, the Longlands Hotel. There is always a pub, this is England! Why, the English have been notorious since mediaeval times as the biggest boozers in western Europe.

A path leads round the embankment and the canal continues on the other side, heading north. Here are the old locks. These have no gates, though the stonework looks in good condition. There is plenty of water flowing through the canal and right under the embankment which blocks it, into the navigable part of the waterway. By this time I was utterly shagged out, having come a long way from Lancaster, and I was quite unable to face the prospect of the steep-looking locks, so I turned round.

I returned to this same spot on another day, keen to explore this hidden world where a boater cannot go. The locks at Tewitfield lifted the canal 75 feet, which makes them pretty deep locks, and as there are eight of them in half a mile, shall we say that the return journey was a lot easier than the way out. At the top of the locks the canal runs on for half a mile or so until it hits the buffers again, in this case the M6 itself. However there is a bridge and a motorway sign announcing "Lancaster Canal". Well yes, there was a canal till someone built a motorway over it! Over the other side of the motorway, the canal resumes, still very pretty. It opens out into rustic pools overhung here and there with drooping conifers. As it was by now May, everything was fresh and green, and the many hawthorn trees on the banks hung heavy with white blossom. Big yellow irises grew in the canal, and the water reflected the blue sky above. Lambs gambolled in the fields. Swans sat on giant nests right by the canal, and on the water were mother ducks, surrounded by whole flotillas of tiny, fluffy chicks, twelve or thirteen of them at a time. Terrific.

On reaching the village of Holme Mills, I once again arrived at one of those spots that made me wish I was an artist. The canal runs along the side of the hill. The village with its duck pond nestles below, and away to the north-west the hills rise in successive waves, each one higher and more rugged, the last of them the Old Man of Coniston. Though the village is certainly not chocolate box, the setting is idyllic. Were it not for the village this would definitely merit a place in my Top Ten Sights of the North British Canals. Although it is only nine miles from my previous Top Ten Sight at Hest Bank, it is a completely different view – you can't see Morecambe Bay from here – but it is difficult to beat, anywhere in England. And previously entirely unknown to me, and also no doubt to the millions of tourists crowding into the Lake District only a few miles away.

I carried on for a mile or two until I began to approach the M6 again when suddenly and right out of the blue, the canal was blocked once more. Someone had had the brass neck to build a road right over it, not even an important road either. That is the third blockage I have found. A mile or so further on, I ran into the M6 again. Exasperated, I turned round. This canal is completely screwed up! I am beginning to see why it might cost £30 million to restore it. Further to the north, if they refill the canal on its original line, I reckon there are four more blockages.

A pretty girl of 18 or so passed me on the bank just here and completely ignored me. One of the things that saddens me about getting older is that I now appear to be invisible to pretty young women, whereas once, I was not. This invisibility did not start until I was into my forties, but I become more and more transparent every year now. There must be something about me which sends an instant signal to young women that I am of no interest as a mate. I returned to my car and prepared to reload the bike. Just then I got a cheery Halloo, an approving glance and a big smile from a pretty lady biker, aged about 30, and I thought, maybe I'm not so invisible after all! It was only then that I noticed that my flies were open, and must have been open all afternoon.

I picked up the canal again on the other side of the M6 blockage. At one point I was charged by a big grey-brown dog with evil-looking eyes but I stood my ground and he pulled up, called off by a worried-looking owner who immediately put a muzzle on him. If you are afraid of dogs, do not attempt to ride a bike on a towpath! I have been charged dozens of times, but not bitten yet! Just after crossing an aqueduct, the canal suddenly ended, right under a bridge. From this point on it was filled in and grassed over. There was a sign just here - Tewitfield 9 miles, Kendal 6, so really it isn't far to Kendal.

In a way I am surprised that the restoration of this canal has had to wait so long, and is still incomplete. To me the top part of it at least has fulfilled its reputation as one of the fairest waterways in the country. However because it was cut off from the rest of the network it has had to queue behind other projects, some of them completed 30 years ago.

CHAPTER 28

I now decided to do something I should have done a long time ago – to take a holiday in a narrow boat, instead of watching everyone else do it. After all, it looked simple enough. What could possibly go wrong?

I selected the Shropshire Union Canal and its branch line, the Llangollen Canal, as these are known to be two of the most scenic routes in the English canal network, with plenty of hire boats available. The Shropshire Union is the modern name for the canal which runs from Ellesmere Port on the River Mersey, via Chester and Nantwich, to the Staffordshire and Worcestershire Canal at Autherley Junction near Wolverhampton. It is 68 miles long. Different stretches of it were built at different times. The earliest part was once called the Chester Canal, running southwards from Chester to Nantwich, and dating from 1772. The main run from Nantwich to Autherley Junction was not completed until 1835, being the last major civil engineering achievement of the famous Thomas Telford. There was some debate at the time about building a railway instead, but a canal was built, probably because it fitted in as the last piece in the jigsaw of canals linking the north-west and the Midlands, so no messy trans-shipment of goods between rail and canal would be needed. Amongst others, there are links off to the Trent and Mersey via the Middlewich Branch, at Barbridge Junction, and to the Llangollen Canal at Hurleston Junction.

The Llangollen Canal dates from 1795 and connects the Welsh town to the Shropshire Union via two tremendous aqueducts at Pontcysyllte and Chirk. We have come across Pontcysyllte before, of course, as it is one of the most famous structures in the whole English Canal system. Again, it is the work of Telford and his supervisor, William Jessop, who also worked on the Rochdale Canal. It is just over 1000 feet long, eleven feet wide and five feet three inches deep. It consists of a cast iron trough supported 126 feet above the River Dee on nineteen slender stone pillars. Despite some public skepticism, of the type received by Brindley on the Bridgewater, Telford was confident the construction would hold water – he had built one before! Completed in 1805, it is the longest and highest aqueduct in England, a Grade I listed building and a World Heritage Site, so it seems Telford was right after all. However, it does seem odd that this tremendous structure was built – at the equivalent modern cost of £2.9 million – just to get to Llangollen! However, that was not the original plan. It should have joined up with the rest of the network beyond Llangollen, but never did.

Our party consisted of myself and Christine plus my son Nicholas, aged 28, and his girlfriend Julie. Our boat was a 45-footer, the Eleanor. All I can say is that 45 feet seemed barely maneuverable, so handling a 70-footer must be a real problem! We picked up the boat from Chas Hardern Boat Hire at Beeston Castle Wharf near Tarporley, half-way between Chester and Nantwich. Our plan was to make for Chester, then turn round.

"Not possible," said Chas.

Oh.

"I have to show you how to turn the boat round. I can do that at the pond just down there, then walk back."

He pointed in the direction of Chester.

"Then you will be heading for Nantwich."

Well all right then. We soon got going, first lock, no problem. I was at the tiller. Observing the narrow boat drift towards some moored boats on our right, I confidently swung the tiller to the right, expecting the boat to swing left. No response. This can't be right! So I put it hard left. Suddenly the boat swung right over. Christ! Wrong again! A panic-stricken couple tried to head our boat away from their moored craft:

"What the hell do you think you are doing?!!"

To no avail – we hit them fairly hard. I apologised. They told me to slow down near going past moored boats. Come to think about it, I think Chas said something about that! Still it only happened to me once.

Everything then went smoothly. Passing the Barbridge and Hurleston junctions, we moored up for the night just outside Nantwich. Now there is this thing about narrow boats – they are indeed narrow. Our boat would sleep four, no problem, but there was a lot of squeezing past! The following day, we went into Nantwich itself. This is a pleasant town, like a mini-Chester with lots of old, black and white timber buildings. I thought it would be good, because I know a number of Oracle consultants from the north-west, and most of them live here rather than in Manchester or on Merseyside. On our travels that day, we saw three kingfishers. I'd only ever seen two before in my entire life. It wasn't the same one three times as we could see them all together – in fact they flew alongside us for quite a time, tiny, but colourful.

After Nantwich we turned the boat round – I allowed Nicholas to do that, it's not so straightforward as it sounds! – and headed off up the Llangollen Canal. We seemed immediately in a different world. The Shropshire Union had been a big, busy, bustling canal, full of boats heading in both directions (a lot of them with dogs on board). The Llangollen was a much narrower affair with lots of tiny locks. In fact there can easily be long queues at these locks, but we went straight through. Eventually we reached the village of Wrenbury where there are a couple of really big restaurants, but they were full up! So we had to traipse a couple of miles up the road in the pitch dark to find another, but find another we did.

You can't get far on a narrow boat in three or four days so we didn't make it to Pontcysyllte in the boat, but found other means to get there. It is an impressive structure, no doubt about it, much more slender and graceful than a railway viaduct, with lots of tourists. Really the most impressive thing is the scenery up the valley, where the River Dee pours of the Snowdon massif in a deep gorge.

It was on the way back that the trouble started. Each lock has a fast race to one side where the spare water rushes through. Instead of going straight into the lock, we had to wait for another boat to come up. I was at the tiller again. It was very hard to keep the boat still. It had drifted over towards the race and threatened to go down it! There was no room for manoevre – I was right up against the bank, which was full of brambles. I reversed into the brambles – nothing else for it. It got me into a real sweat! Eventually I got the thing clear.

Back on the Shropshire Union, we came to a pair of staircase locks, two locks back-to-back with no clear water between them. These had seemed absolutely no problem on the way up. We made our way in, Julie and I on the boat, Christine and Nicholas on the banks. Crossing between the two locks, we hit the bottom. What the hell was going on? Suddenly a man rushed out of the British Waterways office. It was pouring with rain. He looked into the lock, where the water was rapidly draining away.

"If you don't do something in a couple of minutes, that boat will sink!" he cried, then rushed off!

Shit! Do something....but what? The water was clearly emptying from the lock. We were on a sill and would soon tip over. Nicholas spotted the problem. The people in the lock before us had failed to close one of the sluice gates. We had shut the lock gate at the top behind us and should have passed smoothly from the top clock to the lower lock, but we had got stuck because the water was draining out of the bottom gate. I've never seen Nicholas move so fast.

We got through and moored up at the foot of the locks. We needed time just to stop shaking – this could have taken some explaining back at the boatyard! Eventually we got going again, on the smooth run past Beeston Castle to Chester. I was quite familiar with the city, having stayed in a hotel there whilst working for Oracle in 1998 and 1999. The job was at a factory on the site of a former coal mine, a few miles away across the Welsh border. When I arrived at the start of 1998, the job was already under way, supervised by a group of 20 American consultants from Deloittes. The company was American-owned. There were also four American Oracle consultants, and a new team of seven UK Oracle people. The Deloittes were a scruffy-looking lot, but desperate to stay on the job. They were sent home at the end of February, The US Oracle team went as well. By May we were down to four UK Oracle consultants. By September there was only one man left standing, and that was me. I stayed till the end of the year.

Looking around, the city – one of the jewels of the north – looked much the same: the black and white timbered, ancient-looking shops, the red sandstone cathedral, the city walls, by which the canal runs in a deep cutting in the red sandstone, and best of all, the Germanic-looking town hall. A group of Italians on the project had been amazed at how good it was. They said they'd never heard of it.

CHAPTER 29

I had become so fascinated by the canal system that I now found myself exploring further afield, in fact into the depths of the English Midlands. I though I would try a day out in Stourport. This place is famous in the canal world because it was built as a canal town, and remains very much just that. It was later bypassed by the railway network and apparently has not grown greatly since, so what is left, according to the publicity, is a virtually untouched Georgian town. But have you ever heard of an ugly Georgian town? Think of the glorious suburbs of the Edinburgh New Town, or Bath. Could that era have produced urban blight as well? Go to Stourport to discover the dismal truth.

The famous engineer James Brindley was the man responsible for the Staffs and Worcester Canal, connecting the Trent and Mersey canal near Wolverhampton to the River Severn. This link created an inland waterway all the way from Bristol to Liverpool. Approaching the Severn from nearby Kidderminster, Brindley was very much put upon to end the canal at the town of Bewdley. Here river transshipment and porterage up the difficult stretch above the town was already an important business. However, Brindley was a contours man, and he did not like the look of the hummocky terrain between Kidderminster and Bewdley. Instead he sited the exit point of the canal four miles downstream where no town existed, so one had to be built from scratch, and this was Stourport.

However on the day of my visit the whole place, apart from the canal basin and exit to the Severn, presented a depressing air. Amongst the buildings were the Tontine Hotel, overlooking the canal basin, and a long red brick warehouse with a photogenic white clock tower. However the Tontine Hotel was boarded up, presumably awaiting redevelopment. The town was crawling with fat, plebby Brummies on a day out. However, if Bewdley was bypassed by the Staffs and Worcester Canal, and Stourport itself was later left stranded by the Birmingham to Gloucester railway, then I can only say that Bewdley got the better deal. This town snuggles by the big river, either side of a grand bridge, and it is fully of quirky old building. It also attracts a slightly better class of Brummie tourist.

Moving on southwards I arrived at Worcester, terminus of the next canal in the competing network built in the second half of the eighteenth century. This is the Worcester and Birmingham canal, which got right to the heart of the matter by connecting Birmingham directly with the Severn. I was slightly taken aback in the city centre by my first sighting of "Goths", young people with dyed black hair, pale skins, black and purple clothing and an alarming penchant for suicidal behaviour. Worcester had a post-industrial air with a number of old warehouses and factories near the canal now converted pretty smartly into hotels, restaurants and flats. The canal exits close to the cathedral.

The way was barred to the exit basin, so giving it up as a bad job, I turned round and headed northwards in the general direction of Redditch. Here near the village of Tardebigge, the Worcester and Birmingham takes a deep breath and hauls itself up from the Severn Valley to the 453-foot level at which Birmingham's canal network is built. There are 58 locks involved in this, the last 30 of them at Tardebigge. The canal moves stepwise up the hillside, but there is no grand prospect in the way there is at Wigan. Also the canal is a narrow one, and the locks fill quickly.

About half-way up I found a boater to tell me about the locks.

"How long does it take to get up? I asked.

"About three and a half hours," he replied.

"Have you come far?"

"From Bath."

Like so many boaters, this man soon warmed to his subject.

"We sold our house and bought a place in Spain, to live near our daughter - we have children and grandchildren. She moved somewhere else in Spain, so we rent our place out to supplement my meagre pension. Then we bought this boat a couple of years ago – I took retirement at 60. We live on it now. It's best to do this sort of thing while you are still active because it is fairly physical. There is quite a bit of work humping sacks of coal or gas canisters, emptying out the ash and what not, hauling on ropes and pushing lock gates, scrabbling around down in the engine. It's not suitable for anyone frail."

"I was thinking of doing a similar thing myself."

"Well make sure you try it first, on a holiday. It isn't for everyone. Sometimes when it's cold and wet and you have to stay at the tiller, you wonder what you are doing there. But we have no regrets."

"Ever tried it abroad?"

"Yes, on the Canal du Midi in France. There are a lot more facilities there. It's not like the folksy English canal system."

"What happens in wintertime?"

"We spent last winter on the Kennet and Avon. You can moor up for nothing if you avoid the hotspots, though you can only stay two weeks, then move on, and you can't go back to the same place for two more weeks. Silly really – you pass the same boats shuttling back and forth along one stretch of canal."

I wandered on to the top of the lock flight, where the canal disappears under a tunnel over 500 yards long, without the benefit of a towpath. Along the way I marveled at the sagging red brick bridges which cross the canal at many points. When you look at these things, you behold something which is genuinely old. Not like say the gleaming, magnificent and huge Worcester Cathedral, which I had seen earlier in the day. Some part of almost every cathedral you see nowadays is covered in scaffolding. These churches are beautifully and expensively maintained in England. The drawback is that when you look at the outside of one of them, what you see in not actually an 800-year old building at all. Almost every part of its exterior will have been renewed in the last 50 years.

Having seen one end of the Worcester and Birmingham, I thought I might as well go and look at the other terminus in Birmingham city centre. In fact I took my wife:

"Darling, would you care for a romantic weekend looking round Gas Street Basin in Birmingham?"

She said yes – there was a cheap rate at the hotel, £26 at the Travelodge!

The nominally-challenged basin, so-called because it was the first place in the city to be lit by gas, lies at the southern end of a run through the centre of the city, which begins at the Bullring shopping centre in the north. The Bullring has been reconstructed in recent years after the disastrous urban nightmare of the Sixties and Seventies. It is now has a mall, department stores and modern shops built over several levels in steel and plate glass. The most remarkable building is the modernist Selfridges store, which appears to have no windows, and looks like half a sugar loaf coated in clams. Moving away from this end of town, the next place of note is New Street Station – well, my son suggested knocking it down and starting again. Then there is a run of decent buildings including the Athenian-style town hall and the Victorian city art gallery and museum, the best building in the city centre. After this there is a large square with a war memorial and the Rep theatre off to one side. Beyond here lies the International Conference Centre, not a bad modern building but strange in function, as it straddles the main pathway, so everyone wanting to walk southwards must pass right through it. Beyond here, in a land dotted with slender skyscraper hotels, lies Gas Street Basin. At one end of this is another modern monster, the National Indoor Arena.

The most dominant theme of the city centre is its desperately provincial air. Liverpool is much more impressive, and I am not surprised that Manchester wants to call itself England's second city, having seen both of them by now. Or think of Newcastle, a big industrial city but still much smaller than Birmingham. It has the wonderful Georgian Graingerstown and the iconic Tyne Bridge. Birmingham lacks anything iconic, unless it is the Gas Street Basin. There are just so few good, old buildings of the muscular type so common in Leeds, Manchester or Liverpool. What happened to them? Were they ever there? I think so, yes, but there aren't many there now.

One very striking thing about Birmingham is the apparently very large population of West Indian origin. I hardly saw a black face in say Sheffield, which after all is the same type of place. But I will say this – the West Indian population in Birmingham looks comfortable with itself, and well-integrated. Another observation, following many visits to places like Tipton and West Bromwich in the Black Country over the years, is that some of the friendliest people in Britain live in this region. I find that the people are always the most welcoming in the places which have the worst self-image.

Gas Street Basin itself is now a regular tourist venue, surrounded by new or renovated property including two well-known pubs, the Tap and Spile and the James Brindley. There is a shopping and restaurant complex at one end of it, the Mailbox, and the canals are criss-crossed with cast iron pedestrian bridges, painted black and white. This is certainly worth a visit and it is much busier than Castlefield in Manchester, its equivalent in the north. I have seen a photograph of the way it looked before the redevelopment and the transformation is dramatic. Another one for my top ten sights of the north British canals.

Also the basin has an interesting history. The Worcester and Birmingham canal enters the basin from the south, and today flows seamlessly into the next canal in the network, the Birmingham Main Line, which heads off northwards to Wolverhampton. However, it was not always like this. The Birmingham Main Line was build first, and its owners refused to allow a direct connection to the new canal from

Worcester and the Severn. The reason was fear of competition, and the fact that each time the lock was opened into the new canal, the Birmingham main line would lose a lock of water! So it was that the "Worcester Bar" was constructed to keep the canals apart. This is only a few feet wide, and it is still there, today in the middle of the waterways. But it meant that all goods had to be manhandled over it from one barge to another. In 1815, 24 years after the new canal was authorized by act of Parliament, both canals came under common ownership and they were physically joined together.

CHAPTER 30

Well, I had finished my tour of the north British canals, but do you know what? They have canals abroad as well. So I decided to take a look at one of those, the Canal du Midi in France. We English are generally quite familiar with this country, and I am more familiar with it than many, having spent nine months there back in the early seventies, and having returned there a number of times since then.

The cultural divide between the French and the "Anglo-Americans" starts at the dining table, as it is well- known that the Frenchman is a slave to his stomach. I recently read a book by an American undersea explorer, Robert Ballard, the man who discovered the Titanic, who did quite a number of joint expeditions with the French. Lunch on an American ship was burgers and French fries washed down with coke, which they just scoffed down, but on a French ship it was a long drawn-out formal meal with tablecloths, several courses and careful discussions about the choice of wines. This was even more marked back in the Seventies, when there was little fast food anywhere, and none in France – Quelle idée!

I found many other differences between the French and the English, but things have changed somewhat now, as a further generation has passed. A lot more French people speak English now than they used to do, and many Frenchmen have come to England to find work. Thirty years ago, few true Frenchman would have dreamed of doing that. Some of these French people have enriched our dull island life, such as the footballer Eric Cantona.

Despite their reservations about the English, going back to the time of Joan of Arc, the French simply love the English royal family, and the behavior of that family is extensively reported by the French media. The French got rid of their royal family, the Bourbons, several times, so they really must not have liked them, but they certainly like ours.

So, the first major modern European canal was started in 1666 and competed in 1681 during the reign of Louis XIV. This was the

Canal du Midi, connecting Toulouse on the Garonne (which flows into the Atlantic) in south-western France to Sete on the Mediterranean, so avoiding the long sea voyage around Spain. This canal is 141 miles long and up to 12,000 men were employed at any one time on its construction. It was well-known to English travelers, which goes to show that it was not technical know-how which delayed the construction the English canal network. This same technology was in fact used in the drainage schemes in the Fens in the seventeenth century, but the English canal system had to wait for industrial demand to become established.

My first sight of this canal was at a very pretty spot called Le Somail, outside Narbonne. Walking along the bank, I found it not at all like an English canal. It was lined on both sides with huge, mature plane trees, and there was a terrific racket coming from thousands of invisible crickets. Also the water was a milky green, a colour I had never seen before, and not very healthy-looking at that. At least if you fall in at Hebden Bridge you know you are going to get a lungful of Yorkshire water, the finest water you can drown in anywhere.

My next stop was outside Beziers where there is a flight of nine locks called the Ecluses de Fosneranes, tumbling down to the river Orb, where there is a long stone aqueduct for the canal. This is exactly the same arrangement as at Marple on the Peak Forest Canal, and at Maryhill on the Forth & Clyde, but of course, the Canal du Midi is the original. The locks on this canal now have steel gates which are operated electrically – what, Les Anglais operate these things manually, how quaint!

The Canal du Midi has a good towpath and bikes can be hired to ride along it at several points. Many cyclists are said to do the whole thing in two days (it would take me at least two weeks, but I wasn't going to try it. I was with my wife and she does not ride bicycles.) Stopping again at Carcassonne, there were plenty of cyclists. However I don't think many of them were going very far. Stopping once more at the summit pool at Seuil de Naurouze, half-way along, there was no sign of either bikes or boats.

The boats we did see elsewhere were much larger and less quaint than the traditional English narrow boat, and they must have travelled at least twice as fast. Probably the rules for speeding are the same as in England (maximum 3 mph), but equally probably the French simply ignore the rules. It is well know that in France the law is for other people. For example I came away from this tour completely confused about what exactly the rules are about smoking cigarettes. It is supposed to be banned in public places. As far as I could see, you just have to ask for an ashtray to reverse this law.

Passing along the middle stretch of the canal, the impression it created was in some ways similar to that of the Forth and Clyde, or better still the M8 motorway. It is doing the same thing, crossing a low divide between waterways leading into widely separated seas.

My last stop on the canal was in Toulouse itself, where it had at last lost its milky green colour. So it's OK to fall in here. But having seen quite a few miles of it, this canal was frankly disappointing. So much less colourful and lively than an English canal.

*   *   *   *

Canals were also built in Ireland, in fact at much the same time as they were in England, so I thought I might take in one of these as well – the Grand Canal.

Many of the Irish themselves have the dark, Welsh appearance of the ancient inhabitants of these islands, deriving originally from Spain, but there is a strong Norse element as well and I have never seen so many ginger-haired people in my life. Isn't it strange how the individuals of our islands retain the physiognomy of one racial group or another after living together for so long? We are not mixed up at all well really.

The Republic of Ireland is quite a large small country, at 27,000 square miles more than half the size of England (50,000 square miles), but the population is less than four million, less in fact than the population of Yorkshire, so in terms of people per square mile, it is like a vast rural England with a few coastal cities tacked on. This low density was partly achieved by the voluntary but quite drastic measures taken after the famines of the nineteenth century when people married very late, if at all.

The vast majority of the Irish seem genial enough by nature, and not antagonistic to the English in the way that many Scots certainly are. After all, a lot of them have relatives in England. In fact I did detect a certain ambivalence towards the Scots. Chatting to one old man, we got talking about Glasgow.

"I was married to a Scottish woman," he said. "She wanted me to go to Scotland, but oi never went dere. Oi didn't like the look of dem Scottish fellers!"

Perhaps the main Irish hostility is to the Protestants of northern Ireland, originally Scottish and still very much bound of with the Scots.

If Scotland gets its independence it should be made to take this province with it. In fact I had the impression that England was regarded as the local centre of the universe, and English horse racing featured on the main news (something that rarely happens in England itself). In fact horse racing and gambling on the horses and dogs are big business in Ireland, far more so than in England.

Of course, there must be a reason why Ireland is called the Emerald Isle and is know to be full of bogs and big rivers. There is - so don't forget your umbrella. When I arrived there the place was in the first full flush of summer, at the beginning of June, positively bursting with chlorophyllic vigour.

The Grand Canal was built between 1756 and 1803 to connect Dublin and the Shannon, a distance of 80 miles. One of the principal engineers was William Jessop, who had a hand in many canal projects. There are 36 locks and the canal is still navigable, with a well-maintained towpath. The main goods carried on the canal were grain and the canal water itself! This is a most unusual canal because the water is crystal clear, and weeds grow vigorously on the bottom of the canal due to the direct sunlight they receive through the water. I took a walk on the canal near Celbridge, a few miles east of Dublin, and this feature was most marked. Now I always understood that real Guinness had to be made from the waters of the Liffey, but looking at that river, which is just as murky and unattractive as the Aire at Leeds, I now know that this is not the case. Guinness is made from this wonderful clean canal water, even today.

There was just one thing about the canal – why was it called "Grand"? Because it is not at all grand, in fact, the Rochdale Canal is grander than this. But from what I saw of it, it is pleasant enough.

*   *   *   *

I have one final waterway left on my journey, but this is no canal – it is none other than the Yangtze River, the greatest waterway in China, and now converted into what we in England call a navigation, made navigable to ordinary craft along its middle reaches. This has been achieved by the construction of the notorious Three Gorges Dam, which has caused the rapids though the mountains behind it to be drowned and effectively made safe for navigation. But how much has been lost here? Until recently the mighty river narrowed to fifty yards wide, and there is a tradition of boats being hauled up through the worst of the rapids by straining, naked men. Those days have now gone, and with them much of the attraction of the gorges themselves. The fifty-yard stretch is now over two hundred yards wide. At its deepest, the dam banks up 175 meters (570 feet) of water, so the gorges are also much shallower and less spectacular than they used to be.

I started my journey at the monstrous city of Chongqing (formerly Chungking), home to at least 6 million unfortunate people and towering over the confluence of the Yangste and Jialing rivers. The waters from the dam will back up to here and beyond – in fact a total distance of 375 miles. Our guide in Chongqing called himself "Steve". His Chinese accent when speaking English was so strong and his articulation so difficult that he sounded like a spoof Chinaman. Have you ever heard a Chinaman try to say "archeological"? Don't try it on Steve. Nevertheless, he was a sympathetic, middle-aged man, with some strong views.

"The Cultural Revolution was a disaster for China. And it was a disaster for my family!"

Millions of people had been sent into the countryside for "political reeducation" for the crime of being middle-class. Once there they were repeatedly humiliated and made to repent their "crime". Steve had been unlucky enough to be caught up in it. He was sent out to learn how to plant a rice paddy at the age of 17. His mother, father and younger sister were also sent, but the family was split up. His sister went mad and is still institutionalized to this day. His parents never recovered from the shock.

Steve didn't have any strong opinions about the dam, but many of the locals are certainly as skeptical as the rest of the world about it. In fact it is principally a hydro-electric project. They worry about its unknown ecological effects, such as landslides occurring in future years as the local geology is undermined by rising groundwater. But some ecological effects are already known. First, the river is full of rubbish, both vegetable and man-made (polystyrene and flip-flops, mostly). The Chinese are a very clean people and they do not like this. The local authorities along the route try to clean it up, but the task is evidently beyond them. In the old days most of this rubbish was smashed to smithereens in the rapids or disappeared somehow, and never bothered anyone. Secondly, Chongqing, already a furnace in the summer, has become even hotter. House prices in the much more pleasant upstream city of Chengdu, capital of Sichuan province, are much higher than in Chongqing, and that premium is increasing. The locals are very cynical about the "Government temperature", which rarely goes higher than 39.5 degrees Centigrade, when everyone with a thermometer knows that is has reached 42 degrees in Chongqing. The reason is that the workers are allowed to down tools when the temperature rises above 40 degrees.

Along the route of the rising river, there was very little agriculture, as it passes through mountains all the way. However there are many towns and these have all had to move uphill. The locals do not mind this much as the old blocks of flats have been replaced by new ones with better facilities, though the older people fret about the graves of their ancestors. Altogether, 1.3 million people have had to be rehoused.

The river cruise took three days to reach the dam, which nowadays is more of a spectacle than the three gorges themselves, and crawls with tourists. Once at the dam our ship entered the top of the locks. There are five of these, of ship-canal size, 280 metres long and many meters deep. With the ships crammed in like sardines, we slowly descended over a period of just over three hours. The engineering is all very impressive, massive concrete walls and steel lock gates.

*   *   *   *

As I reached the end of my canal tour, I found that I had slowly become converted to the cause of the usable canal – in fact I had stopped being a phony canal person, just like I have stopped being a phony bike person. I would go so far as to say that from being a complete canal skeptic, I have become a real canal fan. These once-great engineering works deserve restoration for they are national monuments, just as much as cathedrals and palaces, which are also heavily subsidized, and I think the canals are just as deserving. I read that British Waterways, which exists on a government subsidy, has invested £237 million of mostly other people's money in restoring and renovating canals over the past ten years. Now that might sound a lot, but it isn't as much as all that when you compare it with the amount spent on other forms of transport, for example on subsidies to the railways. It is worth noting that the local authorities are even now contemplating spending £30 million to restore the northern reaches of the Lancaster Canal, so there must be some evidence that this type of expenditure actually pays off.

Now look at the benefits of a usable canal. Not many boats may use it, but there will be some boats, so the canal will be alive and maintained, and it will not become derelict. From the number of canalside developments I had seen going up on virtually every canal I had visited, this must have had a dramatic effect on the value of the land overlooking these canals, and it has generated an awful lot of building work. I suppose you could argue that those buildings could have gone somewhere else, but they have gone on the canals, haven't they? And why is that? Because these living canals are seen as desirable places to build and restore property. Also, re-opening old canals must have some kind of snowball effect, because the greater the network, the greater the scope for the boatman and the whole canal industry.

Anyway I am not one to complain. Look at what the canals have done for me. I have been to many lovely and fascinating places that I had never even heard of before. Better still, today my blood pressure reading was 150/70 and that was after five hours at work followed by a long and tiring journey home to Halifax. I'll bet you that would have been 185/90 before I started on the bike.

I only wish I'd got those goggles sooner.

Top Ten Sights of the North British Canals, in order of discovery:

Gauxholme Railway Bridge, Todmorden, Rochdale Canal
Standedge Tunnel, Huddersfield Narrow Canal
Priest Holme Aqueduct, near Gargrave, Leeds and Liverpool Canal
Wigan Locks, Leeds and Liverpool Canal
Worsley, Bridgewater Canal
Marple Aqueduct, Peak Forest Canal
Avon Aqueduct, Union Canal, near Linlithgow
Falkirk Wheel, Union and Forth and Clyde Canals
Morecambe Bay, Lancaster Canal
Gas Street Basin, Birmingham Main Line Canal

Also highly recommended: Bingley Five-Rise Locks, Leeds and Liverpool Canal

Lightning Source UK Ltd.
Milton Keynes UK
UKOW050605181211

184007UK00001B/98/P